PENGUIN BOOKS

EVERYTHING YOU EVER WANTED TO KNOW ABOUT BUREAUCRACY BUT WERE AFRAID TO ASK

T.R. Raghunandan is a consultant in decentralization, anti-corruption and heritage conservation. Formerly in the Indian Administrative Service, he quit in 2010, after twenty-seven years, to concentrate on his pet passions of strengthening local democracy and governments, and working on anti-corruption. He currently handles several national and international assignments, including serving as adviser to the Accountability Initiative of the Centre for Policy Research, New Delhi, and adviser to Login Asia, a network of practitioners in decentralization from countries in South, central and South East Asia. He is an avid scale model maker, industrial heritage archivist, steam railway enthusiast and classic automobile restorer. He lives in Bengaluru with his wife, Aditi.

ADVANCE PRAISE FOR THE BOOK

'In this incisive account, T.R. Raghunandan captures the intricate details of bureaucracy with amazing insight. He sprinkles several anecdotes in his book that make this journey through the corridors of power a fascinating trip for all. In Chapter 3, "How to Get into the Civil Services", he carries readers through the rigorous procedure of selection that is spread over a year. He touches upon controversial issues such as posting and transfer of government functionaries, their promotions and ambitions, and the much-debated issue of "Generalist versus Specialist". In sum, an engaging, brilliant read, brimming with sparkling humour. Raghunandan deftly decodes bureaucratic jargon, culture and processes to present a comprehensible and intelligible script on the Indian bureaucracy'—Amitabh Kant, CEO, NITI Aayog

'A trenchant appraisal of the elite echelons of India's civil services by a highly perceptive insider. It stops just short of being cynical and provides valuable insights into how bureaucracy works, and why it falters'—Navtej Sarna, author and former ambassador of India to the USA

'Tempered throughout with self-deprecating humour, here's an unusual insight into the bureaucracy observed from within: attentive, honest, funny, thoughtful and in the end hopeful. For those frustrated with India's slothful bureaucracy, this account humanizes it without ignoring its warts'—Harsh Mander, human rights and peace worker, and author

'This illuminating and often humorous book takes us deep into the heart of the Indian state. With his trademark savvy, intelligence, and wit, T.R. Raghunandan brings the black box of the bureaucracy to life'—Milan Vaishnav, senior fellow and director of the South Asia Programme, Carnegie Endowment for International Peace, Washington, DC

'This book is an insightful insider's account of the functioning of the elite bureaucracy in India. It is lucidly written and eminently readable. The anecdotes are often hilarious and keeps the reader engaged'— M. Govinda Rao, former director, NIPFP, and member, Fourteenth Finance Commission

With an Afterword by
RENUKA VISWANATHAN

EVERYTHING YOU EVER WANTED TO KNOW ABOUT BUREAUCRACY BUT WERE AFRAID TO ASK

T.R. RAGHUNANDAN

PENGUIN BOOKS

An imprint of Penguin Random House

PENGUIN BOOKS

USA | Canada | UK | Ireland | Australia
New Zealand | India | South Africa | China

Penguin Books is part of the Penguin Random House group of companies
whose addresses can be found at global.penguinrandomhouse.com

Published by Penguin Random House India Pvt. Ltd
4th Floor, Capital Tower 1, MG Road,
Gurugram 122 002, Haryana, India

Penguin
Random House
India

First published in Penguin Books by Penguin Random House India 2019

ISBN 9780143442271

Typeset in Bembo Std by Manipal Digital Systems, Manipal

Printed at Repro India Limited

www.penguin.co.in

MIX
Paper from
responsible sources
FSC® C047271

To
Aditi, Ishaan and Ammachy

Contents

1. Overview or Lay of the Land   1

2. Files, Red Tape and the Art of Confusion   29

3. How to Get into the Civil Services   56

4. Postings, Transfers and Government Dysfunctionality   80

5. Promotions and Ambitions   100

6. The Civil Services and Leadership   118

7. Generalists versus Specialists   142

8. Problem-Solving, Technology and the IAS   159

9. Ethics and the IAS   198

Afterword by Renuka Viswanathan   241

Acknowledgements   277

Annexure I: Gardens or Garbage   281

Annexure II: The Vanishing Vote Trick   289

Annexure III: Identity Crisis   297

Notes   303

1

Overview or Lay of the Land

One of the first things that I did when I sat down to write this book was to google the meaning of the word 'bureaucracy'. One needs some impetus to write a book and googling is the mental equivalent of leaning a scooter so that precious petrol flows into the carburettor. The Cambridge dictionary website—as good a place as any on the Internet to search for the meaning of words—defines bureaucracy as a system for controlling or managing a country, company or organization that is operated by a large number of officials employed to follow rules carefully. I would narrow down that meaning for the purposes of this book to the people who run the government, excluding the elected representatives. There is no disagreement with the 'lots of people' part of the definition. A wait at the Central Secretariat Metro Station in Delhi during rush hour will leave nobody in doubt that the Indian bureaucracy comprises lots and lots of people.

Whatever its faults, the Indian bureaucracy cannot be accused of bias when it comes to confounding those who have to deal with it. Veteran insiders who return to it with their petitions after retirement are as clueless as freshly minted supplicants about how it functions.

While autobiographies of bureaucrats extract plenty of amusement from the mysterious ways of the bureaucracy, such reminiscences have little practical value; readers gain no practical tips from them on how to coax government officers to actually function. Outsiders in any case have little knowledge of who is responsible for what and why, or how to navigate that critical proposal through the treacherous shoals of a secretariat or directorate.

At the top of the bureaucracy heap is the fast-tracked elite civil servant, who belongs to a group of generalist and specialized services selected through competitive examinations. While no one of the several services that comprise this exclusive club is officially considered superior to the other, the Indian Administrative Service (IAS) is generally regarded as the most powerful and, therefore, the most desirable by aspirants. The aura of the IAS has remained intact over the years. Their tribal loyalties, handed from one generation to the other like a sacred fire, ensure preferential access to positions from where they not only construct policies for the country, but also develop rules, precedents and conventions that set them apart from the rest. Therefore, the IAS still remains the primary aspirational goal of all those who take a shot at the competitive examination year after year.

Yet, like every elite and powerful group, the IAS vehemently denies the concentration of any power in it. 'We have no powers, "saar". We have to do whatever politicians ask us to do,' they say, shaking their heads ruefully. The most one can extract from them is a reflection that things are no longer like they were before, a refrain that has been heard so often over the past seventy years that it has no meaning whatsoever.

This book aims to deconstruct the structure of the bureaucracy and how it functions for the understanding of the common person. For that purpose, it focuses on the IAS, but not entirely; it uses the IAS as an entry point to describe how the government does and does not function. While the book won't be a do-it-yourself manual of dealing with the bureaucracy, it hopes to replace the anxiety that people feel when they step into a government office with a healthy dollop of irreverence. Lack of awe, bordering on civilized disrespect, is a most effective learning tool. If a reader, when confronted with a gravely articulated excuse by a government officer, is able to instantly discern it as an insane one, the purpose of this book would have been achieved.

Since the civil service has been around for a century and more, one would expect that there is plenty of data available to analyse how it has evolved and changed over the years. Even as I steeled myself for the task of collecting and analysing this data, two excellent and incisive papers were published that more or less traverse the same areas I intended to cover. The first, written by K.P. Krishnan and T.V. Somanathan titled 'The Civil Service',[1] attempts to answer four questions, namely, how the civil service has changed since Independence, how effective it has been and how changes from its original design affected its effectiveness, what were the impacts other institutions and social trends had on its effectiveness and what could be done to improve its effectiveness. Krishnan and Somanathan are no strangers to these questions, having written an earlier paper[2] on similar issues and positioning the later paper as a continuance of their explorations. Since both are senior serving members of the IAS, they place certain caveats on their methodology as 'loyal civil servants and faithful adherents to the conduct rules'. While they acknowledge the advantage they had to insights not available to an outside researcher, they also draw attention to limitations in the degree to which they could use such information.

In order to assess the effectiveness of the civil service, the paper uses four interrelated criteria. The first two are the preservation of India's constitutional order (which include democracy, secularism, national unity and the rule of law) and the impartial implementation of the rule of law in day-to-day dealings with the citizenry. The third and fourth criteria relate to creating public value, namely, faithfully translating the will of elected governments into policies and implementing these effectively and promoting economic development by reducing transaction costs and providing effective and efficient public services. They also identify certain traits that civil servants should cultivate and follow in order to effectively perform tasks that enable them to score well against these criteria. For criterion one, preserving the rule of law and suchlike, it is neutrality and a sense of national spirit and larger purpose; for criterion two, integrity (lack of corruption); and for criterion three, political neutrality, competence and capacity, flexibility and willingness to change, social sensitivity, idealism and empathy. For criterion four, it is capacity and competence.

Krishnan and Somanathan comprehensively outline the design of the All India Services and describe the various changes that the examination system underwent over the years, such as the increase in reservations from 22 per cent for SCs and STs to nearly 50 per cent, including those for the other backward classes. They also meticulously record the evolution in changes in the eligibility age and the number of permissible events at the entrance exam. The wealth of data that they present—which covers the profile of candidates who appear at the examination, the numbers selected, their ages at entry, the number of attempts that successful candidates take at the entrance examinations, the shares of different community categories in the list of successful candidates, the medium of the examination preferred by candidates and the universities of origin of selected candidates—gives more than a worm's eye view of those who constitute the civil services. However, the more interesting section of the paper is where the authors assess the effectiveness of the civil service. They draw a number of conclusions on its current state based not only on a wide range of published reports and research papers, but also on their own considerable insider knowledge of the civil service and some quick assessments of their own design.[3]

Tested against the four criteria that they describe, Krishnan and Somanathan assess that the civil service have been quite effective, 'outstandingly so', in the preservation of national unity and constitutional rule, but far less effective in implementing the rule of law and in dealing with individual citizens, even if this is mitigated by the impressive work of many individual officers who have stood for the fair treatment of the disadvantaged. They note that the number of such upright crusaders for justice and fairness is large enough to find place in popular media and thus motivate young and idealist aspirants to appear at the entrance examinations. On the third criterion of faithfully executing policies, the authors conclude that the experience is mixed. Officers are seen to have obstructed and delayed the implementation of good policy, though sometimes, they have to take the blame for delays and confusions caused by political ambivalence in this regard, where there are contradictions between the political executive's 'publicly proclaimed lofty intentions and privately expressed specific instructions'. Yet, they point out that where the political executive has a 'clear and genuinely held policy view and expresses it consistently, the civil service usually delivers' well. On the fourth criterion of the effectiveness of the civil service in promoting economic development, Krishnan and Somanathan unequivocally conclude that it has not done well. They not only blame policy uncertainty, delays, inconsistent or arbitrary application of known policy, corruption, ineffectiveness in law enforcement and regional or communal parochialism, but also lack of competence as coming in the way of effective promotion of economic development.

The second paper that provides several useful insights into the nature of the IAS (the paper consciously focuses on the IAS alone and not on all civil services) and its effectiveness is Milan Vaishnav and Saksham Khosla's 'The Indian Administrative Service Meets Big Data'.[4] As expected from the title, Vaishnav and Khosla mine through a large number of research studies to compile and analyse data in order to address three questions: a) what determines the career success of officers in the IAS? b) to what degree can individual officers influence tangible development outcomes in areas such as poverty, health and education? c) what impact does politics have on bureaucratic functioning?

With respect to the first question, Vaishnav and Khosla assert that examination scores and education levels are 'highly predictive of future success' for IAS officers early in their careers. As a corollary, they also conclude that older officers who enter the service as part of larger cadres face limited career prospects and are less effective at improving economic outcomes. This is largely a comment on one of the streams of entry into the IAS, which is through the promotion of state provincial civil service cadre officers. They have good news too: officers who systematically invest in training or acquiring specialized skills can expect to receive clear rewards in their career trajectories.

On the second question as to whether individual officers can favourably impact development outcomes, they glean from the research studies that they examine and answer in the affirmative: 'individual bureaucrats can have strong, direct and measurable impacts on tangible health, education and poverty outcomes'. A further finding in this regard is that officers with strong local ties are often linked to improved public service delivery. This is contrary to the oft-repeated perception that IAS officers, in order to be effective, have to be aloof to local pulls and pressures, which is best achieved when the officer is an outsider, unattached to local, social and political dynamics. On the final question of whether political interference adversely impacts the effectiveness of IAS officers, Vaishnav and Khosla concur with Krishnan and Somanathan that political interference 'generates substantial inefficiency; the best officers do not always occupy important positions, while political loyalty offers bureaucrats an alternative path to career success'. Yet, they finally conclude, 'greater political competition does not necessarily lead to better bureaucratic performance'.

One of the most useful exercises undertaken by Vaishnav and Khosla is a literature review of numerous studies—this is where the IAS intersects with big data. Each of the studies delves into career records of IAS officers in the thousands, which is an obvious place to start. However, what makes some of these studies stand out from the ordinary are the linkages they draw, or attempt to discover, at the very least, between the career characteristics of IAS officers and various development indicators.

Take for example, a study by Rikhil Bhavnani and Alexander Lee,[5] in which they study the executive record sheets of 4793 IAS officers serving as of 7 March 2007 and draw correlations with the proportion of villages in their districts that have high schools and health facilities. This study leads to the conclusion—a counter-intuitive one as Vaishnav and Khosla remark—that 'locally embedded officers increase public goods provision, but only in districts with high literacy and newspaper circulation'. Similarly, a study by Jonas Hjort, Gautam Rao and Elizabeth Santorella,[6] who studied the executive record sheets of 2790 district collectors (DCs) serving between 1996 and 2013 and the beginning and completion of capital expenditure projects and satellite night-time luminosity data as a proxy for economic development, concludes that 'bureaucrat value-added explains a significant share of variation in project outcomes and luminosity, and that education, local language proficiency, direct recruitment predict a high-value-added officer'. Surprisingly, the study also finds a negative correlation between high-value-added traits and future empanelment of officers.

As both these studies—'The Civil Service' and 'The Indian Administrative Service Meets Big Data'—rely upon large databases to draw their conclusions, it is interesting to compare and contrast their recommendations as to how the civil service overall (in the Krishnan–Somanathan study) and the IAS in particular (in the Vaishnav–Khosla study) ought to be reformed to extract the best from them.

Krishnan and Somanathan identify ten reasons for the poor performance of the civil service:

1. Political interference
2. The weakening of dual control in recent times and the inability of the Union government to protect All India Services officers
3. The reluctance of IAS officers to make full use of the legal protections available to them due to the costs involved
4. Arbitrary transfers and short tenures
5. The non-transparency of and weaknesses in the empanelment process through which IAS officers are identified for senior postings at the Centre
6. The use of a random roster system to allocate officers to cadres
7. Drastic pay compression, that is to say, a reduction in the ratio of senior officers' pay as compared to the junior ranks
8. Spectacular increases in private-sector salaries and a culture of conspicuous consumption, which has led to the temptation to be corrupt
9. Judicial leniency to civil servants who perform inefficiently through a wide interpretation of the protection due to the latter under Article 311 of the Constitution
10. The dearth of successful prosecution of the corrupt, which reduces the risks associated with turning corrupt

Of these reasons, they clearly identify political interference as being the most pernicious factor that undermines the performance of the IAS. Needless to say, some of the other factors listed above, which affect the performance of the civil service, are also clearly connected to political interference, even though Krishnan and Somanathan do not explicitly state so.

Vaishnav and Khosla also dwell upon the deleterious effects of political influence. They conclude that the 'most visible and lamentable aspect of political interference in the civil service has been the phenomenon of punitive transfers'. The first study to which they refer is by Lakshmi Iyer and Anandi Mani,[7] who studied the career histories of 2800 IAS officers, along with 'data on political changes, proxy measures of bureaucrat ability and a measure of the perceived importance of different IAS posts'. This study reveals how politicians use frequent transfers to force bureaucrats to buckle under pressure. The findings of the study paint a grim picture: an average IAS officer faces a 53 per cent probability of being transferred in a given year, with a further ten per cent increase in the year in which a new chief minister is elected. The average tenure of an IAS officer in any given post is just sixteen months.

Switching back to the Krishnan–Somanathan study, the authors attempt to unpack what constitutes political interference and what does not. They define political interference as:

Acts of politicians—whether formally part of the Executive or not—intended to compel a civil servant, by means of threats or blandishments or both, to follow the course desired by them on decisions which ought to be taken by the civil servant impartially under government policy.

They go on to also observe what does not constitute political interference, saying that:

> It does not refer to the legitimate role of the political executive (ministers and politically appointed heads of agencies) in exercising powers duly vested in them—a role which may indeed lead them to legitimately overrule advice tendered by civil servants.

They conclude that political interference 'is almost always oral, with the civil servant usually pretending that he took the decision of his own volition'.

Why do bureaucrats buckle to political interference, in the view of many, without even the semblance of a fight? Krishnan and Somanathan acknowledge that bureaucrats can come under legitimate fire for not boldly accepting the adverse consequences of sticking to their guns and behaving in an upright fashion, but also point out that things have changed a great deal over the years. Politicians have realized that punitive transfers are an effective stick with which to beat the civil servant who shows spine into submission. It is well known that frequent transfers can disrupt the personal lives of officers, separating families and affecting the education of their children. They also point out the emergence of a lesser-known phenomenon, the one of arbitrary demotion, by which a post that carries lower level responsibilities is arbitrarily upgraded to a higher level and a senior officer placed there, specifically to humiliate him or her. That is indeed a pertinent observation. In at least one Indian state, which specializes in political punishments of this sort, the post of the director of the state archives is the usual equivalent of *kaala paani*. It is not unusual for those who occupied critical posts such as the chief secretary or secretary to the chief minister to find themselves in the basement of the archives when the political dispensation changes, amongst old and decaying manuscripts that they can read and imbibe at their leisure. Krishnan and Somanathan also point to the rising importance of another phenomenon that always existed: the power of politicians to hand out sinecure post-retirement jobs in a plethora of regulatory bodies and miscellaneous commissions, which can turn out to be a strong incentive for bureaucrats to form unholy alliances with politicians and do things that they ought not to do, particularly in the evening of their service tenures.

Vaishnav and Khosla surmise that punitive transfers can drive two kinds of inefficiencies. First, they conclude that 'important bureaucratic positions are not necessarily filled by the most qualified officers available' and second, 'junior IAS officers systematically underinvest in skill acquisition because loyalty to powerful politicians, as opposed to merit-based advancement, offers an alternative path to career success'.

Vaishnav and Khosla also point out to another interesting counterintuitive finding from a study authored by Anusha Nath in 2015.[8] This study focused on the speed and efficiency with which development activities were approved and implemented from the local constituency development funds of members of Parliament by district collectors. After studying the professional histories of all IAS officers who served as district collectors between 1999 and 2009 and the data on the implementation of projects through the constituency development funds of the MPs, the study revealed that bureaucratic performance was most efficient in party strongholds where the re-election of the MP was a foregone conclusion. Officers tended to go with the flow when faced with the prospect of political certainty and approved projects 11 per cent faster than average. In constituencies where the delimitation exercise resulted in the constituency being barred for the current incumbent by virtue of being reserved in future for a particular ethnic category, the study discovered that the collectors took 13 per cent more time than average to sanction the current MP's proposed project, probably dragging their feet, secure in the knowledge that the current MP was debarred from standing for elections in the same constituency in the next polls.

Amongst the large number of suggestions made by Krishnan and Somanathan, four are clearly focused on reducing political interference. First, they re-emphasize that a decade-old proposal for increasing the tenure and prevention of arbitrary penal transfers must be implemented. They point out that the Supreme Court has already noted the idea of a minimum tenure in a post in T.S.R. Subramaniam v. Union of India[9] and required the Union and state governments to notify and adhere to prescribed minimum tenures. Second, they advocate for a reassertion of dual control, under which the Union government intervenes to prevent the capricious use of powers for transfers and postings by state governments, including curbing of the arbitrary creation, upgrading and downgrading of posts in order to punish officers. Third, they endorse, even though somewhat sceptically, the Second Administrative Reforms Commission's proposal to create civil services boards by enacting civil services acts, in order to oversee personnel management at the Union and state levels. Fourth, they suggest that the lure of post-retirement opportunities can be eliminated by aligning retirement ages of regulators with that of civil servants, thus destroying their attractiveness as post-retirement sinecures.

Vaishnav and Khosla too echo these recommendations and suggest that the government enact a plethora of legislation, namely, the Public Services Bill (2007), the Civil Services Bill (2009), and the Civil Services Standards, Performance, and Accountability Bill (2010), which may have the result of constraining politicians from using transfers as a punitive tool. They are less optimistic than Krishnan and Somanathan about the effects of the Supreme Court judgment in the T.S.R. Subramaniam case. The judgment is toothless, they say, given that very few states have complied with the directive to fix a minimum tenure of two years for civil servants. Vaishnav and Khosla, therefore, endorse a suggestion by N.C. Saxena, a retired IAS officer, that a stability index could be developed for key posts, on the basis of which a minimum tenure of, say, two years can be fixed. While this may not work as a blanket ban on premature transfers, it is expected that they would invite raised eyebrows and adverse reactions.

Yet, will all these recommendations actually be implemented? Not if the track record of the government is any indication. The simple and obvious fact of the matter is that politicians do not want to restrict the opportunities for political interference. They see their ability to interfere in the actions of bureaucrats as a legitimate way of furthering the mandate of the people that they secure through winning elections. Only by control—in as blunt and brutal a fashion as they perceive—of officers, can they hope to receive the obedience that they need to execute both their legitimate and illegitimate aspirations. Yet, the resistance to diminishing the scope for political interference cannot be blamed entirely on politicians. What is less obvious is that a significant number of civil servants profit from the current system where political interference is rampant, and, therefore, would not want a change in the status quo. Arbitrary and frequent transfers, while they harm the prospects of many upright officers, also benefit those who fish in political waters for positions where they can exercise more power and influence. Officers who play the political game to be picked for influential and powerful jobs are pragmatic about their prospect of success or failure. First, those in the boondocks can always hope that their chastened change of behaviour and willingness to play ball can be rewarded and they can once again be in the good books of politicians. Second, frequent transfers often are an excellent alibi for non-performance; ineffective officers, who did not have the slightest chance of succeeding in the first place, however long their tenures, can use a premature transfer as a legitimate excuse for why they were unable to deliver the goods.

This may look as an unduly cynical view of matters, but there are reasons for taking a dim view of the reforms suggested to improve the quality and effectiveness of the civil service. Many of the elaborately worded suggestions made in the Krishnan–Somanathan and the Vaishnav–Khosla papers are meticulously thought through, adequately researched and reveal a strong reliance on reason. However, these suggestions have been around for ages; they have not only been echoed in weighty committee and commission reports on which plenty of taxpayer money has been spent, but also asserted in Supreme Court judgments. Many of them, for example, suggestions of the fixation of cadre strength, cadre allocations, promotions, empanelment, disciplinary proceedings and suchlike, are not matters in which politicians, unless provoked to think, are particularly interested to oppose. Yet, hardly have a few of these been implemented thus far. Surely, the blame for this level of lassitude on the part of various departments of personnel at the Union and state levels cannot be entirely attributed to obstruction by politicians.

The blunt fact of the matter is that the bureaucracy, and particularly the IAS, is inherently suspicious of and, therefore, resistant to changes that introduce imponderables into the way the officers' careers progress. Theirs is a bipolar reaction to reforms. Officers will enthusiastically discuss various reforms and even proactively fight for them, particularly after they retire and have nothing to gain or lose. However, inherently, they prefer to deal with the known evils of political interference, frequent transfers and non-transparent empanelment procedures, of cadre inconsistencies and ever-changing examination policies, than lay themselves open to strange new ideas such as lateral entry, frequent evaluations and weeding out of incompetent officers through compulsory retirements. These are nice things to talk about; but please, let's implement these after I retire, is the common but silent refrain.

Nowhere is this more apparent than in the matter of how the IAS has resisted devolution to the local governments. Indeed, the behaviour of the IAS as a class, barring a few honourable exceptions, to the idea of devolution to local governments, goes counter to the opinion of Krishnan and Somanathan, that it has been successful in upholding constitutional values.

The Constitution of India was amended in 1993 by the seventy-third and seventy-fourth constitutional amendment acts. Apart from the infamous forty-second amendment and the forty-fourth amendment that reversed a great deal but not all of the damage done by the former, no amendment of the Constitution has been as detailed as the seventy-third and seventy-fourth amendments. Often decried as writing in municipal law into the provisions of the Constitution, these amendments mandated the constitution of three levels of panchayats in the rural areas, at the district, intermediate and village levels, and municipalities, nagar palikas and town panchayats in urban areas. Elections were to be held to these bodies every five years, with no gaps in between the tenures of two elected bodies. While not celebrated enough, the amendments were of deep political significance: the number of elected representatives mandated by the Constitution increased from the few MPs in Parliament and a few thousand MLAs in the state legislatures, to around 3.2 million elected representatives in nearly 2,50,000 local governments across the country. An elaborate system of reservations written into the Constitution—the clauses that invited the criticism of the Constitution resembling municipal law—ensured that significant numbers of these seats were reserved for women, Scheduled Castes, Schedule Tribes and Other Backward Classes. Since the subject matter of local governments comes within the legislative domain of the states, they were mandated to pass laws that devolved powers and responsibilities to local governments. The Constitution mandated that the responsibilities for planning for economic development and social justice ought to be entrusted to local governments, and helpfully indicated a list of twenty-nine matters for rural local governments and eighteen for urban local governments, in respect of which the states could entrust schemes for implementation to rural and urban local governments respectively.

States were also mandated to constitute finance commissions that would recommend to them as to how the state financial envelope could be carved out to provide adequate financial resources to local governments to carry out their devolved responsibilities. Local governments were also expected to be given tax handles, such as property tax, which would enable them to raise enough flexible resources to address local needs.

More than a quarter of a century later, implementation of the provisions of the amendments remains tardy and incomplete. The political revolution envisaged is probably upon us already. Barring a few exceptions, due to vigilance from civil society and court intervention, elections are held regularly to local governments every five years. The large body of local government elected representatives are, for better or worse, affecting the way political parties conduct their affairs. There are many leaders who have climbed the stepladder to political success and prominence after first cutting their teeth as panchayat representatives, sarpanches, municipal corporators or mayors.

Yet, from the administrative angle, the local governments have virtually no elbow room to function as devolved entities that are able to exercise a modicum of control over their staff and organizational capacities. The blame for this impasse has to be laid squarely at the doorstep of the IAS, which, barring a few exceptions, has stoutly resisted the devolution of administrative control over local officials to local governments.

When an IAS officer is confronted with this allegation, almost immediately, they fall back upon the familiar alibi of placing the blame for tardy devolution on higher-level politicians, who they say, do not want increasing competition to emerge from the local governments. However, a closer study of the details of how local governments are hamstrung will reveal that much of the resistance emerges from the notes and opinions of IAS officers, who fear the dilution of powers of positions they hold dear to their heart.

One such hoary position is that of the district collector, a generalist do-it-all rank that continues from the colonial era till today virtually unchanged in the range of formal and informal powers that he or she exercises. The district panchayat and empowered municipalities, if allowed to flower in the true spirit of the seventy-third and seventy-fourth amendments (and the state laws that actually devolve powers and responsibilities to them, which are, surprisingly, very generous and sweeping in the extent to which they fulfil the constitutional mandate) would seriously impact the scope and range of the responsibilities of the district collectors. That would change the IAS forever, much to its dismay. No other reforms, in cadre strength, pay compression, pensions, lateral entry, specialization, training and suchlike, would shake the IAS to its very foundations like the reduction of the scope and range of the powers of the district collectors. It, therefore, comes as no surprise that the IAS has stoutly, and successfully, resisted any invasion of the domain of the district collectors by local governments.

Only in one state, Karnataka, did the government try to unseat the collector from his exalted position. In 1983, nearly a decade prior to the seventy-third and seventy-fourth Constitutional amendments, the government passed a landmark law setting up a two-tier panchayat system consisting of zilla parishads (ZP) and mandal panchayats.[10] The law reserved 25 per cent of membership in panchayats to women. It also gave the zilla parishad president the status of a minister. This framework was conceived and piloted by Abdul Nazeer Sab, the then rural development and panchayati raj minister. After a four-year wait for the legislation to secure presidential assent, elections to zilla parishads and mandal panchayats were held in January 1987. Devolution was matched by several administrative reforms. On the fiscal side, a district sector was carved out of the state budget to match functional assignment. A state finance commission was set up. However, the decision that sent ripples of fear and consternation through the ranks of the IAS was the one to divest deputy commissioners (collectors) of their development responsibilities and to post officers senior to them as 'chief secretaries' of zilla parishads, answerable and accountable to the elected local body and its president. The confidential reports of chief secretaries were to be written by the ZP *adhyaksha*. The system resulted in a radical and fundamental shift in the power structure, both amongst politicians and bureaucrats. First, a new class of local politicians emerged. While there was some tokenism in women's representation, numerous independent and committed women took on leadership roles in ZPs and mandals. Second, particularly impressive strides were taken in rural infrastructure, such as water supply, roads and school buildings. Yet, at the first opportunity, this new paradigm was done away with. In 1992, when ZP and mandal terms ended, elections were postponed and deputy commissioners were appointed as administrators of the ZPs. In a policy turnaround, officers junior to the DCs were posted as CSs, thus restoring status quo as to who was the de facto head of the district. That position continues today too, with the chief executive officers of the zilla panchayats—the term 'chief secretary' of the ZP was abandoned—being vastly junior to the deputy commissioners, who wield as much formal and informal power in Karnataka as their counterparts in other states.

There are several examples of IAS officers across cadres and levels uniting to protect their turf. A stellar one is the loyalty shown by IAS officers to the idea of autonomous district rural development agencies. Much prior to the seventy-third and seventy-fourth amendments, the Union government decided that they ought to intervene directly at the district level to accelerate agriculture and rural development. In 1979, the Union agriculture ministry created SFDAs or small farmers development agencies at the district level to implement special new initiatives for agricultural development, which were funded directly by the Central government. Given that state treasuries were often cash-strapped and the money deposited with them was likely to be diverted for emergent uses such as the payment of salaries, the Union government hit upon the idea of configuring the SFDA in each district as an autonomous body corporate with its own bank account. That enabled the Union government to deposit its money directly with district-level front-line officers. Flexibility and freedom were the results, as the society could rapidly draw funds and use them without fear of treasury bans and money lapsing back to the government at the end of the fiscal year. States too played along, depositing their contributions to these schemes in the SFDA bank accounts and secretly relieved that their own fiscal stress would not starve these programmes of their funds. The SFDAs were replaced by the district rural development agencies (DRDAs), which enlarged the idea of a direct financial conduit from the Union government to the district administration. The DRDAs smoothly integrated with the district administration, by the simple expedient of mandating that they be chaired by the district collectors. For the IAS mandarins at Delhi, this seemed the most natural arrangement to devise; who else could be entrusted with the direct responsibility of looking after the Union government's grassroots-level initiatives at the district and sub-district levels than district collectors? For the IAS, this opened up a fulfilling opportunity to guide rural development work at the district level. In most states, young officers who cut their teeth as subcollectors[11] were promoted to serve as the project directors of the DRDAs. These were happy times, as they functioned as a good level of delegation of authority from the district collectors. Many old-timer officers rate their experiences as project directors of DRDAs as their best, even sometimes surpassing their stints as district collectors in terms of job satisfaction.

With the emergence of district panchayats as the district-level local governments entrusted with many responsibilities relating to rural development, Karnataka state, as part of its big bang decentralization reforms, obtained approval from the Government of India to merge the DRDAs with the zilla panchayats. However, for many years, that remained an exception to the rule. Only a few states, namely, Madhya Pradesh, Chhattisgarh, Rajasthan, West Bengal and Kerala, followed the example set by Karnataka.

IAS officers who served in the rural development ministry in Delhi, a few honourable exceptions apart, were loath to do away with DRDAs, fearing that it would undermine the position of the district collectors and project directors, and place the entire gamut of local rural development in the hands of locally elected representatives. In order to avoid that horrendous possibility, they threw all notions of serving the Constitution and the law to the winds. This was a bit of a contradiction, because officers did not seem to mind political interference from a district minister or an MLA, but recoiled at the thought that they should be subservient to a zilla parishad adhyaksha and a bunch of elected representatives at that level. Funnily enough, they also did not mind more powers being delegated to village panchayats, which were at such a distance away from them so as to not threaten their powers of patronage and as long as they retained powers of oversight over them.

The IAS has not recognized the potential of the panchayats to change the political paradigm of the country by being a method of distributing leadership. Anxious to protect their own domain of power and discretion, the IAS, with notable individual exceptions, willingly plays into the hands of higher-level politicians, who fear competition from the panchayats and, therefore, are keen to impose all kinds of preconditions that prevent people from standing for elections to the panchayats. Bureaucrats who are driven by the limited vision of making panchayats parking slots for lower-level government officials who engage in 'efficient' service delivery, also support such moves to restrict entry of people with political ambitions into panchayats. So they support hare-brained and elitist ideas like putting educational qualification, ownership of toilets and two-child norms as preconditions for eligibility to stand for elections. Even when such restrictions are not in place for eligibility to stand for higher-level electoral offices!

What IAS officers fail to recognize, in their anxiety to preserve things as they are, is that panchayats and municipalities are about local government. Their constitution is a political action, and they are far from being agencies meant to run the programmes of higher-level governments. The problem is that bureaucrats don't recognize the real significance of panchayats as instruments meant for distributing political power. They see them as merely instruments of service delivery. For that reason, IAS officers instinctively react favourably to arrangements that position panchayats and municipalities as unpaid agents to do what those at the top determine is best for the country. Look at the fiscal position of the panchayats and you'll understand the abysmal state they are in. Less than 16 per cent of panchayat finances come from its own revenues. More than 60 per cent of GP expenditure is of rigid schemes that come from the Union government. In total, less than 7.5 per cent of the country's public expenditure comes from the third tier of government, and that includes municipalities too. Staff are appointed by higher levels of government to the panchayats. So the entire purpose of 'devolution', which is the objective stated in the Constitution, is completely lost and negated after twenty-five years of the constitutional amendment.

In 2012, a committee constituted by the Union government[12] headed by the late V. Ramachandran, a former member of the Second Administrative Reforms Commission and a former chief secretary of Kerala, reiterated that ever since the Constitution mandated that planning for economic development and social justice and implementation of such plans should be the responsibility of the panchayats and provided for transferring schemes in the relevant functional domains to them, the role and relevance of bodies like DRDAs need to be reconfigured. The committee said that the, 'Constitution envisages harmonization not only of laws but also of institutional mechanisms with the Panchayati Raj system,' and that 'the principle of concomitance cannot be limited to just laws but it extends to institutional arrangements as well.' Viewed in this sense, the committee said that such institutions have to be harmonized with the panchayat set-up, or else they become ultra vires of the Constitution.

Citing the example of states that merged the DRDAs with the zilla parishads without suffering any negative consequences on the flow of funds from the Government of India, their proper utilization and timely submission of accounts, the committee asserted that 'as parallel bodies pose a serious threat to the growth and maturation of PRIs as institutions of Local Self Government as envisaged in the Constitution, it is necessary that they are fully harmonized with the Panchayat Raj set-up'. The final suggestion of the committee was eminently practical. It recognized that DRDAs provided both a professional and an autonomous-institutional component and opined that while the former is absolutely indispensable, the latter has no relevance when democratically elected bodies are in existence and entrusted with the same responsibilities. Therefore, in conclusion, it recommended that 'DRDAs are suitably restructured by changing their institutional structure and character as charitable societies and converting them into a high quality professional group, preferably placed in the District Panchayats, but with the specific mandate to service the District Planning Committees.'

The Union government declared that it has accepted the report of the committee. Beyond that, nothing happened.

No orders were issued to restructure the DRDAs. The internal grapevine had it that a few officers dug in their heels and refused to move the file, even as the minister chafed and pressed for an early decision. The government changed since and the matter was given a decent burial.

There are several other examples of how IAS officers can block reforms that have the potential to erode their employment opportunities or open their encadred positions—a quaint term to denote positions that are exclusively reserved for IAS officers—to competition. Take the positions of municipal commissioners in metropolitan cities. Here too, the Constitution mandates that municipalities are a layer of autonomous government in their own right, with legally devolved powers and responsibilities, a fiscal window and with direct accountability to the people for the performance of their functions. Yet, no metropolitan city has the power to hire their CEO, the corporation commissioner. The job is reserved for an IAS officer who is deputed by the state government, often positioned or transferred without as much as a genuflection in the direction of the mayors. Discussions with friends in the IAS result in the usual horror as to what might happen if the powers to appoint the corporation commissioner were with the mayor or the elected council. 'How can that be?' The mayors and corporators are all corrupt thugs, they say.

Not any more or less than the state urban development minister is a thug, is my answer.

So, if the IAS is doggedly resistant to reducing their monopoly on various powerful jobs, are they confident about whether they possess the skills and knowledge to do well at these diverse jobs? Krishnan and Somanathan speak about the increasing perception of the reduced competence of civil servants, but are candid enough to admit that they have difficulty in assessing this issue. They observe that the exposure of civil servants to modern management concepts and to training in highly regarded international institutions has increased, yet, there is a decline in the ability to decide or make specific policy recommendations. They come up with several caveats, that such deterioration may be either due to a lack of ability, or more often than not, because there is no incentive to be decisive; indecisiveness is safe. Yet, they conclude, as insiders, that there is a 'lack of competence in several areas of government and that many civil servants in key positions do not have the necessary subject matter and decision analysis skills'. Having said that, they can only suggest capacity building as a relatively non-controversial area where reforms are easier to implement.

All that is cold comfort for, say, a well-intentioned corporator or a mayor, thug or law-abiding, who has to struggle with the challenges of finding a competent professional team to deal with the problems of a large metropolis.

The IAS, therefore, resembles a vehicle driven with one foot on the brake and the other on the accelerator. On the one hand, it reacts with commendable candidness when the issue of whether it can cope with the wide range of policy and execution tasks is discussed, as Krishnan and Somanathan do. Yet, when it comes to the actual execution of these reforms, it not only holds back, but also actively resists moves to reduce its monopoly and entitlement to certain positions. While it often and successfully raises the bogey of political interference as coming in the way of its fulfilment of its potential, it also prefers to deal with the known risks of political interference rather than submit itself to a brave new world of increasing and lifelong competition, harsher standards of judging of effectiveness and being accountable for governance successes and failures.

Policy changes are what we will prescribe for others, but we prefer to be where we are; thank you very much.

2

Files, Red Tape and the Art
of Confusion

The most important tool of the government is the government file. If one wishes to understand how the government functions, one must understand everything about these files. All decisions of the government and the deliberations that lead to them have to be written down to ensure who is accountable and for what. Furthermore, the records of these decisions have to be preserved so that we have a memory of when what was done. Therefore, files and filing systems are the bedrock of government functioning. Even though paperless systems are being considered for adoption, they do not away with filing; they merely shift the medium from paper to electronic recording and storage.

Outsiders know very little of the filing system in India, but hesitate to ask why a file has to go along a convoluted path, because they fear being regarded as ignoramuses. Little do they know that the government has a time-honoured system of working on files, which has hardly changed in over a century. All aspects of dealing with files—how they are to be created, how decisions are to be made and recorded on them, how they are to be closed and for how long they

29

are to be stored—are described meticulously in manuals of office procedure issued by every government.

The *Karnataka Government Secretariat Manual of Office Procedure*[1] is a typical example of such rules of red tape. The first edition of the *Secretariat Manual* was issued in 1904 by the Mysore princely state and was reviewed in 1915, 1925, 1947 and 1956. This manual was recast into a manual of office procedure in 1958, just after the Princely State of Mysore was enlarged. The 1958 *Manual* was revised in 1967 and in 1985, following which there was a twenty-year hiatus; probably it was thought that the *Manual* was then perfect in all respects. The latest revision was made in 2005. While there are some significant changes in the 2005 *Manual* as compared to the previous one, fundamentally, it remains, like most holy books, a cumulative text. Even as new processes are brought in, bureaucrats are sentimental about retaining the wisdom of their ancestors. Very little has changed in how files are created, dealt and disposed of. What we have then, is an impressive and weighty book, with 287 rules, that describe what is to be done in every conceivable circumstance.

Pic 1: A government file

A file is a collection of paper held in close proximity. It is maintained in a file cover, which is usually made from harder, inflexible cardboard. The *Secretariat Manual* orders that no file shall be submitted to a senior officer without being wrapped in what is known as a file board and with its cover closed, a bookmark inserted at the particular page where the latest note or minute has been recorded. A file board comprises a stiff cardboard with two flaps. One flap has the words 'urgent' written on it and the other 'ordinary' and these are randomly placed one over the other while enclosing the file within the file board. Since government files, unlike the government, tend to be very flexible, they are wrapped within the board and the two flaps to retain their shape.

The *Secretariat Manual* has detailed rules on how to use file boards. For instance, the officer examining a file may need to refer to a book, law or rules. In such cases, Rule 176 (vii) mandates that such publications should be placed on top of the file board flaps and then bound neatly and strongly by means of the string attached to the board in a bow tie. However, when two files are linked, the manoeuvre with the file board is a tad more complex. Rule 177 (ii) informs us that in such a circumstance, strings of the file board of the lower file, but not its flaps, shall be tied round the upper file. The strings of the file board of the upper file shall be tied underneath it in a bow out of the way. Each file, we are confidently informed, will thus be intact with all its papers properly arranged on its board.

That was easy.

Pic 2: A file board

Yet, a description of the knotting technique to hold file boards in place, however detailed, still does not explain why file boards are required. Is it some English quirk, derived from a long forgotten tradition, which was imported into India and then retained here, long after its original utility was forgotten?

Someone vastly more informed than I, told me that file boards owe their existence to mules.

Apparently, when the British took to the Himalayas to escape from the searing heat of the plains, the entire secretariat of the Government of India was transported to Shimla. Before the advent of the narrow gauge hill railway that wound its way up from Kalka, the preferred mode of transport for government files to Shimla was on muleback. The saddlebags that were slung over the unfortunate mules were not kind to un-boarded files. Hence, file boards were introduced to offer stiffness to the files. The mules left, the train came, the British left, the Indians came. But file boards carry on.

Contents of the file, which, contrary to popular public perception, might not always be paper, are typically bound by a multicoloured woven cotton thread, which is bound by metal clasps at both ends to prevent it from unravelling. These threads were earlier manufactured by prisoners as part of their rehabilitation activities in jail, but I am told, after liberalization and globalization, they are purchased from the lowest tenderer. It is of utmost importance that the thread does not unravel, because if it does, the file does too and along with it, life itself.

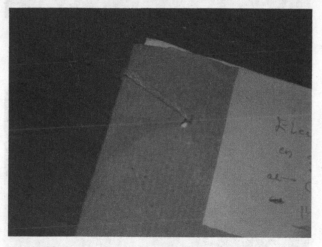

Pic 3: The string that holds papers, policies and decisions together. The phrase 'life hangs by a thread' was derived from the Indian government file.

A hole is provided at the top, left hand corner of a closed file cover, through which the cotton string is drawn in a manner that enables papers to be strung within the innards of the file.

Pic 4: The right way to string the string through a file
wrapper (inside view)

Pic 5: Close-up to show how papers are 'filed', elegantly
using the multicoloured string

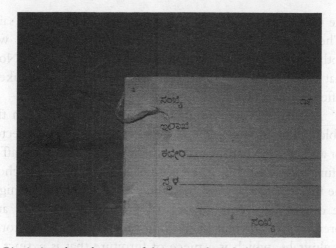

Pic 6: Another close-up of the string threaded through the file wrapper. In a far-reaching measure of administrative reform, holes in file wrappers were provided with metal eyelets, sometime in the mid-nineties.

Since all decisions in the government are taken on files, if your petition or subject is not on a file, you are scum. This is a sobering reflection for activists who protest against government decisions, or have a request to make of the government. Following my exit from the cozy confines of government, I once participated in a strike, following which we went in a delegation, yelling rousing slogans, to the state governor to submit a memorandum. His Excellency, having been adequately warned beforehand, had asked for the undersecretary of the department concerned to be present. It is easy to recognize the undersecretary in any gathering: he is the one who clutches the file. Following the ceremonial deposition of the memorandum to the governor, we repaired to his living room for biscuits and tea. The governor turned wordlessly to the undersecretary.

He raised the dog-eared sheaf of papers, waved it and said, 'The matter is being examined on file, saar!' There was nothing more to say. Subdued and satisfied, we left. Now that we were being considered on file, we would make a difference and change the trajectory of this country.

All files are dog-eared. Leave a neat, new file on the table and by the next day, its corners are frayed. I suspected for a long time that the government employs surplus staff in a furtive second shift, their sole occupation being to chew the four corners of files. In reality, this phenomenon might be caused by a combination of prosaic factors. First and foremost, files do not fit in filing cabinets. They are stored in almirahs, which is a piece of furniture that is extinct in the private sector. Almirahs are made of the finest teak (again provided by the lowest tenderer) and are thoughtfully perforated to permit the ingress of rodents. In fact, a really good file smells of sweat and rat's urine.

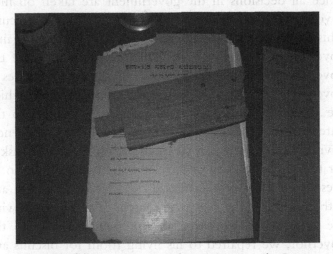

Pic 7: A file following some tender ministrations by Rattus, a rodent that lives in government offices in great numbers

Pic 8: A close-up showing the aesthetics of the fine art of dog-earing, courtesy rats

Wooden almirahs are now being replaced by ugly metal ones, painted in grey Hammerite, referred to as 'Godrejes'. This has not brought down the phenomenon of rats attending to files, for the reason that Godrejes are not used to store files, but typically contain tiffin boxes, cartons of cotton strings, pins, new file covers, file punches, exhausted laser printer cartridges, obsolete extension phone receivers and other essentials. In the new age government office, files are usually stored on top of the Godrejes, or on the floor, a practice that is much appreciated by rodents, big and small.

Astute observers of Pic 5 would have noticed that there were papers tagged on to the right side of the file, but not on the left side. The papers on the left side were removed to show you how papers are tagged on to a file. In reality, no side of a file is wasted.

The right side of the file is termed the correspondence side. This is where all objects that are received in the office, which pertain to the subject matter of the file, are tagged. The oldest object is numbered one and progressive additions are then numbered serially, so that the one on the top bearing the highest number, is the most recently added object to the file.

Observant readers will notice that I have used the term 'object', rather than 'paper' to describe what gets filed. I once enthusiastically pursued the idea of creating databases of panchayat bank accounts and wrote to all states to send the information to us on CDs. In the first decade of the twenty-first century, that was state of the art. I began to promptly receive couriered CDs, neatly wrapped in bubble wrap; they were too precious to be sent by lowly India Post. I sent them down to my office staff; the correct term is to 'mark them down' for being compiled and promptly forgot all about them. A few months later, I inquired what had happened and the file was submitted. All the CDs had been neatly impaled and strung up on the correspondence side, not having, in their passage to the file, been anywhere near a CD drive.

Yes, every object of worth gets filed.

The left side of the file is termed the note sheet. Typically, note sheets are pale green in colour and are longer than the cover of the file, which in turn, you will recall, is larger than a filing cabinet. These time-honoured measures are intended to ensure faster dog-earing. The note sheet is where decisions are taken and recorded for posterity. Language is an important matter here. In most states, file decisions are written in the local language, except by some decision-makers, schooled in the old ways, who have a chronic dread of doing so. I worked with one such individual at a time when the state of Karnataka switched over from using English on the note sheets to recording decisions in Kannada, the local language. Overnight, my suave, all-knowing colleague turned into a blubbering nitwit, being unable to read or comprehend anything, even a note recommending an application for leave. His terrified response on seeing a Kannada note was to painfully scrawl in Kannada '*da cha*' and his initials below as an apology of his Kannada signature.

'Da cha' stands for '*dayavittu charchisi*', which in turn, means, 'please discuss'. This is the long-standing escape route for the indecisive bureaucrat. Once 'da cha' or its equivalent in any language is written, a standard operating procedure follows. The underling who submitted the file is called in to explain its contents to the officer in question, who, when he understands the matter, writes '*charchisiddene*' (I have discussed) and then approves the file. If the officer does not approve the suggestion made, the underling records a sanitized note that contains the proceedings of the discussion and the modified decision. When all is agreed, the boss writes charchisiddene and the deed is done.

You would be surprised how high someone can go, by just being able to write 'da cha' and 'charchisiddene' on file.

Once, my wife, then employed in the government, brought a large file home for examination and I watched her as she wrote a long note late into the night, muttering curses through clenched teeth. She had just undergone a change of boss and the new head of the office was a suspicious man. The file pertained to the purchase of soaps for the washrooms in my wife's office. From the time of the Mysore Maharajah, the office had purchased Mysore Sandal Soap. These are unmistakable objects for anyone familiar with Karnataka, pale, oval-shaped and emitting the pleasant fragrance of sandalwood. What's more, they are manufactured by the government soap factory, fully owned by the Government of Karnataka, so they can be purchased without floating an international tender. Yet, my wife's boss was not convinced of the propriety of the purchase. So he wrote 'da cha' and called her in to enlighten him. After having convinced him that purchasing Mysore Sandal Soap did not involve any serious financial impropriety, my wife was asked to prepare a 'self-contained note', which would begin with a description of the washing habits of government staff in the state of Mysore from the time of Tipu Sultan till modern times and end with an audit-proof justification of why the office should continue to purchase Mysore Sandal Soap. My helpful suggestion that one could buy a bar of cheap blue detergent from a wholesale bazaar and proffer slim slices of these to senior officers was greeted with a volley of abuse from my wife, not appropriate for recording in this book or being put up on file.

The subject of 'self-contained' notes brings me to the role of staff in government offices, whose job is to create files by tagging objects on the correspondence side and submitting the introductory notes on the note sheet. Once every government file is 'built', it then has to be 'put up'. These are technical terms that anybody dealing with a government office needs to understand; they are bandied about across India. Visit a government office in Bengaluru and you will hear people solemnly affirming in meetings, with expressions of great gravity, 'File put up *aagide* [has been done]'; or 'File build up *maadtha iddene* [am building up the file]'. The same statement is made in countless government offices across India in several languages.

Every file has to be titled, for which there are elaborate rules. Rule 182 of the *Secretariat Manual* explains this as concisely as it is possible. We are told that the subject given to a file is called its 'title'. It should be as brief as possible but should give, at a glance, sufficient indication of the contents of the file so as to serve as an aid to its identification. The title should be divided into (a) head, (b) subhead or subheads and (c) content.

That is when things get a bit fuzzy.

Subrule 182 (i) (a) enlightens us that the important word that is placed first in the title, by which its alphabetical position in the index is determined and on which primarily depends the possibility of finding the title in the index, is called the 'head'. The head must be a word or words that naturally occurs to anyone who wants the papers. It must not be too wide. Subrule 182 (i) (b) says that the head is to be followed by a subhead or subheads, which should be more indicative of the precise subject of the file than the head. In selecting subheads the consideration to be borne in mind is to be the same as in selecting the head, namely, that the word or words selected should be such as are likely to strike anyone in need of the papers contained in the file. Where it is necessary to have more than one subhead in a title, the *Manual* informs us that 'the wider and more abstract generally come before the narrower and more concrete'. Finally, subrule 182 (i) (c) says that the content, which is a brief expression of the exact subject of the file, is to come next.

Just in case we were not sure of how to use words like heads, subheads and content, subrule 182 (iv) says that the whole title head, subhead and content should consist mainly of substantives, adjectives, where necessary, and participles. Minor parts of speech should be excluded, as far as possible, to make a strict alphabetical arrangement practicable. The title should be articulated or broken up into parts, each consisting of as few words as possible and each expressing an element in the subject matter. Each is to begin with a capital letter and separated from the preceding one by a bold dash.

As far as possible, I have used the exact words from the *Manual*.

In case you are clueless how that worked, the *Manual*, most helpfully, provides examples. For example, if the question examined on the file is on whether it is necessary under the Public Service Commission (PSC) (Consultation) Regulations to consult the PSC in proposals regarding the extension of service of officers holding tenure posts, then the title of the file would be PSC (Consultation) Regulations – Tenure Posts – Extension of Service – Consultation Whether Necessary.

Still clueless? Never mind.

Putting up a file commences with the writing of a note on the green note sheet, tagged on to the left hand side of the file as seen when you open it. Stuff is written on the left side based on an examination of the objects and papers tagged on to the right side—the correspondence side—of the file.

Let us say that you have written a letter requesting a government office to do something it is supposed to do, say, sanction a scholarship for you. Your letter will be received by the receipt and dispatch clerk, who will take a cursory look at it and forward it to a dealing assistant—a clerk for the old-fashioned—to whom it is to go. The dispatch clerk does not have the most exciting job in the world, but performs a critical function in the office. Once the receipt and dispatch clerk deals with all the letters opened in the morning, these are handed over to the office attendant (or peon, as this individual was known in the old days), who delivers them to the clerks concerned—in your case, the one who deals with scholarships. That individual then tags your letter on to a file—he either creates a new file for dealing with your case or if yours is a pending matter, tags your letter to the already existing file.

Presuming that yours is a new case and a file has been created to deal with the issue of giving you a scholarship, the dealing assistant has to write a note on the note sheet. The first note has to be self-contained and must relate the gist of your letter, examine whether you are eligible for the scholarship and then suggest whether your application is to be accepted or rejected. The file is then submitted to the next level and so on, till it reaches the level at which a decision is taken, following which the file is returned to the person authorized to communicate the decision to you. There are rules that say no file should be delayed for more than five days at any level. So if a letter is received by a dealing assistant from the receipt and dispatch clerk, a file should be built up within five days.

All this sounds perfectly logical and does work in many offices.

If things go wrong, the genesis of the problem is often a badly drafted self-contained note. The villains of the piece are 'flags', which are strips of paper pinned to things tagged on the correspondence side to identify them. The stodgy old pinned flags have now undergone makeovers; they are now sleek Post-it multicoloured stickers. These flags are numbered or identified by alphabets.

Flags make dealing assistants lazy. With their advent, dealing assistants have taken to writing notes such as these on files:

'Please peruse letter at Flag B and the circular of the government at Flag C. In accordance with the rule at Flag C (AA), kind orders are solicited on items B (a), (d) and (m).'

These are not self-contained notes. A friend of mine, weary of receiving notes of such remarkable brevity, once spent a whole afternoon de-flagging a file that had more flags on it than a porcupine has quills and then sent it back with the admonition, 'Where are the flags?'

You should be thankful that was not your scholarship file.

There are a few unwritten rules on how you should write on files that are meticulously followed. One is that the note should always be written in passive voice. You cannot, on a government file write, 'I believe we should do blah and so, I recommend blah.' That is rank bad form. The correct way to express your view is, 'It is believed that blah and so it is recommended that blah be done.'

Another rule was related to me by a crusty senior several years ago. 'Never commit yourself, even if you are certain about something,' he said, 'always say "perhaps". It is a useful word.' He never deviated from this rule. He once wrote on file, 'As the sun may perhaps rise in the east at 7 a.m. tomorrow, it may be prudent for the minister to advance his tour by an hour. For kind orders to instruct the tehsildar accordingly.'

Some people take their note writing very seriously, to the extent that after a few years in the government, they become human manifestations of self-contained notes. I have come across many such specimens in the government.

We often wondered how one of them, the Roger Federer of file noting, might have proposed to his fiancée. We were sure he would have popped the question thus:

'Please refer to our discussions of the seventh ante where inter alia, I had invited your attention to the pending reference concerning the issue of our entering into holy wedlock at an opportune moment in the near future. This is a reminder to your kind self to solicit your attention to the need to pass kind orders on this pending proposal. This may be considered mutatis mutandis to my expression of undying love to you at the secretariat bus stop on the evening of the aforesaid date.'

But perhaps, the most telling note was also one of the shortest that I saw on a file. It was written by Mani Shankar Aiyar, a gentleman with a strong bias for English as the English uses it. Aiyar snorted with irritation at a note sent by Montek Singh Ahluwalia, the then deputy chairperson of the Planning Commission, that was written in the latter's breezy, American style and marked it to me with a terse note, 'Please examine the full Monty.'

Finally, when decisions emerge from files, they have to be communicated to the world at large. This is where the drafters of the *Secretariat Manual*, alive and living, have shown their prowess. The *Secretariat Manual* contains no less than ten forms of written communication that emerge from a secretariat department or office. These are letters, proceedings, official memoranda, circulars, demiofficial letters, unofficial notes, press communiques or notes, notifications, endorsements and telegrams. After stressing that each of these forms has a specific use and phraseology of its own, the *Manual* helpfully points to an appendix that gives specimens of each one of these forms of communication.

The letter is the most usual form of formal communication to authorities outside the government. It has nine parts, namely, the letterhead bearing the names, addresses and contact details of the state government and the department concerned, the number and date of communication, the designation of the sender, the designation of the addressee, a salutation, the subject, the subscription and the signature. All letters to authorities to start with the salutation 'Sir'. However, letters to individuals and associations of individuals start with 'Dear Sir'. All official letters terminate with the subscription 'yours faithfully' followed by the signature and designation of the person signing the letter.

Authorities have every reason to be peeved that they are not dear to the letter writer.

If letters were not enough to oil the wheels of the government in order that they revolve smoothly, the government also has the delightful instrument of the demiofficial (DO) letter. The *Secretariat Manual* informs us that such a letter is used 'in correspondence between government officers for an interchange of communication of opinion or information without the formality of the prescribed procedure'. It is to be used 'when it is desired that a matter should receive the personal attention of the individual addressed or when it is intended to bring to the personal notice of an officer a case in which action has been delayed and official reminders have failed to elicit reply'. Thus, a DO letter is written in the first person singular in a personal tone to an officer and using the salutation 'My dear' or 'Dear' and terminating with 'yours sincerely'. It is to be signed by the writer without mentioning their designation.

In other words, a DO letter is written when nobody has read the letter that was written in the first place on the subject concerned.

There are strict rules about when DO letters are to be written. A bureaucrat cannot write, according to the *Secretariat Manual*, a DO letter to a minister. This prohibition is certainly not based on the rationale that ministers read everything—they don't—but because for a bureaucrat to consider a minister as 'Dear', or even worse, as 'My dear', would be rank bad form.

The next communication form in order of importance is 'proceedings'. This is the sombre, portentous style of communication of financial sanction, disciplinary proceedings involving imposition of a penalty on government servants or orders or decisions of general applicability on important questions of policy. The *Manual* prescribes that 'all proceedings shall be drafted in the third person and it shall contain a preamble that explains the circumstances or reasons why the proposal concerned was actuated, followed by a crisp and self-explanatory decision'. Proceedings usually end with invoking the name of the formal head of the government and are signed on behalf of whoever that might be.

A notification may look similar to 'proceedings' at first sight, but it is not quite the same thing. A notification is an introductory statement that accompanies legal enactments to be published so as to come into force or an information sheet that promulgates to the world that someone has been transferred or posted or has had leave granted.

The final form of outward communication is the endorsement, which is used when a paper is returned in original to the sender or is referred to another department or to an attached or subordinate office for necessary action.

Official memoranda (OM) are used for correspondence between the departments. There is a breezy air to an OM; they are written in the third person and without a salutation or a subscription, like how one would engage in banter in a WhatsApp argument. A circular differs from a memorandum in that it is often addressed to many people or offices and the subject matter does not warrant the formality of the proceedings form.

If that was not delightfully vague and confusing enough, we have another form of internal communication between government departments, namely, the unofficial note. This method is generally employed in secretariat departments for obtaining the views and comments of each other on their proposals.

Just as modern metropolises are built on the ruins of earlier settlements, manuals rest on a foundation of old wisdom that is not easily given up. Thus, the 2005 version of the *Secretariat Manual* recognizes that telegrams may be used, albeit only on occasions of urgency. While they should be concise, the *Manual* tells us that clarity should, however, not be sacrificed for brevity.

What is the status accorded to emails as a formal means of government communication? The *Manual* does not throw too much of light on this matter. None of the precision with which it describes how file boards are to be knotted is apparent. One can only infer the status of emails from two lines in the *Manual* that refer to them.

Section 127 (ii) of the *Manual*, which follows after the detailed descriptions of all the different modes of communication, says that these communications can be sent both by normal modes of delivery, such as hand delivery or post, but depending upon the availability of facilities and keeping in view the urgency, these can be sent or transmitted by email as well. We are also informed elsewhere that no telegram should be sent where email can serve the purpose.

Clearly then, an email is not a communication that is in the same league as letters, DO letters, proceedings, circulars or OMs, but is merely a mode of conveyance of these communications. They are, however, a substitute for telegrams, which is listed as a form of communication. It does not matter that telegrams have now passed into history, with the postal department having given up this century-old mode of message transmission.

So we stand at a crossroads now. Does or does not an email constitutes a formal communication from the government? As far as I can infer, an email is only a mode of communication and not a communication in itself. Thus, if a 'communication' as defined in the *Secretariat Manual* is to be communicated through email, it is best sent as an attachment.

Please note that the *Manual* has nothing to say about the official status of Twitter handles, Facebook posts and Instagram pictures of government departments or government offices. Perhaps, we shall have the answer in a decade or two, when the *Secretariat Manual* is next revised.

Since files are the lifeline of governments, filing systems assume great significance. The government system has remained more or less the same since the British left. Every individual who deals with a file is to maintain a dispatch and receipt register for noting the movement of files to and fro through her hand. Various abstracts are maintained and reviewed every month to ensure that such housekeeping measures are followed. Thus, the dealing assistant notes in her register the date and time when the file was handed over to the next level, say, a section officer or an undersecretary. That officer too, when the file leaves her hand, notes down the date and time when the file moves on to the next level. At senior levels, every officer has a private secretary whose job, along with intimidating and obstructing any lay individual who wishes to meet the officer concerned, is also to maintain the dispatch and receipt registers to record the route of travel of the file.

This system has been streamlined a great deal through e-governance, with states such as Karnataka now having computerized file dispatch and receipt registers. This enables reports to be generated on who are delaying files, which is occasionally reviewed within the government. Other improvements include automatic alerts on phone for senior officers when files are delayed beyond prescribed limits. These changes have been formally recognized in the latest version of the *Secretariat Manual*, which contains screenshots of the various computer-based formats to track file movement.

Some departments make file movement information available to the public through their websites. At one stage, touchscreens were proudly installed in the foyers of government offices to show file movements. These stand-alone touchscreens looked very smart and instantly upgraded the décor of government offices. However, very soon they began to malfunction, resulting in signboards hung across their faces, made from discarded file covers and strung with the same string used to hold files together, saying 'under maintenance'. This was not pleasing to the eye. Therefore, most touchscreens were banished to the same place where old almirahs and Godrejes go—underneath the staircases or in stairwells.

For long, the holy grail of red-tape reformers in the government was to aim for government offices to go paperless. Early efforts towards building a paperless government file system mimicked the conventional paper system to the T, with correspondence and file noting sides appearing on the monitor. Electronic filing began with scanning of all paper correspondence and then uploading those documents into the correspondence side. Officers were expected to electronically write their notes on the note-sheet side and then forward the note to the next in line in the decision-making process. On its return journey, decisions were finally printed on paper for the record of people concerned, but all processes in between did not require the preparation and recording of notes on paper. However, even though the first vendors of such systems to the government were able to make impressive presentations about how a paperless office would function, the idea of going fully paperless never caught on. Though several efforts were made to convert files into electronic documents in an effort to go paperless, these did not fully succeed, except in a few departments or services.

The government is stubbornly loyal to the paper file. Unless a government office is buried under paper, preferably with fetid odour, it does not look and feel like a government office. Paper lends gravitas to the doings of a government office, in ways that images on a computer screen cannot match. There are many reasons cited by the government as justification for not going entirely paperless. Citizens, we are told, are immensely satisfied if their file is called for, momentous decisions are taken in front of them and recorded in the file, and endorsements and letters written on paper are handed out. The second reason cited for retaining paper is that the paperless filing system cannot transcend the boundaries between departments or between them and their field offices. Thus, letters will necessarily have to be printed to convey instructions from one office to the other, we are told. That reason does not hold water, because if the paperless system is configured as a continuous chain of decision-making that flows without obstruction from the field unit to the department concerned, or between departments, then the paperless system can work across these artificial boundaries. The third reason, which is equally fallacious, is that paper data can be stored securely whereas electronic data is vulnerable to being hacked.

That brings me to the next part of the filing story, namely, how files are stored and protected. All files are divided into four categories from the perspective of how long they need to be preserved. Files classified into the 'A' category—known as 'A-dis' files—are to be stored forever. B-dis files are to be preserved for thirty years, C-dis for ten years and D-dis for one year. This classification is so ingrained into government jargon that insults too are patterned on this. I have seen government officers referring to others that they do not care for very much as E-dis: not worth keeping even for a minute.

Not for a moment should one be naïve enough to believe that because files are on paper, or are stored in accordance with strict protocols, they are not vulnerable to being tampered. Instances are numerous, particularly in cases of a sensitive nature, of important files having disappeared. A file need not disappear in toto; it often serves the nefarious purpose concerned if parts of the file go missing.

Many years ago, while serving in the health department secretariat, I had to deal with a file that concerned a criminal case filed by the drug controller, the regulatory authority that kept a close watch on the quality of drugs sold in the state. The controller had nabbed an Ayurvedic practitioner whose magic remedy for asthma—he prescribed sixteen doses of it for a complete cure—was laced liberally with steroids. It was an open-and-shut case as the test reports were clinching evidence. However, the chief minister, who was also holding charge as the health minister temporarily, was influenced to take a lenient view of the matter. In my opinion, there was no way that the man could have been condoned. The Drug Control Act prescribed severe punishment, including a minimum period of incarceration in jail for the selling of misbranded allopathic drugs. When I submitted the file to my boss, recommending prosecution under the Drug Control Act, he, having been suitably briefed by interested parties, conducted an inquiry, established that there was prima facie evidence of adulteration, but recommended action against the Ayurvedic practitioner for the crime of having sold a misbranded Ayurvedic drug—an offence that carried a small fine as punishment. The chief minister approved the latter action. When the file was returned to me, I was horrified. Considering that the active ingredient in the concoction sold as an Ayurvedic drug was an allopathic off-the-shelf corticosteroid, I pleaded for a reconsideration of the case, that it must be treated as a case of misbranding of an allopathic drug. To my boss's credit, he sent the file back to the CM for his reconsideration. The chief minister overruled me and reiterated his earlier decision—to let the Ayurvedic practitioner off with a rap on the knuckles. We were ordered by the CM's office to take action as instructed and return the file to the CM's office to prove compliance.

Soon afterwards, the government fell and president's rule was imposed. The file was promptly returned from the CM's office. The last inch bit of the file note sheet, where the CM had endorsed a thoroughly wrong decision, was neatly snipped out with a pair of scissors. The matter did not end there because I had taken the precaution of photocopying the file before sending it to the CM— an unauthorized action on my part, but necessary in the circumstances. The photocopy showed the CM's signature. The matter was then handed over to investigation agencies for an inquiry, but as usual, nothing came of it.

What then, of the future? How long will India continue to grapple with the problems of twenty-first-century governance using nineteenth-century tools? How long will paper files continue? Clearly, incremental reforms such as computerization of a few registers that track file movement, while still retaining files in paper, have run their course. Dreams of leapfrogging to a paperless filing system have also been abandoned; too many officers firmly believe in the standard excuses against paperless systems, for instance, that these are incapable of straddling departmental boundaries. Besides, most officers think that there is no time for the government to pause and switch processes. There is no glamour associated with managing the uncertain transition to a new system. While solutions based on block-chain technology are being discussed enthusiastically, no one seems to know what precisely they mean. One of the dilemmas is whether one should go in for an overall reengineering or whether decentralized process reforms are the answer. Going by the government's record, decentralized software deployment for process streamlining, while giving it initial, celebrated success, soon reached a dead end and left it with the problem of dealing with inter-operability of different systems. Something popular with the government is to sponsor hackathons for process reforms and invite young innovators to participate. But all too often, these focus narrowly on single-process solutions, which means that the government still does not move forward in a manner where it knows where it is going.

All in all, it looks as if knowing when to use the salutation 'Sir', 'Dear Sir' or 'My Dear Sir', and when to sign off 'faithfully', or 'sincerely' will be the key to effectively running the government for some years to come.

3

How to Get into the Civil Services

People enter the civil services through selection processes supervised and conducted by the public service commissions, which are mandated by the Constitution for the Union and each state respectively, and whose status is circumscribed and protected from interference. The chairpersons and members of public service commissions are appointed by the Union or the respective state government. As far as possible, half of the members of each public service commission ought to have been experienced officers of the government, either of the state or the Union. They are to hold office for six years and up to the age of sixty-five or sixty-two years, in the Union and state commissions respectively. During that period, they have special protections; they can be removed only by the President of India on the ground of misbehaviour, after having first referred the matter to the Supreme Court and obtained their opinion. Members and chairpersons of public service commission are considered to be guilty of misbehaviour if they become interested or concerned in any government contract or agreement. In order to ensure their impartiality, members or chairpersons of these commissions are prohibited from any further employment, other than to be the chairperson or member of the Union Public Service Commission. Likewise, the chairperson of the Union Public Service Commission is ineligible for any other government employment. All expenses of the public services commissions are directly borne on the Union or state consolidated funds, as the case may be.

The Constitution says that public services commissions must conduct examinations for appointments to the services of the Union and the services of the state respectively. Barring a few exceptions stated in the Constitution, the government shall also mandatorily consult the public service commission concerned on matters concerning recruitment to the civil services, principles to be followed in making or checking the suitability of candidates to appointments, promotions and transfers from one service to another and disciplinary matters.

So, as systems go, the arm's-length distance at which the public service commissions are placed from the government is to ensure that selection processes are free from bias. One cannot fault the system design.

The selection process itself has undergone change over the years, which means that most advice based on the experience of successful candidates of the distant past is irrelevant for current aspirants. The entrance examination to the pre-Independence Indian Civil Service (ICS) was highly biased towards the selection of candidates who had a thorough knowledge of the British system. Even though these examinations were open to Indians from the late 1880s onwards, nobody in their right minds thought of selecting Indian Indians. The choice was exclusively in favour of those Indians who, for all practical purposes, were Englishmen except for their darker skins. Since the written examination would not reveal the breeding of the candidate, the interview was of prime importance; it would reveal to the imperial government whether the candidate, in spite of a good performance in the written exam, had sufficient English ways and manners on which to build upon. My father, though having suffered untouchability in his early days, acquired enough skills and knowledge to get through the written examinations for the ICS. But he did not make the grade at the interview. Conducted at Metcalfe House in Delhi, my father recalled that there was a rueful shaking of the head when he mentioned that he was the first generation of those who had obtained a graduate degree in his family and that his father was illiterate and his mother barely literate. No; his antecedents and family background was not of the type that would do the ICS much good.

By and large, the ethos of the ICS examination continued well after Independence. The examination tested verbal skills—in English alone, mind you, one could not write the examination in any other language—and was biased in favour of the humanities subjects. There was clockwork regularity in the conduct of the written examination; they always started on 30 September, with three general papers that everybody had to write. The first test was a general essay, where the candidate had to write an essay on a subject chosen from a list. The same afternoon, a general knowledge examination was held. The next day, in the forenoon, there was a general English paper, which included a section on logic. In the general knowledge and general English papers, there were no objective or multiple-choice questions. One could not tick mark one's way through. These papers were for 150 marks each.

Following upon the general papers, each candidate was to appear for three 'lower' papers, which he could choose from a list of twenty-three subjects mostly tilted towards the humanities. A wider choice was available with respect to some academic disciplines. For example, those who wished to write their lower papers in history could choose from Mughal history, to ancient Indian, European and British history and so on. In contrast, subjects such as engineering and medicine were not offered as choices. The lower papers carried 200 marks each.

After a three-month gap, the Union Public Service Commission announced a list of candidates, selected on the basis of their performance in the general and lower papers. These candidates were eligible to appear at the next level of examinations, which comprised two 'higher' papers, again to be chosen from a list of fifteen subjects and with each paper carrying 200 marks. Both the lower and higher papers were of a postgraduate standard of syllabus. The next milestone was the interview. These started in March of the year following that in which the examinations were held. Every day, ten candidates were interviewed, five before and five after lunch. If any woman candidates were on the interview list, they were the third to be interviewed. The interview carried 300 marks.

The examination system also provided for a separation between the rigour applied to the selection of a few key services that were considered to be higher in the hierarchy and other services. Thus, the higher paper marks were taken into account for the selection into the Indian Administrative Service and the Indian Foreign Service (IFS), while not being considered for selection into the Indian Police Service (IPS), the revenue service, the audits and accounts services and so on.

In 1976, the D.S. Kothari Committee,[1] set up the previous year to recommend reforms in the selection process for the civil services, gave a detailed report. The committee stressed the need for the government to cast the net wider to secure talent in various fields, rather than continuing to focus, as the British did, on securing those who imbibed and lived an Anglo-oriented culture. With this focus in mind, the committee recommended that the selection examination ought to be held in more towns, apart from the major cities. Continuing its focus to enable those from the weaker sections of society to write the examination, the committee recommended increasing the age limit for writing the exam to twenty-six years, with further age relaxation in the case of those from the Scheduled Castes and the Scheduled Tribes. Examinations could be written in any of the languages listed in the Eighth Schedule of the Constitution. The differential rigour applied to the selection of the IAS and the IFS was given up and a common entrance examination mooted for all civil services, on the ground that all entrants into the civil services needed the same strong foundations of ethical values and service orientation. The Kothari Committee recommended that the combined civil services examination ought to be a four-stage selection process, comprising a screening test to determine eligibility to write the written examinations, followed by the main written examination, an interview and finally, another written examination following the common foundation course conducted by the Lal Bahadur Shastri National Academy of Administration (LBSNAA). The government did not accept the last recommendation on the ground that a post-training test could be fraught with undesirable subjectivity given the hierarchies of caste and class prevalent in India. However, the rest of the recommendations were put in place for the examinations commencing from 1979 onwards.

The system as recommended by the Kothari Committee was in place when I wrote the examination. There was an objective type preliminary examination to screen the large number of aspirants and reduce the field to a more easily handled ten thousand or so. This preliminary examination was completed in a day, and comprised a general knowledge paper and a paper in a subject of the candidate's choice. There was no negative marking, which meant that if one did not know the answer to any question, there was no risk involved in guesswork, either educated or wild. For those who cleared it, the preliminary examination marks did not matter any further in the selection process. Those selected for the main examinations had to write eight papers. These were two papers each in general studies—the term 'general knowledge' had become old-fashioned by then—and two optional subjects. In addition, there were papers in general English and one Indian language, which had cut off marks that needed to be cleared in order to be selected. The actual marks obtained in the language papers did not matter any further in the selection process. Finally, if one cleared these examinations, there was an interview. There was no minimum cut-off level of marks for the interview, so even if someone did abysmally badly in it, he could make it through if he had enough marks in the written exam. Studious, shrinking violets stood a chance.

I did not particularly want to join the IAS; I was more interested in becoming a marine biologist. However, opportunities were very limited in the early eighties and I meandered, as usual, to sitting for the civil services. Another motivating factor was that I wanted to marry my girlfriend and I thought this would be the best way to get over any potential objections in a cross-country romance. On a much later date, a conversation with two high performing officers in the government of India confirmed that such motivations are all too frequent. A lot of people, at least in my generation, wrote the exams to win over girlfriends or boyfriends or to spite them.

I started studying for the exam in 1980 or thereabouts, even though I was a few months too young to appear for the exam in 1980. I took my first shot at the exam in 1981. Those days, Delhi University—at least the humanities stream classes was suffused with the civil services madness. Everybody was preparing for it, except some misguided souls that—horror of horrors—wanted to join the private sector or those in professional courses like law who had set their minds on becoming lawyers. Preparations for the civil services exams darkened one's carefree existence like a billowing grey cloud. Everything about the civil services was considered a black art. Classmates and seniors, particularly those who had already appeared for the examinations, failed and continued their preparations for the next stab, undaunted, had their valuable insights into what would definitely click. The array of subjects on offer was also vast and that led to intense discussions on what subjects were 'scoring' and what were not. Thus, some sagely concluded, even if one was an economics student it did not make sense to choose economics as a subject. Public administration was a better choice. Psychology ruled for several years as a 'scoring subject', till the UPSC awoke to the inordinate number of those who opted for it and engineered a genocide of candidates who opted for psychology one year. Personally, I did not think too much about selection of subjects. The tactic of choosing scoring subjects and learning them from scratch did not appeal to me. So I chose an oddball combination of zoology and law. I had an honours undergraduate degree in zoology from Delhi University, liked the subject and was a reasonable whiz at it and law; I was in the final year of my undergraduate course in it, when I wrote the exam.

The preliminary examination was a cakewalk, given that I was a quiz freak, my general awareness was pretty good and I had reasonably good reading habits. I chose zoology as my subject of choice for the preliminary examination, because I felt it was a more precise subject than law and better suited for an objective, multiple-choice test.

Studying for the main examination started with looking at past question papers; there were bookstores in Connaught Place and a pavement vendor outside the UPSC office who sold these in slim volumes. Since the examination system had been changed in accordance with the recommendations of the Kothari Committee in 1980, the question bank for the new system was not too large. Initially, I joined a group of friends, seniors in the Campus Law Centre, who were studying for the exam. However, I realized soon that they were confusing and scaring me; all the time they were talking about trends or worrying about the large number of people writing the exam. I soon began to study alone, juggling my preparations for the examination with studying for my final two semesters of the law course.

I wrote the exam along with my law classes, got through the prelims, mains and finally, following the interview, I got a rank of 963, which meant I would make it into the group 'B' services. I was disappointed and vowed that I would do well next time around. I also realized that while my knowledge of the subjects of choice was reasonably good, I needed to be more systematic and organized in my presentation. I decided to join a good coaching school to prepare better for my next stab at the examination.

The classes at the Rau's study circle, in Delhi, were a revelation. Old man Rau, a hoarse-voiced bachelor who reeked of stale cigarette smoke, was a laconically precise coach. He rarely repeated himself, so one had to pay full attention to his low and sometimes indistinct voice. Not much was taught; the focus was on precision in stating out what one already knew. Rau had a few instructors who were ruthless in their testing of mock papers. His monologues on preparation for the examinations were often peppered with strategic guessing of topical information that might find their way into the current affairs section of the general studies paper. Some of Rau's tips for preparation were useful and stayed with me long after I ran the gauntlet of the examinations.

Rau's advice was as follows:

- Always pay attention to the question and answer to the point, in grammatically correct language. Whatever the language medium in which you write your answers, one must have top-class language skills. Science students needed to pay particular attention to their language, because often they did not fare well as their language skills, even while explaining their own subjects, were poor.
- If there is a word limit, stick to it. The questions are so designed to be answered in exactly the time provided. If one exceeds the word limit, not

only will one lose marks for the question, but one will also not have time to finish the examination paper.

- An answer paper is not only to test one's knowledge of the subject in question. It is also a test of how well one can organize and articulate one's thoughts on paper. So, do the little things that show that one is systematic and neat. Improve one's handwriting; leave a neat margin all around on the paper. Write question numbers prominently. At the end of an answer that has a word limit indicated, count the number of words and write them down in brackets. If the answer is about 5 words less than the limit, one is in a good zone and there will not be any negative marking. If one exceeds the word limit, one will lose marks.

- If one has a choice between attempting short-answer questions and writing a discursive answer to a single question, always choose the former, even if one may not know the answer to a few short-answer questions. For example, one may be faced with a choice between answering ten subquestions with two marks each (answers limited to two sentences) and writing an essay of 250 words on a subject that one thinks one knows well, also for twenty marks. One may discover that one knows the answers to six subquestions. Of the remaining four, one may not be sure about two questions but may be able to make educated guesses as to their answers and one may be clueless about the remaining two questions. One's uncertainty about four questions may drive one to choose to attempt the longer essay-type question. Yet, even if one writes an exceptional essay, one may not be able to get more than twelve to fourteen marks out of the possible twenty. However, if one attempts the short-answer questions, one would certainly get twelve marks for the six questions for which one knows the answers for sure. In addition, one also stands a good chance of raising that to sixteen marks if one's educated guesses are right. If the wild guesses turn out to be right, one may get the remaining marks too, Furthermore, answering short questions also leaves one with time to ponder other tricky questions and answer them in a measured fashion.

- Always answer the questions that one knows well, first. Displaying one's strengths in the first half of the paper gives the examiner a good impression and these things matter in the overall context. One will not lose marks for not answering questions in sequence, provided one mentions the question number prominently on the top of the answer.

To drive his point home, Rau's study circle conducted frequent mock exams, at least twice a week. His instructors were relentless in their criticism of our answers, laughed derisively at us and destroyed us with their strict marking, lending a new meaning to the term 'mock answers'. I started with a mere 30 per cent score initially and never crossed 52 per cent. In the final analysis, the mock examinations at Rau's were tougher than the final examination papers.

Rau's advice went beyond the technique of answering the general papers to cover the optional subjects as well. I believed that language skills mattered a great deal in all the papers. I took great care to write my zoology papers as if I were attempting an English paper, writing as if I were explaining scientific concepts to an intelligent novice, avoiding jargon as far as possible.

For the content of the subject papers, Rau was not of much help. So I studied alone at home. I did not stress myself too much. I slept well, nearly ten hours every day— eight hours at night and two hours for an afternoon snooze. I also went for an hour's walk in the evening.

I talked to myself all the time. As I was reading, I also wrote revision notes, constantly doodling as I wrote. I regret not having kept my revision notes; they were works of art, very elegantly prepared. I drew elaborate patterns, cars, monkey faces and wove anagrams from key words and acronyms that would remind me of things that I had to remember. I even made songs out of some concepts. I converted nearly everything to a visual or an audio content and then attempted to commit an entire page to memory. The idea was that if I had to answer a question, I would try to recall the entire page and read out from it in my mind's eye. The more the colour on the paper, the better it was for creating a visual memory of my notes.

Even apart from the Rau's mock exams, I wrote more of them. I wrote up the questions, timed my answers, stuck to word limits and marked myself.

For the general studies paper, I studied from the India yearbook published by the Ministry of Information and Broadcasting, Government of India. This book is invaluable for preparation and along with a few other yearbooks, for example, the *Manorama Yearbook* published by the Malayala Manorama group tells you almost everything contemporary that one needs to know about governance. I read that book every night too; there is no better cure for insomnia than publications of the Ministry of Information and Broadcasting. I abstracted relevant points from those yearbooks into my own notes.

I avoided other acquaintances appearing at the examination like the plague. Only two other friends, one my future wife and the other from my school, came over every now and then. Since both of them did not go to any coaching classes, I translated what I had learnt in class to them. That was useful for me as well. I did not speculate too much on the question paper or waste time with a larger circle. In the last days of preparation, I did not look beyond my own notes, with their calligraphy, cartoons and other attention-grabbing graphics. I slept well before each examination day.

One always knows when an exam goes well. I got that sense for all my papers, except one. In my second law paper, I finished four and a half questions out of five at first. For the last half question, I was flying blind. It was a case study and I did not recollect any precedent cases to quote. So I wrote the answer relying on my own pure reason and language. I was very upset after I finished that paper, I recollect. I had to pull myself together to prepare for the zoology paper. Since papers were arranged in the alphabetical order, I had about ten days to prepare for it. When the results came, I was utterly surprised that I had great marks for that law paper. On the other hand, in the first law paper covering constitutional and administrative law, I got low marks even though I felt I had done very well in that paper.

I had no problems with the interview. I have always had the gift of the gab and growing up in a large family meant I was always arguing a lot. I attended interview coaching classes in Rau's study circle only for three days, mainly as a pep talk. I was then working out of station and had to return to Delhi for a short while for the interview. Rau told us the usual things; to be neatly dressed and to be pleasant, even if one was asked a tricky question. One was also told to think for a couple of seconds before attempting an answer.

I recall very little from my interview. I dimly recollect that I was offered tea and after a question on Mother Teresa, I was asked to point out where Albania was on a map of the world. I got reasonably good marks for the interview, I recollect.

Did the post-Kothari Committee system achieve its objective of making the civil services more inclusive? Did it widen the field and increase heterogeneity? If so, at what price was this objective achieved? To answer these questions, regard has to be had to the extent to which the recommendations of several committees were considered and accepted or rejected. True to type, the government makes it as difficult as it is possible to make sense of the recommendations of these committees. While the reports of the Professor Yoginder K. Alagh Committee[2] and the Hota Committee[3] are available in the public domain, those of the Satish Chandra Committee,[4] the S.K. Khanna Committee and the Baswan Committee are not. The last mentioned is the latest and only rumours fly around as to what this report contains.

Suffice to say that these committees usually considered four or five aspects related to the entrance examinations, namely, the syllabus of the papers and the pattern of the examination, the extent of reservations of seats for various categories of aspirants, the age limit set for them to take a stab at the examination and the number of attempts they could take at it.

From a reading of the reports of these committees, or reports about the reports of these committees, one is struck by the extent to which the major recommendations were not accepted promptly, rather than the other way around. Take the Yogendra Alagh Committee, for instance. Of all the committees other than the Baswan Committee, the recommendations of which are still not released to the public, the Yogendra Committee stood, well, *alag* from the rest in terms of the paradigm changes it suggested. While its recommendation that the general studies paper ought to be replaced by a civil services aptitude test with emphasis on comprehension, logical reasoning, problem-solving and data analysis was partly accepted,[5] the one that the preliminary examination must carry a 25 per cent weightage in the overall scheme was not. Also rejected were the recommendations that the four optional papers ought to be replaced by three compulsory papers on sustainable development and social justice, science and technology in society and democratic governance, public systems management and human rights. That the interview should be replaced with an extensive testing comprising a personal information form, psychological tests and group tests followed by an interview was also not accepted.

With respect to the age limits and the number of times that candidates could write the examinations, both the

Satish Chandra and Yogendra Alagh committees preferred not to upset the apple cart. They recommended an upper age limit of twenty-six years for general candidates and age concessions for other categories.[6] Both concurred that general candidates could continue to have three attempts at the examination, and that SC, ST, OBC and physically handicapped candidates could have more.[7] The Hota Committee, which explored the wider area of civil services reforms, recommended a reduction of the upper age limit to twenty-four years and this was promptly rejected. In other words, the Hota Committee *nahin hua*.

What is undisputable is that the competition for entering the civil services has increased manifold. Furthermore, in the pre-Kothari Committee system, the IAS and the IFS were not in competition with the other services because those aspiring for these services had to write two extra 'higher papers'. In the post-Kothari Committee era, all aspirants had to appear for the same set of papers, even though the optional subjects could be chosen from a wider range of options.[8] This change meant that the levels of competition involved grew overwhelming. As I remember, in the early eighties, post the Kothari Committee report, the number of people writing the examination had risen to around two and a half lakh people. Of these, about 10,000 were declared eligible for the main exams, about 1800 were called for the interviews and 450 made it to the Group A civil services, with about 120 in the IAS. These are approximate figures. I have added a more detailed and contemporary reference below. The latest figures show that the competition is as intense, if not more. Less than 1 per cent of those who appear at the main examinations get through into any civil service.

	2013–14	2014–15	2015–16[9]
Number of applicants for the civil services preliminary examination	7,76,604	9,47,428	9,39,763
Number of aspirants who appeared for the civil services preliminary examination	3,24,279	4,46,623	4,63,418
Number of applicants for the civil services main examination	14,800	16,706	14,927
Number of aspirants appearing for the civil services preliminary examination	14,178	16,286	14,626
Number of candidates interviewed	3001	3303	
Number of candidates selected	1122	1363	
Number of women candidates selected	261	313	
Number of OBC category candidates selected	326	369	
Number of SC category candidates selected	187	196	
Number of ST category candidates selected	92	98	
Number of physically handicapped candidates selected	30	54	

One phenomenon that became apparent following the introduction of the new system was that of several aspirants obtaining the same number of marks. While typically there is a large gap in the marks obtained from top rankers and the rest, from around the fifteenth rank or so, for every mark less, one's ranking in the combined merit list dropped by ten positions. In such circumstances, a formula was adopted to rank people who get the same marks in the examination; those who get more in the interview are given a higher ranking, then the marks in the general studies paper become the determinant, and so on. Thus, every single mark counts towards one's final position and may mean the difference between the services allocated, or within the service, the application of other choices such as the state to which the officer is assigned.

In my own case, in the 1982 selection process, I secured 1020 marks out of a possible 2050. I got the 963rd position. In 1983, I got 1180 marks, which were just 160 marks more, bettering my percentage marks by a shade less than 8 per cent. However, the effect on my ranking in the merit list was dramatic; I rose to the sixteenth position.

The phenomenon of the bunching together of several candidates with identical marks was corroborated by S. Venkat Ramani, a good friend, who had secured the first rank in the very first examination conducted to the pattern as recommended by the Kothari Committee. Ramani is something of a legend in the civil services examination; I believe he holds the record for the highest marks secured in the main exam and the interview; 1441 marks out of a possible 2050. Legend goes that Ramani's marks in the written examination were so high that had he got zero marks for his interview (he got 180 out of a possible 250) he would still have topped the list of successful candidates. Ramani, being the modest person he is, said that was not right; he would have got the fifth rank or so, according to him.

Ramani was a student of the Delhi School of Economics when he decided to write the civil services exam. He began his preparations for the old system of examination, but in 1979 he wrote the first examination after the government accepted the Kothari Committee recommendations. Ramani recalls that he welcomed the new system; he always felt that the old one, with its focus on the humanities, had a huge bias towards those educated in Delhi University or Jawaharlal Nehru University. Delhi School of Economics also contributed a steady stream of candidates for the civil services, even though economics was not considered a scoring subject. Ramani felt that the way Delhi University approached the subject of economics was ideally suited for the civil services exam in the pre-Kothari Committee days. Furthermore, when it came to how the compulsory papers of general knowledge were set, there was a strong upper-class bias. Those who studied in the hallowed environment of Delhi University knew by word of mouth and association how to crack the paper. In particular, Delhi students, in his opinion, excelled in writing answers within the parameters prescribed—answering a question crisply, in three lines or forty words, was a cakewalk for the Delhi-educated student, who was conversant with this style.

The new system opened up the field to more aspirants from the hinterland, away from the more highly regarded universities and colleges of Delhi. Many of the more upper-class aspirants from Delhi were unhappy with these changes; they did not realize the huge opportunity that the new system provided to those from lower-middle-class backgrounds to appear at the examination. These were people who did not secure the advantage of a Delhi, upper-class education, but who had made the grade through dint of sheer hard work and application.

And yet, the new system, as it threw open the doors to a wider range of aspirants, also exacerbated the phenomenon of close bunching of those with identical marks. Ramani recalls that when he wrote the examination, the first twenty-five rank holders were clustered into a range of 200 marks, but the next 100 were clustered together in a range of just thirty marks out of a possible 2050, a wafer thin range of just under one and a half per cent. In other words, if one had a bad day at the interview, it could be curtains to your aspirations to joining the IAS or to be in the civil services altogether. Ramani believes that the interview was the weak point in the selection process. Marking in the interview, according to him, was random and haphazard. Much depended upon the interview board that one faced; some were considered strict and intimidating, others were more cordial and went to great pains to put the candidate at ease. However, it was not necessary that the intimidating interview board marked candidates more strictly; there were no such trends seen.

The current pattern of the examination shows the cumulative effect of the recommendations of the plethora of committees set up since the Kothari Committee. No committee's report has found full favour with the government, yet bits and pieces of their recommendations have been accepted. At present, the preliminary examination comprises two objective type papers, one termed the general ability test (GAT) and the other, the civil services aptitude test (CSAT). These papers comprise eighty and hundred questions each and are valued for a total of 400 marks.

0.33 marks are deducted for every wrong answer. A minimum score of 33 per cent is necessary for a candidate to be eligible to appear at the main examinations, subject to the broad pattern that their numbers don't exceed, roughly, about twelve times the numbers of candidates proposed to be selected.

Many incremental changes have accumulated since the immediate post-Kothari period to make the main examinations quite different from what they were. The language qualifying papers continue comprising an English paper and an Indian language of the candidate's choice, from amongst those listed in the Sixth Schedule of the Constitution. The marks from the language papers do not count for the overall merit, they are merely qualifying papers.

There are seven merit papers in the main examinations, each valued at 250 marks. Five of these are now common to all candidates, unlike in the past. To that extent, the broad rationale of the Yogendra Alagh Committee's report—that a large number of optional papers raises the problem of how performance across these may be assessed—has found favour. Three of these papers traverse the gamut of general studies as one conventionally knows it. Paper I covers Indian heritage and culture and world history, geography and society. Paper II focuses on Indian governance, the Constitution, polity, social justice and international relations and paper III on technology, economic development, biodiversity, environment, security and disaster management. One of the remaining papers is an essay and the last, termed the general studies paper IV, is on ethics, integrity and aptitude.

The last mentioned change, introduced a few years ago, intrigued me. While I explore the subject in more detail in Chapter 8, it did fascinate me that someone was convinced that one's ethical and attitudinal strengths could be tested through an examination. Since I speak to the officer trainees at the Lal Bahadur Shastri Academy, I did notice, very fleetingly, I must admit, a more attentive, questioning and inquisitive class than the ones I was part of, back in the day. We, or at least I, were a bored lot, believing that we knew all and that classroom sessions were better spent in dreaming with our eyes open or furtively writing letters. Not so, I felt, were these young entrants of today.

Has the introduction of the ethics paper changed the ethos of the civil services? I asked an experienced insider colleague and friend steeped in the business of training and personnel management. She hoped it did, but preferred to reserve her judgment. Cracking the ethics paper is a game, just like cracking any other, she said. The coaching camps are on to it, and soon, candidates will know the right things to say. It is possible to build enough of a façade to sail through an ethics paper, she said.

The remaining two papers in the main examinations cover two optional subjects of the candidate's choice. The range of subjects from which to choose has narrowed in certain aspects and widened elsewhere. In a partial acceptance of the recommendations of the Satish Chandra Committee, gone are the foreign language papers and the slivers into which history was sliced—Indian, European, British history and suchlike. In their place has appeared mechanical engineering, civil engineering, electrical engineering and medical science.

Those who clear the main examinations appear for the personality test, which is valued at 275 marks. There is an interview board that interviews each candidate, much in the manner of the past.

Whatever may have been the examination mode that one faced, no aspirant who has made it through the examinations is likely to forget the day when the results were announced. Shortly after writing the civil services entrance examination in December 1982, I had joined a bank and was working in a dusty town in Saurashtra. As the days passed, I grew increasingly anxious about the result. I had not begun to prepare for the next round of examinations, which I would have to inevitably undergo in case I did not make it. After much procrastination, I decided to commence preparing for the exam on a hot day in May. That afternoon, I played hooky from my bank desk to take a short nap, before opening my books once more. I was sapped of all motivation, but bowed to the inevitable grind.

I snapped awake at a knocking on the door. '*Aapke liye trunk call hai*,' said the boy at the door of my tiny room, deep in the rabbit warren of a ramshackle lodge where bachelors lived.

It was my sister at the other end. 'Welcome to Karnataka,' she said. She herself was an IAS officer and posted as the deputy commissioner of a district. 'You've made it. Sixteenth rank. You'll get your first choice of state: Karnataka.'

She disconnected. Trunk calls were expensive those days and her three minutes were up.

My first feeling was one of immense relief. I would not have to undergo another year's backbreaking torture of preparation for the examination, I realized.

Then I thought of my girlfriend in Delhi.

A few days later, I backpacked to Delhi, again absenting myself from office, taking advantage of the newfound indulgence of my boss. Train tickets were booked full for the next three months, so I hopped by bus to Baroda and then boarded a crowded unreserved compartment of the Frontier Mail at the dead of night. After twelve hours on my feet, I was finally able to sit down and slip into an exhausted but euphoric sleep. As we steamed into Delhi, I jumped off at a signal, clambered down an embankment and waved down an autorickshaw to take me home.

My father opened the door. He was not particularly given to sentimentality. He smiled his welcome. I sat him down. 'Daddy,' I said, 'I suppose you know Aditi, my classmate, who comes over every now and then to meet me at home? I would like to marry her.'

It was a job swiftly done.

From the day of their success, IAS officers are catapulted to stratospheric heights. They are the objects of adulation and envy, feted by their castes, states, districts, towns and villages. Society celebrates the IAS officer far out of proportion to her achievements.

Luckily, in my case, that did not happen. I spent the next few months backpacking without a care in the world, travelling to meet my friends, visiting relatives and finally, penniless, landing in Delhi to prepare myself for the life of a civil servant. I borrowed money from my father to buy all the essentials: suits, shoes, *bandhgala* coats and riding breeches, stuff that was on the checklist that I received from my future alma mater—Lal Bahadur Shastri National Academy of Administration, Mussoorie. He grumbled but coughed up.

Did it all go to my head? I would like to think that it did not, but that took some effort.

4

Postings, Transfers and Government Dysfunctionality

Bengaluru is now more famous for its polluted lakes that froth and catch fire than it is for its gardens. Perched on a plateau nearly a kilometre above sea level, Bengaluru is so situated that water can quickly flow away to low-lying areas around it. Yet, every time there is a downpour, the city gets flooded and the traffic—bad as it is on usual days—gets into a state of complete gridlock. The city had nearly three hundred lakes, big and small, that enabled it to slow down and absorb sudden water flows. However, over the years, these were filled up to provide land for expansion and only about eighty of them remain now. Paving over of footpaths, the blockage of storm-water drains with garbage, encroachment into public land and the narrowing of streams leading from lake to lake has ensured that rain water has no place to flow in Bengaluru, except on the streets.

The destruction of Bengaluru's natural water storage and drainage system, while it places its citizens in danger, also results in plenty of economic opportunities to profit from dysfunctionality and suffering. Even as after every cloudburst the citizens wait for the water to recede so they can wearily trudge home, the barons of the dysfunctionality business lick their lips in anticipation. For them, there will be disaster relief works taken up, drains that need to be desilted, potholes that have to be filled and broken electric poles and pipelines that must be repaired and consequently, more contracts to be handed out. Dysfunctionality entrepreneurs have ensured a good business model for themselves, through bad city planning over decades.

Lant Pritchett, a Harvard professor who has a penchant for straight talk, refers to India as a 'flailing state' in an article[1] that tends to get every bureaucrat's goat. Pritchett characterizes India as a country with strong laws and weak implementation; where the head is in the right place, but the limbs do not answer to its commands.

I once sat through a fascinating presentation in which Pritchett explored why and how governance in countries might begin to flail. He began by unpacking the concept of accountability into 'thick accountability', which applies to tasks that are discretionary in nature and 'thin accountability' as applying to those that merely require the following of instructions. He then analysed how these forms of accountability would apply to actions of 'narrow' scope, which required only a few players to participate and those of a 'broad' scope, where many players are involved. He visualized his grid in this fashion:

	Narrow scope (involving few people)	Broad scope (involving many people)
'Thick' accountability (requiring the exercise of discretion)	For example, policy formulation, legislation and other such apex activities. **India does OK here; it makes good laws, its policies are well thought out.**	Transaction-intensive service delivery or compliance with quality obligations (for example, healthcare, education). **India is an organizational disaster here, as for example, in curative care, quality of teaching, operation and maintenance of assets, quality of police, etc.**
'Thin' accountability (Compliance with algorithms is sufficient)	For example, maintaining filing cabinets or managing office archives.	The logistics business, such as postal delivery. **India does modestly OK here, it can build decent buildings, collect taxes, do vaccinations, deliver letters, conduct elections.**

Pritchett went on to observe that India has achieved relatively greater success in performing thick, narrow-scope activities (such as law-making) and thin, broad-scope tasks, such as running postal services or conducting democratic elections, where those taking commands had only to follow strictly and did not need to apply their minds on their choice of actions. However, in Pritchett's view, India had failed to achieve similar success in performing thick, broad-scope activities such as healthcare and education.

And that is where the dysfunctionality business booms: in tasks that require the involvement of large numbers of people, interacting through multiple transactions, but where accountability is 'thick'. With respect to those services where delivery quality is dependent on how service delivery agents exercise the discretion they have, sadly, India has weak accountability systems.

Two trends happen here. First, service providers who are tasked with 'thick accountability' functions begin to behave as if these were 'thin accountability' functions. Thus, doctors might land up in clinics if enforcement of attendance is tightened up, but they may still not provide good healthcare because they might not exercise their discretion in that direction. Similarly, teachers might land up in schools, but might not be teaching well. Second, those in thick accountability systems might attempt to position themselves in doing tasks that involve fewer people and where their discretion does not come under excessive scrutiny. Thus, a health minister might not concern himself with whether doctors are delivering healthcare responsibly, but might be spending more time attempting to make money from interfering in the postings and transfers of doctors. Pritchett explained this falling away from the task of performing thick accountability, broad–scope tasks, as the rot spreading from politics into organizations and back into politics, and as higher functions being treated as routinized lower functions. He visualized this as follows:

The rot spreads from politics into organizations and back of politics and from higher functions to lower functions

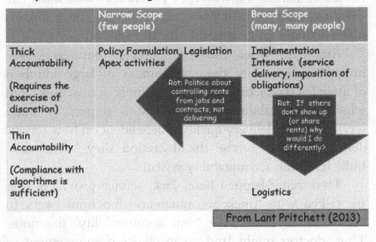

From Lant Pritchett (2013)

From Pritchett's musings, it is clear that public servants in India are more interested in either political meddling in the administration or in the routinization of critical discretionary tasks, thus leading to a rapid fall away from quality service delivery.

Is it possible to stem this flow of interest away from the crucial task of improving service delivery and into political meddling in the administration and the routinization of critical discretionary tasks? Could one force ministers and bureaucrats to focus on performing 'thick accountability' tasks of service delivery better? For assessing whether that is possible, the focus would be to understand the dimensions and ramifications of the industry of political meddling in transfers and postings of officers, which is something that ministers, MLAs and their collaborators love to do.

One of my earliest postings was as the joint director in the gleefully corrupt food and civil supplies department, to manage Bangalore city's public distribution system (PDS). The PDS in Bangalore provided ration card holders rice, wheat, pulses, cooking oil and kerosene at subsidized prices. It was chronically corrupt because there was rampant leakage of these subsidized commodities into the open market. Fair Price shopkeepers used to keep false ration cards based on ghost identities and use these to claim more commodities than they could sell. The profits were shared with departmental staff and payments went all the way up, to political parties, ministers and suchlike.

The food department grapevine was elated to know that I would not take bribes—the presumption was that anyone posted to the department was on the take. It was not that they had any hope (or desire) that I would stop corruption; they believed that they would have one person less with whom to share their monthly loot. Of course, I was not to know that, so they bore my enthusiastic forays into cleaning up corruption with good humour. By the way, lest I tar all my colleagues with the same brush, the director of the department and another joint director, a colleague, were also honest officials to the core, thus multiplying the contentment of the staff manifold. Corrupt departments actually love honest bosses, particularly if they are transient.

So while I went about my job with enthusiasm, conducting midnight raids and suspending officials who I caught engaging in irregularities, the departmental staff bore these minor inconveniences with much indulgence.

But then came the annual transfer season.

In an earlier, more honest era, the task of transferring officers from one position to another was left to senior officers to do. Politicians had little to do with the moving around of administrative staff. However, in the late eighties, the chief minister of Karnataka decided to pander to the itch of legislators and other politicians to interfere in postings and transfers and soon, a trickle of recommendations from them turned into a deluge of demands. MLAs and MPs began to swamp ministers and secretaries to the government with letters of recommendation, suggesting that various government officials be posted to one place or another. Often, they did not have any interest in these positions and sold their influence to corrupt government officers who were increasingly willing to pay to be positioned in lucrative jobs.

When this was the case, I decided to oppose transfers to various positions under my control, except on the basis of norms. I was protected by an honest boss, who not only gave me full rein, but also defended my actions to my minister. That finally got my staff hot under their collective collars. Clearly, I was not playing ball according to the rules of the transfer sport. Suspending a few officers here and there was OK, but interfering in the transfers and postings of staff within the department was clearly hitting at their livelihood options and diminishing their well-stabilized bribe-based economy.

My minister was a warm and decent man. Some people said he was corrupt, but I did not know of any direct involvement he may have had in the shenanigans of the department. He was, of course, very prone to being pressurized to transfer officials, as the latter jostled for the best position from where they could make the most money. Although my minister was consternated at my ignoring his directives on the transfer of staff, he still felt that he needed to reason with me to see sense. On one such occasion, he called me to his office for a heart-to-heart chat on the issue of transfers.

My minister pleaded with me to accept his list of transfers and with me not relenting, he stated his final position. 'I know that you want to post certain honest individuals in certain positions, but please consider my situation,' he said. 'I am your minister after all and I would like to oblige some of the people to whom I am politically indebted.'

'Could you please consider a tiny list of recommended postings, which I will send to you?' He was warming up to the theme. 'Please note, I have no interest in the individuals who are being transferred, but the column in the table on the extreme right,' he said, pointing to a typed sheet of paper, 'gives details of the individuals who have made these recommendations. These people are politically important to me,' he concluded, handing me a list of his recommendations.

I was touched by my minister's politeness and saw no reason why I should not accommodate his requests, particularly when he was being so nice about it. So I glanced at the column on the far right of the table, which contained the names of people that the minister felt were very important to him from a political sense. That right hand column contained the following names:

(a) One head of a religious institution
(b) Two astrologers
(c) The minister's family gynaecologist

(d) The minister's dentist
(e) The chief minister's security officer, known as a 'gun-man' in Karnataka
(f) A deputy director who worked directly under my control in my team

It was a fair cross section of the sources from where the minister derived his source of power and influence.

In a couple of months after this incident, I was transferred from the food department to the department of personnel, which looked at transfers of all senior officers in the state government.

It was a swift transition from the frying pan into the fire.

It was easy to presume that my transfer out of the food and civil supplies department was due to my uncivil behaviour in not accommodating the minister's reasonable request for a few transfers of his choice. However, that was not the case; moving me into the department of personnel and administrative reforms to handle the responsibility of postings and transfers of senior government officers was as random a decision as any other in the government.

To say that I did not like my new job would be an understatement. Poring over large, dog-eared files to suggest a list of postings that nobody cared to consider anyway was as dull as ditchwater. Yet, most of my contemporaries in the government thought it was a great job; I sat next to the office of the head of the bureaucracy, the chief secretary of the state and answered directly to him. I would meet the chief minister every day and be the fly on the wall, listening in to some interesting conversations. Many others would have given an arm and leg to be in my position, to become the chief rumour-monger in the state.

Yet, it did not take long for my disinterest to plummet to disgust.

First, senior officers were moved all the time. There was a transfer season year round. We did not undertake any exercise of human resource planning. Since there were no minimum tenure conditions for any position, people were constantly being transferred to new positions. In such circumstances, undertaking analyses of tenures of individuals, ascertaining who needed to be moved and suggesting the names of individuals with the requisite qualifications, experience and attitude was a redundant exercise. If one had suggested positioning officers on the basis of a throw of dice, the outcomes might have been the same.

Second, officers were not moved on the basis of any criterion of competency or aptitude for the job in hand. Only two questions were ever asked in the secret discussions on transfer lists between the chief minister and the chief secretary. These were whether the individual was honest or corrupt and what the individual's religion and caste was.

It was at these closed-door discussions between the chief minister and the chief secretary that my inadequacies at the job were exposed. Sadly, I do not have a head for names and faces. It was not possible for me to surmise from either what an individual's caste or level of integrity might be. So, when the chief minister asked these dreaded questions, I sputtered and stammered and looked around helplessly for assistance.

I knew the game was up when the undersecretary, my subordinate, was also called in for those secret discussions. He was a veritable encyclopaedia of caste. Soon, I was a silent observer in these meetings, as the chief minister and chief secretary directly discussed the intricacies of individual positions with my undersecretary.

I lasted as deputy secretary, department of personnel, for twenty-eight days before the chief secretary lost patience and moved me. It was my shortest posting ever.

The randomness and frequency of transfers of government officers spawns a huge industry, namely, that of generating and dispersing rumours. In the days when I passed through the department of personnel and administrative reforms like a meteor, rumours of impending transfer lists would be triggered by seemingly disconnected events. I realized this when a battle-hardened senior officer—a predecessor in my job several times removed—called me up to ask if there was a transfer list going to be published that day.

'I don't know, Sir,' I answered, truthfully.

'Raghu,' he said. It was clear he thought that I was an imbecile. 'Have you been asked to keep the cyclostyling guy waiting?'

For those who were born in the eighties, a cyclostyling machine, also known as a stencil machine, is one that generates copies of documents that are typed on a stencil, while also spraying generous quantities of gooey black ink on the operator who cranks it. This was how copies of government documents were generated before the invention of the Xerox machine.

I remembered that earlier in the day, the chief secretary's peon had knocked on my door to inform me that the cyclostyling guy must wait after office hours. I mentioned that to my colleague on the phone.

'Yeah,' he concluded. 'There will be a transfer list today.'

After my brief tenure of twenty-eight days in the department of personnel, where I was totally at sea as I could not remember people's castes, I was transferred to the department of health and family welfare as a deputy secretary. My heart sank as I saw my little room. There was plenty of construction activity going on upstairs and the contractor had not received his payment on time. That meant that he had been at the job for two years. He had just cast the ceiling of the next floor and generously cured it with water.

My ceiling was leaky.

My incarceration in a room that resembled the Count of Monte Christo's cell, with black fungus growing on the walls and ceiling, was worsened by the fact that I was put in charge of—what else?—the transfers and postings of doctors in the medical colleges of Karnataka.

To complete my gloom, my wife, who was expecting a baby at that time, was most thoughtfully transferred by her department to Madras, in violation of the rules that recommended that husbands and wives (married to each other, needless to say) ought to be posted together. I would sit in my damp, sunless cell the entire week and travel over the weekend to Madras to meet her. It was for us, a period of family hell-fare.

The wealth was elsewhere.

There are two kinds of government doctors: powerless and powerful. The powerless ones are the generalist ones, with just an MBBS degree, the kinds you see at remote primary health centres and hospitals across the country. The good ones amongst them do heroic work in their positions, often sans medicines, equipment and electricity.

The powerful government doctors are usually specialists. They derive their power from the fact that they treat the powerful. Most of them are also professors, assistant professors and lecturers in government medical colleges.

One of the key policy issues relating to government doctors, particularly those in the teaching profession, is whether they ought to be given permission to undertake private practice. On the one hand, allowing government doctors to undertake private practice amounts to a significant and obvious moral hazard: it does not take a genius to discover that government doctors would then have a strong incentive to divert patients from government hospitals into their private clinics. Besides, medicines from government hospitals stand the risk of being diverted as well. On the other hand, government doctors argue that after they have invested considerable money and effort into acquiring a medical education, government salaries are too low a compensation.

In Karnataka, government doctors had the freedom to undertake private practice and any effort to curb this had met with stiff resistance. I found politicians and senior government officers to be more than pliant in the hands of doctors. I put it down to the fact that most of them might have been pressurized while on the operating table. As one grows in government service, or in politics, one's health takes a turn for the worse. Therefore, most politicians and senior government officers are dependent upon good doctors for their survival. In such circumstances, one's ability to ignore a gentle suggestion on the issue of continuing private practice is considerably diminished, when the doctor delivering the suggestion is poised over one's exposed posterior, sharp knife or menacing syringe in hand.

I discovered that the same was the case in respect of doctors' transfers.

In the late eighties, there were only four government medical colleges in Karnataka: in Bangalore, Mysore, Bellary and Gulbarga. The opportunity for private practice was ample in Bangalore and Mysore. So no professor, assistant professor or lecturer in the medical education service wanted to be posted at Gulbarga or Bellary. However, there were limitations as to how many doctors could be posted to each medical college, because each one had an approved staffing pattern. It was impossible to post more doctors to a college than those indicated in its staffing pattern.

Or so I thought. But doctors, and their patrons, are a fiendishly intelligent lot.

Once, a professor in the surgery department in Bangalore Medical College came to see me. He had just been transferred to Gulbarga Medical College, 600 kilometres north of Bangalore. He looked pale and distraught. I had just snatched away his lifeline: a lucrative private practice in Bangalore. Please post me back to Bangalore, he said. I explained to him why he was posted to Gulbarga. Bangalore Medical College has six positions of surgeons, I said. All of them were taken. The position from where he was dislodged, was taken by another doctor with greater political and caste clout. On the other hand, Gulbarga Medical College had only one surgeon against five positions. There was nobody to teach surgery to students there, I explained.

He was unmoved. There is a vacancy of a professor in radiology in Bangalore, he said. You could post me against that. I looked hard at him. You are not a radiologist, I said. How can you be posted as a radiologist? Would you do a radiologist's work? I asked. He left silently, but his eyes showed that he would not take no for an answer.

Within the day, I was asked by the health minister to submit the file to him. I did, with a detailed note on why a surgeon could not be posted to Bangalore against a radiologist's vacancy, particularly when there were hardly any surgeons teaching at Gulbarga Medical College. By evening, the doctor walked into my room, just as the file was delivered to me, with orders from the minister retaining him in Bangalore as a surgeon officiating as a radiologist.

The floodgates opened. The crowning glory was a gynaecologist officiating as a dentist.

In Bellary and Gulbarga medical colleges, postgraduate students, lacking professors to teach them, were conducting classes for their juniors. It was medical education in do-it-yourself mode.

Since those early years, the interference of elected representatives in the placement of public officials in key jobs has multiplied manifold. Today, MLAs and ministers have nearly fully centralized the transfer and placement of officials in all jobs. Bluntly put, not one individual in any department can be positioned or transferred without the opinion of the MLA concerned. Over the years, the accommodation of occasional requests made by politicians has turned into a complete and abject capitulation by officers. Recognizing the unchallenged powers of the MLAs to interfere in transfers, the standard operating procedure for any official now is to procure a recommendation letter from an MLA before seeking a transfer.

The most successful example of a revenue model emerging from the randomness of government transfers is the appropriately named website, 'whispersinthecorridors. com'. A private website, all it does is to collect rumours from government officers on impending transfers and postings and put these up as terse one-liners. Its credibility rests on the fact that it has been remarkably accurate in predicting transfers of individuals. It has a most helpful section, termed 'whispers getting louder', in which rumours in their infancy are reported. Finally, when transfers do happen, the site triumphantly proclaims its success rate.

Whispersinthecorridors.com has a huge fan following; many senior officers have it as their home page on the net. Many of them learn of their postings from it rather than the official government website of the department of personnel. The site also offers value-added services such as arranging of marriages between the children of senior government officials—I attended one such wedding in Delhi, where the owner of the site was the very visible master of ceremonies.

Indeed, keeping with the new spirit of minimum government and maximum governance, I strongly suggest that the government outsources the entire department of personnel to whispersinthecorridors.com. At least it has a more easily navigable website than the government one.

'Can I meet with you?' said the cheery voice on the intercom.

I smiled back and invited him in. I liked him, let's call him W.D., he always gave me the impression of being a clear-headed and busy man, which was inspiring to observe for a government officer like me. W.D. worked for an international multilateral agency, which was then engaged in negotiating a huge loan with the Government of India, aimed to provide budgetary support to improve the overall fiscal situation of the state of Karnataka. That had brought a deluge of consultants into the state and soon, in keeping with the times, we were leafing through chubby spiral-bound reports and speaking multilateralese, a curious dialect of English, in order to keep step with these more evolved beings. In other words, we were no longer meeting people, but meeting *with* them, and we never held discussions, because we were *dialoguing*, instead. We stopped preparing minutes of meetings, preferring to craft *aide memoires* to preserve for posterity the results of our incessant dialoguing. The entire environment generated by these discussions with the multilateral agency concerned was delectably foreign and exotic and made us all feel very important.

Since the loan proposed to be taken by the Karnataka government was a large one intended to strengthen its overall finances, the multilateral agency concerned imposed several conditions, aimed to strengthen good governance and service delivery. These included stuff like improving the accounting system, rationalizing taxation, and to my glee, promote decentralization to local governments.

It sounded very good.

I was very enthusiastic, because as secretary, panchayati raj (rural local governments), I was willing to use any pulpit to evangelize about the benefits of decentralization. W.D. was passionately in favour of that.

As I elaborated upon my vision of strong and empowered panchayats to W.D., I spoke about the constraints as well. One of them was that the panchayats were not allowed to recruit their own secretaries and higher-level staff; all of these were posted and transferred by the state government, often with no notice to the panchayats. This, I told W.D., struck at the very root of the concept of accountability of local governments to people. How could the panchayats perform any of their responsibilities if they did not have any control over their staff?

W.D. beamed back in response. He looked like someone who had found the answer and without any ado, he proceeded to explain it to me.

The finance and the administrative reforms departments of the Karnataka government, he said, had agreed to create a human-resources database that would capture every last detail about every government servant. All transfers would be entered into the database and these would be provided to senior officers and ministers so they could take considered decisions to post the right people to the right jobs.

'What's more,' he said, 'the government will upload all details of transfers of officials on a website that would be open to the public.'

The Government of Karnataka signed on the dotted line and obtained the loan.

The website was never created.

Homegrown initiatives for regulating and introducing some norms into the transfer system have been more successful. Back in the nineties—and here, I will mention names—Govinde Gowda, a remarkably honest education minister in Karnataka, introduced a system of counselling for transfers of teachers in the education department. Every teacher could give their preference, which would be classified into a priority list based upon simple criteria such as the length of the current tenure, personal exigencies such as maternity and paternity responsibilities, marriage, and suchlike. Teachers would be invited to a counselling centre, where they could see the vacancies available through a real-time online system and then choose their preferences for postings. The system was met with skepticism, but over time, particularly because Gowda stood his ground and refused to submit to political pressure to bend the rules, it gained credibility.

However, since the system was not formalized through a law, subsequently, another minister of a markedly lower integrity level as compared to Gowda, insisted that he needed a teeny-weeny discretionary quota within the counselling system. When met with stiff resistance by the secretary to his department, he got him transferred and got his little quota sanctioned by the chief minister. Before you could say 'discretion', 35,000 transfers were undertaken through the minister's quota.

That signalled the end of the counselling system and Karnataka went back to the process of MLAs recommending transfers of teachers. This was not a small reversal, considering that of Karnataka's six lakh staff, more than a third were teachers.

The restoration of the power of MLAs to make recommendations for the transfers of teachers was not without its downside. MLAs were faced with a tsunami of requests to recommend transfers. They were approached by teachers of all hues, from those in their constituency to those who belonged to their caste. They were approached throughout the day and night.

'It was not good,' said one of them to me once. 'They would even hand over petitions to me requesting transfers through the ventilator of the toilet.'

I commiserated. Intruding into the privacy of an elected representative in that fashion was hitting below the belt.

It took but a few years for MLAs to realize that they had bitten off more than they could chew by wanting to interfere in teachers' transfers. Long after the redoubtable Gowda had retired from politics, his excellent innovation of a counselling system for teacher's transfers was enacted as a law by the Karnataka legislature.[2]

Sustained disturbance of the bowel movements of legislators by teachers had had a salutary effect on the furtherance of administrative reforms.

5

Promotions and Ambitions

Closely associated with postings and transfers is the issue of promotions and elevations within the government. Since most government servants are recruited on a permanent basis, how they grow within the government is a critical factor in the retention of their motivation levels. The hierarchies of postings are also well entrenched, with terms such as 'plum' posting and 'punishment' posting being well understood in the government servant's lexicon. Closely associated with the promotion system is the government appraisal system through the time-tested method of an annual confidential report. The subject is a rich source of black humour, even as its reforms aim at a more fair and well-rounded approach to assessing performance.

The higher bureaucracy is full of intelligent people, who have gone through layers of tough competition to gain entry. Prior to cracking the entrance examinations, many of them over the years, have trained themselves to be single-minded in their pursuit of excellence, to compete and win. A collaborative spirit is not welcome in the training of such minds. Indeed, since selection is based on competitive examinations, collaboration is anathema.

When a set of driven, competitive individuals gain entry to the stratosphere of the bureaucracy, it is too much to expect them to transform themselves into caring, sharing, tightly knit teams overnight. Of course, if it suits them, they will passionately advocate team building, but there is an implicit precondition: that they will invariably head the teams that they build and the teams will do as they say.

At the start of their careers, the implications of competition are not so readily apparent. There are plenty of jobs on offer at the lower levels for officers to excel. The initial years following recruitment into the IAS, for instance, follow nearly identical pathways in different states. Everybody starts off with a series of field postings, as subdivisional magistrates, CEOs of district panchayats, and that final summit from where they can lord over their far-flung mofussil empires: district collectors. While there is some element of comparison between these positions, it is hard to say that being district collector of one district is not at par with the same position in another district. True, there are so called 'prestigious' districts; for example, in Karnataka, being posted as the DC of Mysuru is to be savoured more than being the DC of Bidar district; but then, the latter incumbent has the compensation of being the minor sultan of a far-flung outpost to console herself.

It is after those first fifteen years that the field narrows down. The general public, accustomed to seeing all officers as exalted, might not discern the difference; everybody is up in their snowy peaks. However, for the insider, the difference between a good post and a bad post, between a sideline position and a mainstream, plum posting, is stark. If one is pushed to a position of relative unimportance, the effect can be as good as being punished.

There are many ways by which these hierarchies and inequalities are recognized and maintained, which only the insider knows.

In Delhi, an individual knowledgeable of the caste hierarchy of the Union government's bureaucracy enlightened me of the criteria used to position officers in social gatherings. 'Who you are, in Delhi,' he said, 'depends upon five things: the ministry in which you work, the colony in which you live, the school to which your children go, the club where you have membership and the breed of your dog.'

By those yardsticks, I reckoned, I lived in the basement of the rankings. I was joint secretary in the Ministry of Panchayati Raj, which ranked low in the pecking order of social sector ministries, particularly when compared with the more prosperous and self-important Ministry of Rural Development. I lived in a colony that was centrally located, but in a house that was two levels below the category to which I was entitled. My son did not study in Delhi, so I got zero marks in the school criterion. I did not belong to any club, since, like Groucho Marx, I would not join any club that would deign to admit me. And my dog, bless the rascal, was a Road Island retriever, which came off an island on the road. If I looked hard at his silly face, I might recognize a shade of Labrador, but that would be cheating.

Hierarchies are important in the IAS as anywhere else in the government. It is not only important as a positioning tool within the service, but also to peg oneself against other hierarchies. There are complicated equivalence codes that equate IAS officers to positions in the armed services or uniformed services, such as the police. In normal circumstances, these are of academic interest, but at times, they can be of critical national importance. For example, whether a joint secretary is higher in rank than a brigadier can determine who sits in front of whom in the Republic Day parade audience.

Closely linked with the hierarchical positions is the protocol of whom you address by his or her name, or respectfully refer to as 'Sir', or 'Madam' (To my mind, the latter has a faintly pejorative tinge to it, but I must admit, that is not so in Indian English). The 'Sir' or 'Madam' rule, keeping in mind India's federal polity, varies from state to state. In some states that have strict hierarchical cultures—bordering on the obsequious—one is supposed to address officers who are even a year senior as 'Sir' or 'Madam'. In other, more relaxed states, you can dispense with this formality for an officer up to certain levels of seniority. In Karnataka, where I worked for the better part of my life, you could risk calling an officer five years senior by her name and get away with it.

However, this is not without its risks. When officers from different states are drawn to work in the Union government secretariat, then havoc can ensue if one addresses an officer not used to it in his state, by his name. This happens quite frequently; government officers are not a close-knit tribe where everybody knows everybody else. Besides, particularly when officers come from different backgrounds and states, the chances are more likely than not that they do not know each other well enough to begin to slap each other's backs.

When two officers who do not know each other meet, a process is set in motion that would put the mating rituals of sarus cranes to shame. Through a set of polite inquiries, often so subtle that they do not raise the suspicions of the one who introduces the two, a positioning game is played.

Let us presume that IAS officer 'A' meets IAS officer 'B' at a wedding. They are introduced to each other by a busy host, with a quick opening statement that merely reveals to the other that they both belong to the IAS. However, that is akin to a biologist describing an airborne creature as some kind of flying thingie, it does not enable the stickler for detail to conclude whether the said airborne object is a bird, a bat, Superman or a UFO.

IAS officers are sticklers for detail. They need to find out quickly as to whether the individual opposite them are (a) senior or (b) junior to them and/or whether they are (c) direct recruits or (d) promotees into the service. The nub of the matter is to find out the status and seniority of the other. However, a blunt approach is considered unsporting. It is distinctly rude to ask each other 'what is your batch?'— referring to the year of recruitment—thereby completing 50 per cent of the positioning game in a flash.

No, the approach is far more subtle. A well-worked gambit is for one person, usually the person who in appearance seems more decrepit than the other, and therefore, presumably the more senior of the two, to seek from the other the whereabouts of his batch mates. Thus, for example, if I were to meet someone who is introduced to me as an IAS officer from another state, and who seems to be in a better state of physical preservation than I am, I would casually inquire from him how my batch mates in his state were doing. That sets in motion a smooth and nearly instantaneous process of positioning. The moment I mention names, the opposite party discovers in an instant my batch and thereafter, can determine whether I am senior enough to him to be treated deferentially, or considered a peer, or that, in spite of my aged looks, I am actually—a ghastly thought—junior to him.

A miscalculation of seniority in that introductory meeting can result in the destruction of one's confidential reports. It is not good for one if the person one has treated raffishly because of a wrong presumption of seniority turns out to be more senior, and worse, is posted as one's boss. In such circumstances, it is prudent for the ambitious officer to err on the side of caution and address any object that looks senior to her, animate or inanimate, as 'Sir' or 'Madam'. I have often been addressed that way (Not 'Madam', but 'Sir') by officers senior to me. The chagrin on their faces when they realize that it ought to have been the other way is delightful to observe. I have not rued going prematurely grey.

An insider friend of mine, a keen observer who records the dynamics of seniority across various services for his amusement, points out that the battles of seniority within the armed forces are easier to settle, because everybody carries their ranks on their shoulders. Yet, confusion can result. He recalled (he himself served as a senior bureaucrat in the defence ministry) that once, when he was attending the funeral of a legendary soldier, there was much jostling in the cordoned off section reserved for senior retired officers, as they attempted to secure vantage positions on the basis of their inter se seniority. All of a sudden, there was silence and the jostling fell away. The crowd parted like the Red Sea. Moses, nay, Moses and his wife, when they emerged, turned out to be a wizened and tiny man in his air force uniform, accompanied by his tiny wife. They walked with great dignity to the foot of the coffin and after the man smartly saluted and paid homage, they laid their wreaths on the coffin, turned around and walked away through the crowd, which once again parted respectfully to make way for them.

'Who was that?' asked my friend, expecting to be told that the wizened man was no less than a former air chief marshall. He is a retired wing commander, my friend was informed. 'A Mahavir Chakra winner.' All rules of seniority fell away in the unanimous and time-honoured recognition of gallantry. While I would not conclude so with certainty, an awarded officer in the IAS would not be liberated from the shackles of seniority in so forthright a manner as in the armed forces.

It is in the government secretariats, which is where most IAS officers end their professional lives, that their designations take on a boring, repetitive tone. Using Linnaean terms, every officer belongs to the genus of 'secretary'. But within that is a wide evolutionary spectrum of positions.

The 'undersecretary' is the lowest member of this genus; the one that has just crawled out from the primeval slime. The next step on the evolutionary chain is the 'deputy secretary'; a slightly evolved subspecies of this level is the 'director'. That is followed by the 'joint secretary'. The secretary sits at the top of the secretariat food chain, the tyrannosaurus rex of the genus. However, the joint secretary is no pushover; she is the velociraptor of the pack. The post of a joint secretary is a powerful position for many reasons. One is that, joint secretaries tend to hold their positions for far longer than secretaries, so ministers tend to rely on them, often bypassing secretaries. This keeps T. rexes on their toes.

Trapped in between the two carnivores is a position that is neither here nor there, which is the position of the additional secretary. Uneasy lies the head that wears the additional crown. This hapless individual is an herbivorous offshoot of the chain, an evolutionary dead end. Basically, when a joint secretary grows long in the tooth, he is promoted as an additional secretary, but continues to perform the same tasks and responsibilities. In earlier days, when stagnation in the higher echelons of the service was not such a serious problem, the position was akin to waiting in a transit lounge. An additional secretary worked as an understudy to the secretary and quickly moved in to take the latter's position. However, as the administrative system has grown to be top-heavy, additional secretaries are often in such suspended animation for up to five years, during which they either become brain dead or drive themselves crazy with the worry of whether they would ever graduate to the exalted position of secretaries. Being additional secretary is akin to being a teenager between the ages of fifteen and eighteen, old enough to sprout a moustache, but not old enough to watch adult movies. Walk in the corridors of power and if you discover people who are jumpy, nervous and shifty-eyed, the chances are that they are additional secretaries. It is because of the long tenures, that many officers have to endure as additional secretaries, that the last ten years in the higher bureaucracy are nerve-wracking.

While these positions result in a natural and well-recognized pecking order in India, havoc can prevail when Indian officers travel abroad. I was once on a training programme in the US, which was also attended by an undersecretary and an additional secretary from the Ministry of Finance. In the US, an undersecretary is the equivalent of a minister of state in India. Therefore, every time the undersecretary introduced himself, the audience did a double take and turned awfully respectful, addressing him not by his name, but as 'Mr Undersecretary'. On the contrary, the additional secretary was slapped on his back and addressed by his name. The undersecretary revelled in the temporary glory; the additional secretary was a nervous wreck at the end of the course.

Because there is very little room at the top in the bureaucracy, there has to be a way to select the best for the top job; a way to separate the wheat from the chaff. The most frequently used method is to use the system of ACRs. Equally popular are playing golf (or joining golf clubs where your boss plays) and organizing temple tours for pious, influential seniors and their families.

But let me focus on the ACR system.

ACR stands for 'Annual Confidential Report'. This is, as is obvious, an annual, confidential appraisal of an officer's capabilities by his or her bosses. Since bureaucracies are organized in elaborate hierarchies, each appraisal comprises three steps. One's immediate boss initiates the report and is known as the reporting authority. The next level is that of the officer who reviews the report of the reporting officer. This level is known as the reviewing authority. However, since the system is deeply distrustful about anything said about anybody, whether good or bad, there is an accepting authority at the top of the pile. After its arduous journey through these three levels, the ACR, in the case of IAS officers, ends its journey in the office of the chief secretary of the state where the officer works and with the department of personnel at the Government of India.

Invariably, the onus is on the officer concerned to start the process of having his appraisal done. In earlier, more irresponsible times, the format in which the ACR was written was vague and capable of variable interpretation. The officer concerned was required to mention his name, his current responsibility and how long he was holding it. A few more terse questions, such as whether he enjoyed good health and had undergone any training during the year under appraisal, and the ACR was set on its way. Since then, the ACR has undergone several changes. Now, the officer is required to mention six to eight thrust areas of his work and give a self-appraisal of how he has functioned over the year in respect of key, relevant targets. He is also required to give an honest appraisal of constraints that he faced in not achieving set targets.

The rules also say that one has to speak to one's boss in advance and fix targets to be achieved before the year commences. That never happened in my time and, I am given to understand, does not happen now.

Writing a self-appraisal is an art. I did it meticulously, and did it in the finest calligraphy that I could muster; I am sure my effort would have drawn gasps of admiration from those engaged in writing entire Qurans into books the size of matchboxes. I drew neat lines in red ink to separate one target from the other and embellished my achievements with numbers. I also developed the fine art of making my non-achievement of targets look like success in the face of adversity. There were always some large calamities that one could draw upon to justify one's lack of success ('I planted 1,28,000 saplings but 2460 survived, because the rest were washed away by Hurricane Kaif,' you get the idea).

Once the ACR is set on its journey, the reporting officer has the task of sieving through one's subterfuge and boasts to get to the root of what exactly one has been up to.

The first question that is asked of one's boss is whether he or she agrees with the targets and the achievements attained. This often catches the boss on the wrong foot, because he knows he did not discuss the fixation of those targets with you at the start of the year (just as he did not discuss his targets with his boss). So, therefore, calligraphy or not, one is likely to get the nod on the targets and achievements that one has reported.

Then come a lot of subjective questions: does the officer show initiative? Does he get along with his colleagues? Is he capable and good at teamwork? How is his oral and written communications? While these questions provide ample scope for the reporting officer to air her literary talents, this is rarely the case. CRs are often written by reporting officers in a terse style. I put it down to the fact that as officers get senior, most of them begin to resemble more and more, in their manner, demeanour and articulation, a government circular come to life.

'Once they have crossed twenty years of seniority,' a boss of mine well versed in these matters told me, 'nobody reads anything, except the civil list and the railway time table.' Replace the latter with airline schedules and you get the general picture.

Then comes the icing on the cake: the question on the integrity of the officer concerned. It stands to reason that if you have agreed with the officer's achievement on his stated targets (which you are barred from questioning) and if you have written some wishy-washy stuff on his team spirit, initiative and communications, you might find it very difficult to write anything more than ho-hum stuff in the integrity column. You might also not want to write paeans to his honesty here, as if he is exposed in a scam later, you will have egg on your face. So, in the circumstances, the accepted bland phrase to use is as follows:

'Beyond reproach.'

However, I have seen some strange comments in the 'integrity column'. One said that the officer concerned was 'fully integrated'. Was he a mathematical equation? I wondered.

The best one that I heard, of course, was the one by a sly reporting officer who wrote in the integrity column, 'The officer, Mr [. . .], sometimes conducts experiments with the truth.'

Once a senior officer endures the tedium of commenting on various aspects of the officer's performance, space is left for her to give her general opinion on the officer being assessed. Even though this presents a window of opportunity for the reporting officer to exhibit her literary talents, not many venture to do so, because junior officers provide little inspiration for effusiveness. While I usually stay away from regional stereotyping, I believe that the typical south Indian officer is more conservative in this regard. Complimentary comments are rationed out by them, as if each of them were only given a limited supply of these. Where a typically large-hearted north Indian officer might launch himself into poetic raptures about his junior's talents, a south Indian is only cautiously optimistic. A colleague of mine complained bitterly about his boss. 'All that my boss could muster while writing my ACR was that "the lad shows some promise". And that too, after I had completed sixteen years of service,' he fumed.

After these general remarks comes the final hurdle to completing an appraisal. An officer has to be graded across five categories: 'poor', 'average', 'good', 'very good' and 'outstanding'. It is rare that an officer is graded as 'poor'. This is considered a 'bad ACR' and a bad ACR has to be shared with its victim.

The Indian Administrative Services in its internal dealings, generally shies away from confrontation. There is the fabled notion of esprit de corps, which, most people believe, will be seriously threatened if we say exactly what we feel about each other, to each other. That is why, even though we might feel that all the brains of our subordinates might fit on a pin head and leave enough space for a boxing ring, we do not give them 'poor' CRs. It is simply not done. We give them outstanding CRs instead.

The norm is that nearly everybody is given an outstanding CR. The reason is that as one goes senior and there are screening processes put in place, the simplest, rough and ready way is to count the number of outstanding CRs that an officer might have and then use this mathematical chart to clear the officer for the next level.

As an example, let me speak of the first such real hurdle in climbing the ladder. Till about the sixteenth year of service, an IAS officer of undistinguished, average performance can make the grade. The words used to describe different levels of IAS officers are traditional jargon of the narrowest kind, which nobody else can understand. Thus, an officer at the lowest level is called as belonging to the 'junior scale'. Mercifully, the stay in junior scale is short—just about four years—after which the officer gets promoted to the 'senior scale'. Then, there is something known as the junior administrative grade or the 'selection grade'. I am told there is a difference between the two, but I could never discern that and survived unscathed for twenty-seven years in the government with this glaring deficiency.

The real big step in the career progression of an IAS officer is a process known as empanelment. Contrary to popular notion, empanelment does not refer to the encasing of an IAS officer in Formica sheets, even though, by the sixteenth year, he might begin to resemble a lifeless sheet of laminate more and more. Empanelment refers to the screening process by which officers are declared as eligible to join a panel of a selected few, from which joint secretaries to the Government of India might be selected. The process of empanelment depends upon a study of the ACRs of officers. While there is no official confirmation of the process, it is widely believed that empanelment requires that of the last ten or twelve ACRs, at least eight or ten should be 'outstanding' ones—nobody knows exactly how many, but everybody is unanimous that some form of cut-off, determined by the numbers of 'outstanding ACRs', is followed.

Joint secretaries are awesomely powerful people. India is a federal country, where every state stands to gain from the discretionary decisions of the Government of India, and most of these decisions are taken by joint secretaries. Most secretaries are burnt out and in senescence by the time they reach that level, so they depend upon their joint secretaries for most decisions.

Therefore, there is a great incentive for states to ensure that many of their officers are empanelled as joint secretaries.

This, in turn, drives the incentive for senior officers to give nearly everybody 'outstanding' CRs.

The question still remains that if nearly everybody is graded as 'outstanding', how might the ACR be used to provide hints of the true talent of the officer? In other words, how can one distinguish the difference between an 'outstanding' officer of average quality and a truly outstanding 'outstanding' officer?

A story I heard in an entertaining lecture by an officer who had worked for years in the department of personnel and had the privilege of reading scores of confidential reports, which was attributed to Natwar Singh, the former external affairs minister and a former bureaucrat himself, described the perfect way to do this. Exasperated at having to see an endless stream of 'outstanding' ACRs for officers who were anything but outstanding, he is said to have remarked on one of them, 'This officer belongs to the category of 90 per cent of officers who are graded "outstanding".'

A few years ago, the system of confidential appraisal underwent some major changes that included an opportunity given to peers and subordinates to comment on the performance of the officer being appraised.

When positioning is all important even in the most informal of contacts between officers, it is difficult to believe that the 360-degree system will work effectively. The reason why a peer-based appraisal system might be compromised is ambition. Everybody has it. When the room at the top is restricted, it becomes the prime influencer of any behaviour of the reviewer and the reviewed; it does not recuse itself when 360-degree appraisals are undertaken.

One of the reasons why I think that peer reviews and 360-degree appraisals won't work is nothing more than my cynicism. The performance appraisal system has undergone several changes over the years, all intended, at least on paper, to ensure that the most deserving reach the top. Yet, the percentages of dunderheads who still make it to stratospheric levels remain the same. Reforms have to be judged not by the effort put into them, but by what they have achieved. By that yardstick, performance appraisal reforms have not worked effectively in the past, they won't work in the future.

Before one sets in place a system of 360-degree appraisal and expects it to work effectively, two prerequisites have to be in place. First, there must be a shared understanding of what integrity is and second, there must be a culture of acceptance of honest criticism up the hierarchy. Both are sadly lacking in the government.

One of the key questions in the system of performance appraisal in the government—the Annual Confidential Report system—is regarding the integrity levels of the officer being appraised.

Let's explore the idea of a shared understanding of what comprises integrity in the government a bit more by considering the scenarios described below:

(a) An officer routinely uses his official car to go to a private club on the way home and stays there late, playing cards, whilst his driver waits outside, without being paid overtime.

(b) Marshy government land, which is considered useless, is arranged to be granted to the club by the officer to set up a golf course. Officers of the civil services are given fast-track membership into the club on the payment of a concessional fee.

(c) An officer knows her minister is making money by interfering in postings and transfers of officials below her. The task of undertaking transfers has been always with officers, but slowly, the minister has taken over by demanding to see the files on transfers. The officer shrugs her shoulders, says that things have gone seriously wrong in the government and looks away.

(d) An officer working in the local government allows the members and corrupt engineers to make some money on contracts for roads, but on the tacit understanding that she be left alone to run a corruption-free programme for supporting farmers with training and technical inputs for water harvesting. This, in turn, ensures that the officer is not moved out and the programme benefits a large number of people.

(e) An officer has a reputation for austerity and honesty of a high degree. Wherever the officer is posted, she investigates who is dishonest and proactively collects evidence against such people. She then submits petitions to higher-level governments against such people. She often leaks such reports to the press and gains a reputation as a David who slays the Goliaths of corruption. The problem is that she is transferred within a few months in each of her jobs and she never stays long enough to complete any of her missions.

I am not going to attempt to analyse or provide answers as to whether the behaviour of the protagonist in each situation comprises behaviour of high or low integrity. However, these situations—and many more that are similar—paint a picture of many hues. We are led to realize that in reality, standards of integrity are not precise or universal, but are made up in the nick of time, as circumstances unravel.

It is not as if the government does not do anything to define standards of integrity. However, documents that aim to do so are usually verbose and vague. Typically, the rules for official and personal conduct of government staff do not keep pace with the circumstances of the day. Catch-all phrases such as 'conduct unbecoming of an officer' can be subjectively interpreted to apply personal biases as to what is acceptable and what is not whilst judging an officer's behaviour. For example, whilst arriving at one's workspace in an inebriated state would be a definite no–no, drinking off hours in a private bar might or might not be considered as behaviour unbecoming of an officer. The exceptions to the rules are also capable of being widely misinterpreted. For instance, while the rule that an officer ought not to communicate with the media without permission is easy to understand and apply, the exception that applies to expressions that are of an artistic or literary nature has been used as a window to express oneself on social media. That would be fine if one were writing about one's hobby or publishing a work of fiction, but when an officer of the government takes sides in a political argument through Facebook or Twitter, it might become decidedly iffy.

Clearly, it is safe for an appraising officer, whether in a supervisory capacity or in a subordinate role, to write that the officer being appraised is 'beyond reproach'. Much safer than saying that he is a 'rotten egg'.

6

The Civil Service and Leadership

Funnily enough, IAS officers don't think it is necessary to explain to anybody what the IAS is. I have seen people introducing themselves as 'IAS officers' to foreign audiences in training programmes abroad. It does not matter if you are Mexican or Mongolian, or speak Aramaic or Yiddish, you are expected to know what those three hallowed letters stand for.

Even though non-Indians are poorer by their lack of knowledge of the Indian Administrative Service, it is a really big deal in India. I would hazard a guess that nowhere in the country would one get 'huh?' as a reply if one announces the fact that one belongs to the IAS. What you will get is indifference turning into action and hostility turning into fawning.

The entry into the IAS is through several hurdles of competition. The year-long process of selection involves three examinations by which a field of nearly two hundred and fifty thousand aspirants is narrowed down to the few individuals who are selected for the IAS. The field is pared down by a preliminary test to about 10,000, who are declared eligible for the main exams. Of these, about 1800 are invited for face-to-face interviews, following which, about 450 of them are selected to join the Group A Civil Services of the Government of India. Of these, selected through a process of individual choice and ranking in a merit list, about 150 join the IAS. As it is rare—but for the occasional exception of a choice in favour of the foreign service—for an individual to seek any other service as a first choice, the IAS comprises the crème de la crème of the merit list.

Therefore, there are ample reasons for an IAS officer to commence his or her career with a swollen head. Yet, this is necessary; before one unpacks why IAS officers tend to have swollen heads, one needs to refresh one's minds with a brief, conceptual understanding of what leadership means. After all, IAS officers are meant to be leaders.

It is difficult to have agreement on the definition of leadership. Any literature review throws up many adjectives that describe or qualify it, each equally convincing. Yet, one must avoid conceptual stretching of the term, because each individual can adopt a definition convenient to support her position, leading to meaningless consensus conclusions in order to accommodate diverse points that cannot be reconciled. In the circumstances, it is useful to start from the point of what leadership might not be.

Leadership is not defined by the purity of the end goal, because what might be considered laudable by one individual might be a reprehensible goal for another. Thus, a terrorist who masterminds an attack or a dacoit who robs people are leaders in their own right because they believe in what they do, even though society at large considers their acts to be deplorable.

'Leadership' is not exactly the same as 'management' either; the latter entails following rules and ensuring that objectives are reached within a defined framework. Leadership might require one to step beyond that framework in order to achieve a larger vision. There might be circumstances in a management role to assume a leadership role, but much of management does not entail leadership. Therefore, taking ideas derived from good management and using them to define good leadership might not always be appropriate.

If leadership is not management, then what exactly might it be? From the plethora of definitions and descriptions, two thought-provoking approaches emerge.

The Leadership Institute of Harvard College has generated cutting-edge thought on the concept of leadership. Ron Heifetz, in his work on 'Adaptive Leadership' (*Leadership without Easy Answers*, by Ronald A. Heifetz, Harvard University Press, 1994), attempted to clarify two important distinctions: between technical and 'adaptive' problems and between leadership and authority. He defined leadership as an activity rather than a position of influence or a set of personal characteristics. He suggested abandoning the idea that leaders are born and not made, as this belief fosters both self-delusion and irresponsibility in those who see themselves as born leaders, and can lead to inaction and dangerous forms of dependency in those who do not see themselves as leaders. Heifetz suggested that leaders are confronted with technical problems, which can be solved by expertise and good management, and adaptive problems, which require innovation and learning. Traditional management strategies are useful in dealing with technical problems, but in situations where beliefs and values come into play, technical 'fixes' tend to exacerbate the problem. Adaptive challenges involve a disparity between values and circumstances. The task of the leader is to close the gap by marshalling energy, resources and the ingenuity to change the circumstances. But just as often it requires that people change their values. Leadership, therefore, consists 'not of answers or assured visions, but of taking action to clarify values'. Good leaders know how to stimulate and contain the forces of invention and change, and to shift the process from one stage to the next, he said.

According to Heifetz, there are five strategic principles of leadership: 1) diagnose the situation in light of the values at stake and unbundle the issues involved; 2) keep the level of distress within tolerable limits for doing adaptive work (he said, 'Keep the heat up without blowing up the vessel.'); 3) identify the issues that engage the most attention and counteract avoidance mechanisms such as denial, scapegoating, pretending the problem is technical or attacking individuals rather than issues; 4) allow people to take responsibility for the problem, but at a rate they can handle; and 5) protect those who raise hard questions, generate distress and challenge people to rethink the issues at stake.

Heifetz explored the phenomenon of *leadership without authority*. He said that leaders without authority 'push us to clarify our values, face hard realities and seize new possibilities, however frightening they may be.' He cited Gandhi as the most celebrated example of this type of leadership. Gandhi tried to force attention to a set of problems in India that the British colonial government refused to acknowledge. He identified many adaptive challenges and used various methods of creative defiance to get people to face them.

Similarly, Nelson Mandela, Lech Wałęsa, Martin Luther King Jr and Margaret Sanger gained considerable informal authority and widespread popular confidence and support through their very lack of formal authority that allowed them to address deep-seated adaptive problems in society.

Heifetz believed that while we usually focus attention at the head of the table, *leadership may more often emerge from the foot of the table*. For example, many women who have been denied formal authority roles in society have developed strategies for leading without authority. The same is true for other traditionally disempowered groups.

Finally, Heifetz cautioned that the stresses of adaptive work are often severe and can bring out the worst in people. Leadership is demanding, even dangerous and strategies must be developed for 'staying alive'. Heifetz pointed out that leaders and authority figures get attacked, dismissed, silenced and sometimes assassinated because they come to represent loss, real or perceived, to those members of the community who feel that they have got, or might get, the bad end of the bargain.

Heifetz's practical recommendations to leaders include getting far enough above the fray to see key patterns, distinguishing between oneself and one's role, externalizing the conflict and *giving it back to its rightful owners*, identifying and sharing the burden with partners, finding a sanctuary, and preserving a sense of purpose.

Heifetz's compelling work has since been followed by much amplification of these lines of thought. Eric Michael[1] feels that leadership is the art of empowering and mobilizing others to want to accomplish a mutually agreed-upon goal while advancing the group's integrity and morale. He acknowledges that everyone has their own style of leadership, much like every painter has his own style of brushstrokes. Some people naturally start off better as leaders than others, but everyone can learn to become better with training and practice. He believes that effective leaders must be able to enable others to do things, as well as get them to do it. A leader is most effective if followers are both able and willing. Hence, 'want to' is also a critical part of this definition. In addition to being willing and able, mobilizing implies getting the group to follow through with action. Leaders must get the group to work towards a mutually agreed-upon goal, in an honourable manner, whilst adhering to moral and ethical principles. An effective leader should also be responsible for the team and its enjoyment and feelings towards others on the team and the work. Michel agrees with Heifetz's point on adaptive leadership and says that leadership does not 'denote position or de jure power. Anyone can be a leader by fulfilling this definition, both an elected head and a member without any official position.' Without occupying a seat of power, if they could 'empower and mobilize others to want to accomplish a mutually agreed-upon goal, while advancing the group's integrity and morale', they could be effective adaptive leaders.

Another thinker on the subject, Dean Itani,[2] further stressed the idea of leadership emerging from anyone. Whilst under traditional understandings of leadership, communities are broken into leaders and followers and leaders make decisions and motivate and the followers do what they are told to do, it is possible that anybody, however humble, is capable of engaging in acts of leadership. Itani asserted that his definition of 'acts of leadership' encourages and empowers everyone in a community to be alert to add what they can to their missions any time that they can. It encourages everyone to be entrepreneurial in their approach to their world.

Itani succinctly stated that 'leadership is moving *sustainable* communities forward *ethically* in their missions'. The words 'sustainable' and 'ethical' (in the definition) are crucial, he said. He reiterated the point that anybody could be a true leader, even if they were not endowed with authority, if they desired to move their communities forward and grasped the opportunity to make a difference. Since nobody would 'want to be neutral towards their communities, much less act in detrimental ways,' he said, 'anybody could not only be a leader, everybody would want to be a leader.' Stressing upon the ethicality of the objective to be achieved and the use of means to achieve it, he said that any practice or mission that cannot be sustained will make the community implode and, thus, no real leaders would ever involve themselves with them. Itani thus said that *'moving one's community towards unsustainable or unethical goals are detrimental to the health of the community itself and are therefore not leadership acts'*.

Another interesting viewpoint on leadership explores further on whether it could bridge divides. Peggy Dulany (1997) pointed out that as the new global environment was beset increasingly by conflicts and potential conflicts that arise from inequities in structures and systems, a different leadership response, which builds upon the *'inherent quality of human behaviour that can be conserving, reconciling, attuned to the connective forces in the universe that imply greater unity and continuity'* was needed. Dulany felt that what was needed were *'bridging individuals'*, who could bridge the gap between, and among, contending organizations and interests. Qualities of such individuals would include the ability to engage different kinds of people; openness to compromise; credibility with his or her constituency; and an aptitude for learning to understand the language used by different sectors of society. She said that the bridging leader's capacity to elicit trust from the community comes from competence, integrity, constancy and empathy. Bridging leaders needed to have the ability to deal with diverse views and ambiguities, capacity to orchestrate coalitions and build alliances. While they needed a strong belief in a vision, they must be willing to amend it to include insights of others.

Inspired by Dulany's work, a corporate named Synergos decided to further inquire into the phenomenon of the bridging leader. In path-breaking research, Synergos studied the traits and strategies of bridging leaders in Africa, Asia and Latin America and came up with startling insights. Synergos discovered common values and characteristics of bridging leaders, regardless of their differing cultures, economic position and gender. These included integrity and credibility, honesty and commitment and values that engender trust. Bridging leaders had access to networks; had wide and extensive relationships with people and the capacity to transform networks into partnerships. Their personal attributes included empathy, capacity to listen reflectively and low ego needs.

Clearly, the new thinking on leadership believes that leadership is not about 'leading' in the conventional sense as understood. Leadership is not about position or authority; there is no need to believe in the limiting notion that it is largely about occupying a vantage position from where greater influence can be applied. Leadership is not about good management either, which narrowly focuses on providing technical fixes to solve problems. Leadership, they describe, is more about adapting to change, of bridging divides, of pursuing goals in an ethical manner, of undertaking and nurturing acts of leadership by others.

Perhaps the most powerful thought is Itani's point, that there are 'acts of leadership', which even ordinary people can, and have, performed.

Before we plunge into the question of civil servants acquiring adaptive or bridging leadership qualities, we must scrutinize the position of civil servants as a class within the overall governance structure and ascertain what the expectations from them are. In the structured hierarchical system of government, the authority of the civil service comes next to that of the political executive. The essence of a civil servant's responsibility is to tender advice to the political executive. Once the political executive considers the proffered advice and takes decisions, the task of a civil servant progresses to implementing the decisions taken. Before doing so, the civil servant, if she disagrees with the political executive's decision, is entitled to an opportunity to resubmit her advice for reconsideration. If the political executive still insists on the earlier decision, then it becomes the task of the civil servant to execute that decision. The political executive's mind speaks through a hierarchical system of decisions and civil servants must take action to follow them in their strict hierarchy of predominance. *Thus, the civil servant's first allegiance is to the Constitution, as it is the overarching expression of decision of the political executive, then to the law, then to rules and other forms of decisions.*

This would imply that most of the time, a civil servant if he has to be effective, has to function as a manager. In an ideal world, *there would be little scope, within a framework that is defined by the Constitution, laws and rules, for anything more than good management.* Thus, civil servants require more skill building in management than in leadership.

The question then moves on to whether there is scope for civil servants to perform 'acts of leadership' in such circumstances. This could lead us to a paradoxical discovery, that *the greater the dysfunctionality in the implementation of governance frameworks and the law, the higher is the possibility for civil servants to perform acts of leadership*. This insight can lead to an uncomfortable realization: civil servants who desire to perform acts of leadership *might overtly or covertly engineer situations where governance frameworks are weak, so that they gain more opportunities for maverick leadership acts, either good or bad*.

The question is whether civil servants consciously design dysfunctional systems so they can have more opportunities to show that they are indispensable. Just one example is sufficient to support my contention that they do.

The post of district collector (also known as the deputy commissioner and the district magistrate, in many states) is the one single position that symbolizes the IAS in the public eye. It is a job reserved for members of the IAS alone. Over the years, the post has gained an aura of invincibility and infinite ability, by the assignation to it of many roles, through Central and state laws and executive instructions. The DC heads the 'district administration' and along with the superintendent of police, the district forest officer, the PWD superintending or executive engineer and the DRDA project director, constitute a group to which the state turns for information, advice and action. The administrative structure of the panchayats and municipalities, which are both constitutionally mandated as devolved local governments, is ignored in the scheme of things, or is considered subordinate to the DC, to whom is entrusted the task of 'getting them to work'. A variety of parallel bodies are set up, to which funds that ought to go to the lieutenant governors are transferred. Worse still, this official system is hybridized with LG administration, creating a vicious web of relationships between the official and political hierarchies that provides plenty of scope for patronage and non-accountable behaviour.

In most states, this ragtag assembly of political and official systems cannot and does not function well. Yet, there is an unchallenged notion that even-handed development can be delivered only by the collector, who is believed to be external to the local system, which is considered to be exploitative and captured by the elite. This essentially colonial mindset has not changed in seven decades of independence.

As a consequence of this huge concentration of power, DCs are currently hugely burdened with development, regulation, protocol, disaster management and election duties. The Second Administrative Reforms Commission listed more than sixty odd committees that the DCs chair. These include chairing several parallel missions that bypass the state and local governments and implement sectoral programmes directly.

The aura of the DC is assiduously promoted and protected by the members of the IAS. Efforts to reduce the burden of the DCs are resisted by the IAS, invariably with success. Yet, in spite of the aura of invincibility and authority that surrounds the position of the district collector, there is no evidence to show that such centralized district administration has yielded development results. In Karnataka, during the 'big bang' decentralization effort of 1987–92, DCs were divested of their development responsibilities and officers senior to them were posted as 'chief secretaries' of zilla parishads. The DRDAs were merged with the ZPs. The chief secretaries of ZPs were accountable to the ZP. Their performance appraisals were undertaken by the ZP adhyaksha. The system resulted in a radical and fundamental shift in the power structure, both amongst politicians and bureaucrats. Documented studies show that there was inclusive participation of women and poor people in development during this period. Rural Karnataka's development accelerated in this time. Particularly impressive strides were taken in rural infrastructure, such as water supply, roads and school buildings. Yet, in 1992, when ZP and mandal terms ended, elections were postponed and collectors were appointed as administrators of the ZPs. Meanwhile, in a policy turnaround, officers junior to the DCs were posted as CSs, thus restoring status quo as to who was the de-facto head of the district.

The overburdened collector's post, with its many grey areas of responsibility, is a good example of a dysfunctional governance system. *However, this position provides ample scope to the incumbents to engage in acts of leadership.* For that reason, the incentive amongst bureaucrats to reform these dysfunctional arrangements is low. One cannot dismiss the intoxication that the wielding of absolute power can bring.

The unnatural concentration of power in the institution of the civil service can more likely than not, permanently transform even the most level-headed individual who joins it. The excessive power that the bureaucracy keeps to itself becomes another form of intellectual imprisonment. Even those who feel uncomfortable with it and are candid enough to admit that they cannot handle these powers, feel obliged to put on a brave front and stoically shoulder the burden. A collector cannot be a sissy. No district collector can stand up and honestly admit that he cannot handle this burden. That would be career suicide.

I, therefore, make the point that *what we need are functional systems and not many opportunities for civil servants to indulge in acts of leadership. The system is to be the leader and if it is functional, most of the opportunities for maverick individual leadership will fade away.* Yet, let me contradict myself straightaway, this is not to say that in a functional system, being a civil servant entirely erases opportunities for acts of leadership. In fact, the contrary would be true. The key opportunity for the officer would be *not to indulge in individual and extraordinary acts of heroism, but to provide the space for teamwork and motivate large numbers of people within teams to perform small, but significant acts of leadership.* It is in this opportunity for nurturing and coaxing leadership out of a team of people accustomed to being followers that an officer could find the greatest effectiveness and satisfaction.

While some aspects of dysfunctionality within the government have been built up through several civil-servant-driven decisions that go against fundamentally accepted principles of federalism and decentralization, the civil servant cannot be blamed for all weaknesses of the governance system. Moreover, it would be unfair to cast the blame on each new crop of civil servants for the mistakes of her predecessors. Today's administrative system is a challenging environment, with many stakeholders and interests that are often at loggerheads with each other. Even as fractured systems are being rationalized, a civil servant on the field has to deal with situations that arise, there and then. This brings us to the next question, which is whether civil servants can consciously cultivate the qualities required to be an 'adaptive' or 'bridging' leader.

One of the key attributes for a successful bridging leader is to have low ego needs. However, here, the civil servant, particularly the IAS, starts off with a distinct disadvantage. There is nothing in the training, upbringing and work environment of the IAS officer that teaches an individual to cultivate low ego needs. On the other hand, right from the day that they clear a tough competitive examination to enter the service, IAS officers are catapulted to stratospheric heights. They are the objects of adulation and envy feted by their castes, states, districts, towns and villages. Society celebrates the IAS officer far out of proportion to his achievements. The fat dowries offered for his hand, the excessive traditional bowing and scraping that still survives in the name of official tradition in many states, the awe in which junior officers hold their IAS colleagues or bosses are very dangerous for the ego. Most officers go into the field to take up positions that are legacies of the colonial era, occupy bungalows left behind by the British and rule the district in exactly the same way that their ICS predecessors had. It takes a very level-headed individual to not allow these factors to go to his head. Thus, it is difficult for IAS officers to imbibe the attribute for having a low ego need. Those who do become bridging leaders are exceptions, having the strength of character to not get carried away by the fuss that society makes over them.

Can the IAS learn bridging and adaptive leadership? Can a programme be devised, which draws from these new insights into leadership, to design a game plan for enhancing the leadership qualities of civil servants, in a wider sense? Can we look at these new diagnostics of leadership, teach budding civil servants a systematic way of analyzing stakeholders and their interests and based on that motivate or provoke people to undertake acts of leadership? Can officers be trained to become adaptive or bridging leaders, who can smoothen out conflict, harmonize diverse interests and also motivate and protect other individuals so that they can perform acts of leadership? Obviously, one single training programme or strategy cannot result in the personality attributes that are required for individuals to imbibe these skills. To become a good leader is a process of daily growth, which happens through a combination of training, response to the environment and internal discipline. It requires a nurturing environment, in which training is but a part for officers to makes these skills a habit.

Here are a few things that could be done in the training space, the overall design and structure of the civil service and in terms of changing the personal habits of individuals in the civil service that if followed, may nurture the kind of qualities required for an adaptive, bridging leader to flower.

First and foremost, the IAS needs to consciously work on curbing swollen heads within their tribe. By all means, let there be a genuine celebration of the fact that people have cleared a tough examination to enter the hallowed service. However, following that, it is important to develop a sense of equanimity and not let pride turn into arrogance. One should not, either covertly or overtly, reinforce or support the belief that IAS officers are a cut above the rest, that they are successors to the ICS and that it ought to comprise strong individuals aloof from the people, able to deliver justice with an even hand and therefore rule over people. This of course, cannot be achieved through delivering homilies on humility. What could be done is to avoid calling maverick officers from the field to boast about their exploits during training sessions. The 'effective SDO' and 'effective DC' seminars in the IAS training academy at Mussoorie tend to do this. They are all about 'I, me and myself' and such displays of unverified examples of IAS effectiveness should not be paraded before fresh entrants.

Second, there is a need to build a genuine respect for democracy within the IAS. There has to be a really good grounding in the concept and practice of democracy. Skills for implementing one or the other programme can be taught, but it is important to build the attitude of respecting democracy. Bureaucrats have always inwardly tended to ignore the importance of democracy, yet there is nothing more valuable for a country struggling to erase years of poverty and discrimination. While the way that democracy is practised in India has many grievous faults, there is a need to stop sneering and scoffing at it and actually plunge into a dispassionate study of what works and what does not, with democratic discourse being non-negotiable. There are some very interesting new practices emerging in informed public democracy, such as deliberative democracy, which offers new opportunities in India and that can be adapted by the sensitive and caring civil servant. Building a positive attitude to democracy and to remain positive, whatever the provocation from the immediate environment might be, is an important aspect of building adaptive leadership.

Within the overall goal of building a respect for democracy, there has to be a good grounding in the theory and practice of decentralization. The LBSNAA does not earmark sufficient time for a deep study of decentralization. I say this with some pain and resignation, born out of experience. In 2008 and 2009, when there was a collaboration between the LBSNAA and the Duke University in designing and conducting the Phase III programme for IAS officers of eight years of seniority, I was tasked to design and conduct a four-day optional programme on decentralization. Internal evaluations and feedback from participants indicated that the programme was much appreciated. Yet, when the

Duke University collaboration came to an end, the time allocated for decentralization was reduced to half a day. I still continued to deliver those half-day lectures!

One of the reasons why IAS training programmes tends to ignore a study of decentralization is because they equate the larger idea of decentralization with the nuts and bolts of running the panchayat system. It is also due to the IAS's unwavering conviction that whatever else one might do for decentralization, it should not topple or undermine the post of the district collector. Therefore, unfortunately, very few IAS officers have read contemporary literature on local government-related institutional design, public finance, politics and democracy in order to develop an objective understanding of how a multi-tier government system is structured and how it runs. Generally, IAS officers have a symptomatic appreciation of decentralization and give up hope on it based upon adverse personal experience, anecdotes and generalization. Nothing could be further from reality. Decentralization is a vast field of study. In its broadest sense, it encompasses federalism and indeed, is a study of inter-governmental relations. Knowing decentralization is as critical as understanding globalization.

In training civil servants on decentralization, they must have several opportunities to be exposed to the elected representatives of local governments, so that they cleanse their minds of the wrong stereotypical images they might be carrying. Civil servants would find it fascinating how local government representatives build their political capital by negotiating through a dysfunctional system full of institutional contradictions and wrong incentives. Exposure to people on the other side will certainly build empathy and an attitude of respect in the minds of civil servants. It will also hopefully wean them out of the steadfast belief in the district collector being the sole benefactor of the district. They will hopefully realize that decentralization means something more than agencification of local governments to do their bidding. They will need to learn the tough lesson that development might flower if they step out of the way. *Above all, they might realize that promoting and supporting decentralization offers tremendous opportunity to develop and utilize valuable skills of adaptive leadership.*

As a part of this training, the field assignment would also need to be reworked, so that civil servants, when they do their attachments with the panchayats, do so not at the behest of district collectors, but are placed with the zilla parishad president for being deployed to the panchayats. There are several panchayats that have achieved extraordinary success in governance and civil servants should be sent to these, independent of the district collector, to gain a true understanding of the grassroots reality.

Yet, the coming years call for adopting the new-age strategies of bridging leadership and adaptive leadership if civil servants are to make a difference. Training alone cannot make a difference in leadership styles and effectiveness. A combination of training, institutional reforms and adopting some simple personal habits might accelerate this transition in leadership.

In the overarching analysis, the IAS needs to be exposed to competition. It is undeniable that once a civil servant clears the entrance examination, whatever might be the discomfort of the job, the IAS tag itself offers a comfort zone to successful entrants. One cannot expect civil servants to retain their sharpness if all they need to do is to pass one exam and then sail along, largely protected from competition. Besides, over the years, the IAS has been nimble in identifying where the opportunities lie and have moved themselves to the right jobs that emerge through changing times, by changing their internal policies on placement. In the licence and public monopoly raj period, the IAS occupied most public sector undertaking postings, particularly in state governments. As many old-style PSUs were disbanded and liquidated in the post-liberalization period, the IAS abandoned these and began to occupy the special purpose vehicles created for channelizing money downwards. For example, new-age institutions such as infrastructure development corporations, health missions and education missions became preferred positions for IAS officers to be posted. Similarly, the proliferation of regulatory jobs has offered ample opportunities for post-retirement employment too, to IAS officers. Again it was the self-serving attitude of the service that queered the pitch. The Fifth Pay Commission recommended increasing the retirement age to sixty with one caveat: nobody should hold any government post after retirement and the break with employment must be complete. The higher bureaucracy engineered the acceptance of the recommendation and ignored the caveat.

One of the ways is to throw open the bureaucracy to lateral entry in a systematic and transparent manner. This was suggested by the Administrative Reforms Commission, in some sense by the Sixth Pay Commission and has been recently implemented, but not without some controversy.

Lateral entry is not a new thing; outsiders have been inducted on occasions in the past as well, largely at the secretary level, in order to bring in fresh thinking and domain expertise into the government. Those continue to be eminently desirable objectives. Bureaucrat skills tend to suffer from lack of competition. Internal competition is not of great worth, because it is restricted and everybody eventually moves up, in some manner or the other, within the tribe. Outside talent can, besides improving the quality of the bureaucracy, shake up the complacent within the government. It can effectively send the message that officers need to constantly hone and improve their skills.

Bureaucrats threatened by the prospect of being swamped and elbowed away by lateral entrants keep stressing the need for having generalists with a holistic view of things, and also those who know to work the system. They say that lateral entrants will have tunnel vision, lack an appreciation of the larger picture and be unable to understand the internal workings of the government. I don't buy these arguments at all. The fears of being swamped are not merely overstated, they are wrong. Second, surely, intelligent people selected through a rigorous process will be able to adapt to a new environment quickly. Besides, it is just as well we dilute the number of loyalists to obsolete processes within the government. If an intelligent lateral entrant thinks that a process does not make sense, it probably doesn't and needs to be junked.

In its recent decision to bring in outsiders into the government through lateral entry at the director and joint secretary levels, the Union government is also aiming to provide a solution to a burgeoning problem. Low recruitments into the civil services during the late nineties and the early noughties led to a shortage of director- and joint secretary-level officers available for induction into these positions at the Union government level. There was a time when IAS officers were in hot competition with each other for the positions of joint secretaries, but now, in the light of the shortage of those of an appropriate seniority, many posts are being filled by officers of other services. In such a scenario, bringing in lateral entrants is a logical solution.

Yet, the manner of the recent selection of lateral entrants leaves much to be desired. Nine posts were advertised, there was a deluge of tens of thousands of applicants and after an initial screening, with no marking or grading of that process being made public, interviews were held to select the successful candidates. Detractors were quick to point out that there were no south Indians nor were there any people belonging to the Scheduled Castes or Scheduled Tribes amongst them. The government clarified that since each post was considered a single post, the question of providing a reservation quota did not arise.

The opaque selection process and the controversy over reservations has clouded and diverted attention from the benefits of lateral entry, which is to bring in outside talent and introduce healthy competition that would keep insiders on their toes. Surely, the valid concerns against the current approach being piloted can be addressed and a more transparent and systematic system of lateral entry can be introduced. Some of the ways that a lateral entry system could be made more systematic are as follows:

First, the positions that are open to lateral entrants ought to be made known well in advance of any recruitment so that candidates can have adequate time to prepare themselves.

Second, lateral entry opportunities ought to be made open to in-service candidates as well. A junior officer who has greater domain knowledge and specialization as compared to an indifferent senior who has managed to rise through the ranks should not be thwarted. I know such an approach will go against the hallowed principle of seniority being followed in positioning bureaucrats, but that is an antiquated and inflexible approach. Lateral entry should enable talent within the government to be fully utilized.

Third, the current single interview system will just not do. It is not transparent enough. There must be a general written examination and possibly two levels of interviews. Marks must be made public, just as they are, for the competitive examinations.

Fourth, and this is a knotty problem, is the issue of reservations. When internal selection to the positions of joint secretaries is made there are no quotas and there have always been wry observations, mostly true, of various caste and regional lobbies that operate to pick officers for glamorous and desirable positions. Yet, no community or region can dominate the selection; even those who show a sly favouritism are conscious that they cannot go very far in pursuing their biases; other lobbies keep watch. Yet, a systematic process of lateral entry will need to consider reservations; sidestepping the issue by considering each post as a single post to which reservation will not apply is fraught with danger and will upset the informal commitment to preserving a wide variety in the selection of offices, which exists at the moment.

We also need to take specific and conscious measures that reduce the ego needs of the bureaucracy. There are many personal habits and personality traits that reinforce the ego, which officers should eschew as individuals. Many of these are either mentioned or hinted at in the conduct rules, but are ignored in practice.

The IAS must learn to give credit where it rests. IAS officers must learn to publicly acknowledge the actual individuals responsible for outstanding development. I have seen many IAS officers receiving awards on behalf of their districts or institutions. Rarely have I seen anybody thank their team or mention the names of those who actually did the hard work. I found it laughable that when NREGA performance awards were given away in Delhi, it was the collector who was called for the presentation, and not the district panchayat chairperson. Under the NREGA, it is the district panchayat who is to approve the shelf of projects and district programme coordinators assist them. I once saw a brochure on the NREGA published by the district administration, in which the collector had put his own photograph and taken credit for a programme that is largely implemented by the panchayats. Such practices of seeking vicarious credit should be discouraged, even ridiculed. Please note that in no NREGA scam unearthed through social audit, has one seen any district collectors taking vicarious responsibility and offering to go to jail.

If IAS officers need to become bridging leaders, they should consciously avoid giving the impression that they are individuals who are destined for a higher order. They will need to give us symbols of separation and power. They could take several steps in their official and personal lives that might look silly, but are deeply symbolic in India's hierarchical societies. These little things go a long way in changing the equation of leadership. Symbolism is important and one needs to bring in a new era by changing the symbolic grammar of daily interaction.

First, they could avoid discriminatory practices. For example, why have separate officers' toilets, or separate elevators? Why not instead, ensure that all toilets in the office are clean? For a start, they could have common toilets for everybody in North Block in New Delhi, occupied by the most exalted of India's mandarins. Similarly, IAS officers must learn not to break queues; even if somebody offers them a place ahead, they need to learn to decline and follow the rules like anybody else.

Second, the IAS could avoid using symbols of rank. The IAS is not a uniformed service. There is no need therefore for symbols of rank to be adopted. For instance, the IAS officers of a state that prides itself on its egalitarian culture has actually managed to design an IAS flag, which flies ceremonially from the flag post of their cars when they are chauffeured! Apparently that was because they were peeved with similar habits of their police counterparts. Such ridiculous ego trips should be abolished immediately.

Third, the IAS could adopt habits that do not require a retinue of hangers on. For example, they could carry their own bags when coming to office. They need not have an army of attendants to see them off or receive them at airports. They could drive their own vehicles on off days. They need not keep orderlies informally at home.

It will be too much to ask that IAS officers should avoid putting the 'IAS' tag after their names, or on visiting cards. I know how inconvenient that is; that tag opens a lot of doors and is very useful to flash about on occasions. Perhaps one will succeed with the suggestion that IAS officers should encourage people to address them by their names, or designations, and eschew the use of 'Sir' and 'Madam'. But I don't think that will happen either.

Generalists versus Specialists

The debate on whether the administration is better served by generalists or specialists is one that never fails to cause friction in official circles. Whenever the administration is put in the dock for bad performance, essays are written about it in the media. However, I suspect that apart from a hazy desire to see some kind of overall change for the better, which drives a general endorsement of the idea that more specialists ought to hold higher-level jobs in the government, the public at large has no great preference either way.

Who exactly are these generalists and specialists that are at loggerheads with each other? One could ask this question from the perspective of the entry-level context concerned, which aspirants have to clear in order to enter the hallowed portals of this higher-level of government, or from that of the services they are destined to join after being selected. The common civil services examination is the entry-level test for the selection of aspirants to join two all India services, namely, the Indian Administrative Service and the Indian Police Service, and also a range of Central services, seventeen at the last count. Of these, some may be the sole service that deals with a particular specialized aspect of government activity, whereas others may serve a common specialized activity, albeit in diverse departments. Thus, we have the Indian Foreign Service, the sole Group A service that focuses on foreign affairs. There are five services that focus wholly or partly on accounting and audits in different wings of the government, namely, the Audit and Accounts Service, the Civil Accounts Service, the Defence Accounts Service, the Post and Telegraph Accounts and Finance Service and the Railway Accounts Service. Similarly, there are two revenue services that comprise the category of those that work in the tax and revenue collection spheres, namely, the Income Tax and the Customs and Central Excise services.

Seen from the angle of which would be their parent departments where those selected are destined to serve the better part of their careers, there are eight categories of Central services as follows:

External Affairs	Indian Foreign Service
Audits, under the Comptroller and Auditor General	Indian Audits and Accounts Service
Railways	Railway Traffic Service Railway Personnel Service Railway Accounts Service Railway Protection Force
Defence	Indian Ordnance Factories Service Defence Estates Service Defence Accounts Service
Post and Telegraph service	Indian Postal Service P & T Accounts and Finance Service

Ministry of Finance (Maintenance of Accounts)	Civil Accounts Service
Ministry of Finance (Revenue)	Income Tax Service, Customs and Central Excise Service
Other departments	Indian Information Service Indian Trade Service Indian Corporate Law Service

However, there are specialists who are selected through other means as well. The Indian Forest Service, the third of the all India services, is selected through a separate examination that compulsorily tests proficiency in the life sciences. Similarly, engineers are selected through separate examinations for jobs in the government.

The debate between generalists and specialists is, therefore, between the IAS on the one hand, the true 'generalist' service of the lot and three kinds of specialists, namely, first, those selected through the common civil services examination—the same through which IAS officers are selected, such as the Audits and Accounts Service, the Foreign Service and the Police Service—second, those who are selected through separate examinations that a priori test them on their specialized competencies—such as the Forest Service and the Engineering Service—and third, outsiders brought in through lateral entry—an oft-touted strategy to bring in completely external talent from outside the government sphere—into the government.

There is a mutual dislike between these three categories of aspirants for the higher echelons of the government and the 'generalist' IAS. The former two resent the IAS for upstaging them and capturing jobs that they believe they deserve. The lateral entrant is bewildered by the general hostility that the IAS shows when they occupy their seats in the government.

In a perceptive piece on the generalist versus the specialist debate,[1] Praveen Kishore observed that though reviews of the organizational structure followed by restructuring of each service are mandated to be done periodically, these end up only tinkering with the edges and hardly ever result in a thorough overhaul. He also noted that the occupation of most senior management posts in the government by the IAS has left others from the specialist services thoroughly demotivated and resentful of the dominance over them by the former. To address that criticism, Kishore suggests three policy options and what he calls, an 'alternative vision'. First, he suggests doing away with the separate service branches for senior management levels, term all recruits into the service as IAS officers and consider them as specialized generalists who could be treated as adept in a certain category of governance functions. He says that such a bunching of everybody into the same category will put out the fire of inter-service rivalry and in any case, is not far removed from the reality of generalist IAS officers holding the predominant number of senior management positions. In place of the current set of 'service branches', Kishore advocates the setting up of broader, domain-based service branches. He goes so far as to say that certain specialist services, such as policing and revenue collection, could also then be headed by generalist officers, whilst also admitting in the same breath that he may be criticized as being conservative and harkening back to an earlier, uncomplicated era.

His second option is diametrically opposite to his first one. It is to treat the informal but visible distinction between the IAS—he also clubs the IPS with the IAS in this regard—and other services as a formal one. This would entail that a separate examination be held for the IAS and IPS so as to retain a clear demarcation between those destined for other services and these two 'specialized generalist' services. This, he maintains, would set clear expectations from the very outset as to the careers as generalists that those who are selected to the IAS can aspire to, whilst also making it clear to those who opt for the civil services (other than the IAS and IPS) selection process, that they will be considered only for the specialized services for which the exam is conducted.

The third option suggested is that the formal equality that exists on paper between the different specialist services and the generalist IAS is enforced strictly. This would mean that the IAS would be restricted in making lateral entry into the senior management positions of each service branch, which would be reserved for those rising from within the service concerned.

Finally, in his 'alternative vision', he suggests that the civil service cadre be organized into 'feasible and worthwhile branches' of 'larger domain areas' demarcated on the basis of a broad congruence of functions and responsibilities. While not giving any examples of what he suggests, he elaborates that these larger domain areas ought not to be created for any specific departments or for narrow purposes. This approach, he says, will lead to the evolution of cadres of 'specialized generalist' officers who are 'capable, competent and exposed enough' to shoulder responsibilities. Kishore lists out several advantages of such an approach, which would reduce, in his estimation, the number of services from the current twenty-five or thirty to about ten broad branches. These include greater flexibility, scope for reorganization and cross-agency expertise even within the functional domain concerned. He advocates that these services could also move from the Union to the state-level jobs with a smoothness that does not exist as of today.

Kishore concludes with some suggestions on how to identify and define these broad domain areas, a prelude to the constitution of service branches. He suggests that there be three categories of functions, namely, first, 'sovereign functions' such as law and order, internal security, foreign relations, fiscal and revenue management, defence, ensuring justice and fairness; second, the provision of public goods, comprising, for example, development administration, education, public healthcare, human development, promoting general welfare, carrying out distributive transfers, protecting property rights and enforcement of contracts for operation of markets; and third, economic and social management, comprising infrastructure development and management, economic and financial regulation and control, urban and rural habitats, and environment, natural resource management, power and energy, agricultural, commercial and industrial management, communication and transport.

While these are good suggestions for the future, as Kishore acknowledges, they need to be fleshed out and developed. For example, I would further categorize the broad categories of functions he lists out. The sovereign function category that he speaks comprises functions that are quite different from each other and are held together only by the fact that they are all performed largely by the Union government. That mere fact may not justify their classification into one category, because the skill sets required to perform these would differ from function to function.

The point remains that suggestions such as those given by Kishore still need to be considered by the government and their adoption would create several winners and losers, both in the long and the short terms. Besides, the administration that has to sagely consider these suggestions would still comprise the very interests they would affect: the civil service. Anybody acquainted with the fractious issue of promotion and career progression of any civil service will know of the vicious and long-drawn-out battles not only between services, but within different routes of selection to posts within a service. If the battle between specialists and generalists is not enough to prevent the administration from acting as one smooth machine, inter se seniority battles can cripple them totally. It is the rare state or service that has not witnessed long-drawn-out court battles between services or between promoted officers and directly recruited officers for inter se ranking and seniority.

So what of the present? It is a chaotic arrangement in which no hard and fast rules can be drawn as to who can go where. That's it, more or less. Specialization, whether acquired before entering service or afterwards, has little bearing on the career progression of those selected into the civil service, and particularly, into the IAS. The rivalries between services have led to resentment, true, particularly in those who are denied the chance to rise to the top level within their specialized services. However, it has also led to certain conventions and practices, which, even in the absence of rules that endorse them, seem to have acquired the force of law.

Let me explain, therefore, how the system works, at least from the perspective of the IAS. A disclaimer: I have a huge mental block to understanding this fully and there may be several errors of detail. Having thus unburdened myself of taking responsibility for any inaccuracies, this is how the system broadly works:

Every IAS officer selected lives three lives in succession. First comes the field life. In the initial years of their service, say for the first ten to twelve years, IAS officers largely serve in field postings. The first of these are the posts of a 'subcollector', 'assistant commissioner' or 'subdivisional magistrate'—all these terms loosely mean a similar set of responsibilities in most states. The subcollector exercises responsibilities within a subdivision, which is smaller than a district, but which comprises several tehsils, taluks or blocks, as the case may be. In earlier times, the subcollector exercised land administration, development administration and law-and-order-related powers, but now, with the establishment of local governments in the form of panchayats and municipalities, there is some variance in the extent to which they handle development administration. In some states where the panchayat system is strong, they have no role to play. In others, where there is no clear separation between local government responsibilities and the administration in practice, the subcollector wields formal or informal overseeing power over the BDOs who work within the panchayat system. Following the subcollector's posting, IAS officers are generally posted as CEOs of the district panchayats. There is also a growing tendency for them to be posted as municipal commissioners, particularly with the increasing urban population. In both cases, the officer functions as the administrative head answerable in varying degrees depending upon the state, to the elected body of the local government. It is rarely that an officer gets posted to the state headquarters to take charge of a specialized department or unit, though some do get posted early after a truncated posting as subcollector or as CEO of the district panchayat, as a punishment.

Generally speaking, when the officer has about eight to ten years of experience in these early field postings and a posting or two in a state-level department or institution, she is posted as the district collector. This is the apex of the field posting era of the IAS. The district collector is still considered as the head of the district administration and the first point of contact for the government in a district. In spite of the formal separation of powers between the state and the local governments, in practice in most states, the district collector wields considerable influence and power over the local governments. Sometimes this power is a formal one, where the district collector is the appellate authority over decisions of the local governments, but in most cases, the collector plays the role of a coordinator, backed by convention and practice. The district collector's position is a convenient level of delegation and, therefore, it is not surprising that she is overburdened in most states with a variety of functions. The Second Administrative Reforms Commission (2010) observed that the district collector in one sample district handled fifty different institutions and review committees, while admitting that many more might have been overlooked.[2] As a coordinator of governmental action in a district, there is no doubt that the district collector's institution is a bad idea in the current circumstances. However, no IAS officer will dare say that; the institution of the collector is a beloved one for the IAS and it is unthinkable to most that this position needs to be rejigged in the interests of better administration. Yet, whatever may be its faults, the district collector's position is the furnace in which the IAS officer's character, work style and capabilities are tested and tempered. It is this position that forges the IAS officer's skills as a generalist who is capable of thinking of the larger picture and provide both the vision to aim at and the coordinating skills to ensure progress in that direction.

Once the IAS officer finishes serving as a district collector, her career changes gear. The field posting era is over and the realm of the techno-manager opens up for the IAS. It is in the next phase of the officer's service that his positioning becomes largely domain-based. An officer gets posted to a functional division of the government, say the agriculture department, the energy department or suchlike. Such postings may also be with specialized corporate parastatal entities, say, for example, the electricity distribution corporation, the Commissionerate for Education or health. Suddenly, the officer has to adapt the rough and ready Rambo style of management acquired over field postings to the more genteel environment of a department. What's more, the officer has to acquire a working understanding of the intricacies of the specific domain in which she is placed; whether it be agriculture, electricity supply or education. Some officers make the transition easily, others do not. Havoc is sometimes caused by officers who cannot read balance sheets and yet, are posted as managing directors of large public sector corporations. Havoc is also caused by those using the overweening commanding style of personnel management in an environment populated by technocrats, sometimes resentful, who do not as readily defer to the authority of an outsider brought to head the organization as those in district-level jobs.

The final rebirth of an IAS officer is when she rises to policymaking levels, usually that of a secretary to the government. Officers do serve in the secretariat and policymaking levels at a relatively junior stage of their careers, but it is another thing when the officer begins to head a secretariat as the secretary. Policymaking requires yet another set of skills that is built on the foundation of the field experience and acquired in an executive capacity in corporate or parastatal positions. Policymaking needs the ability to read, listen, assimilate and understand. It requires the skills of drafting, piloting and articulating policy, followed by monitoring its execution, rather than directly executing it.

Layered within the second and third reincarnations is the opening up of positions in the Union government for IAS officers to occupy. Officers with experience of about a decade become eligible to get picked up to serve in the Union government. The first posting is usually as a deputy secretary in a department, followed by a promotion as a director. Then, following a rigorous screening process, officers can hope to get picked as joint secretaries in Union ministries, or equivalent positions in parastatal organizations. Here too, the officer is confined to dealing with a particular domain—one who serves in the petroleum ministry would be handling a different set of policy issues as compared to a colleague in an equivalent position in the health ministry.

Of course, it goes without saying that these categorizations are broad and that officers do follow atypical career paths too, where they rise into policy positions much earlier in their careers than others or continue to be in technocrat and executive jobs well into the later stages of their careers. In practical terms, each officer is faced with a bewildering array of permutations and combinations of opportunities, in core ministries or departments, parastatals and corporations at both the state and the Union levels. Thus, it is no surprise that there cannot be any generalizations of who specializes in what, as far as officers are concerned. It is not something dependent entirely on the interest of the officer concerned, but strongly influenced by the sectors in which he is posted, which is often a random event.

In an earlier era, the idea that an IAS officer should be a generalist had the makings of a dogma. It was considered bad form for an IAS officer to quote an educational degree in a particular subject to seek a posting in a related department; indeed, it was bad form for an officer to ever ask for a post. Furthermore, if the generalist officer developed an interest in any subject either fortuitously or by design, it was considered suspicious for that officer to ask to be retained in that specialization. Thus, senior officers who managed the careers of others felt that if one worked in the infrastructure sector and was good at it, it was time to post one to the education department. This was done religiously, to ensure that nobody developed a vested interest in any one field or forged contacts amongst the other stakeholders in policy, as that would dilute objectivity and distort policymaking. Over the years, that attitude has diminished somewhat; even the confidential reports now seek to know from senior officers whether the officers whose performance is being reviewed need further training or career placement in one or the other domain of specialization. Such a column would have been anathema to officers now long gone; yet, in today's day and age, this is considered desirable.

With the desire to enable officers to seek and acquire specializations now not considered a crime, officers are indeed doing so. Yet, the decision on which path to take can still be a fortuitous one. An officer that I hold in high regard, Venkat Ramani, has two specializations. Ramani served as a director in the Ministry of Petroleum and in his stint of four years, developed a formidable reputation as the One Who Knew Everything and Who Is Called in for Every Crisis. When Ramani's term ended and he reverted to Maharashtra state, he meandered into the field of nutrition, where he developed an equally legendary reputation. Ramani is an old-school officer; he, I think, believes in the old adage that one must serve wherever one is posted and not ask for anything special. Yet, the fact that he developed expertise in two diverse specializations with no relation to each other, exemplifies that the civil services examination system does bring some outstanding minds to the fore.

In contrast to the Ramanis of this world are those that are intent on specialization from the first day onwards. Usually, such focused souls quell their specialization ambitions as they pass through the early and busy days of field postings. However, they, at the first available opportunity, do work on acquiring the appropriate educational qualifications required to bolster their case for a specialization. Typically, those who have done so have attempted to specialize in the field of finance and economics. This is indeed commendable, because there ought to be no bars on officers acquiring more skills as their career progresses. The government is also rather generous in addressing these ambitions; there are several training programmes offered between top universities worldwide and in India and the government subsidizes and allows officers to attend these on a sabbatical. However, it is when officers return from such training programmes, all ready to use them in their new postings that the government turns inexplicably diffident. One would expect officers trained in a particular area of specialization to be posted to jobs that would utilize their newly acquired talents to the fullest. That is usually not the case. The government comprises people, who are both collaborators and competitors of those who return with specializations. Jealousy and the persistent thinking that officers must serve in a wide variety of unrelated jobs continue to assail the thinking of those who make choices of who should be posted where. And so, more often than necessary, officers who have acquired academic specializations end up being frustrated at not being picked for jobs that would suit them.

There is yet another ingredient in the mix of the decision-making system but the author just said that this does NOT happen. That ingredient is the politician. The final say on who is posted where increasingly depends upon the politician now. At the state level, typically, the decision on the posting of senior officers rests on the chief minister. In earlier days, the voice of the chief secretary had influence, but from what I hear now, this counts for very little. Officers are picked not for their specializations, but for the sake of convenience. Particularly in the state milieu, politicians have only a marginal interest in the specialization an officer may flaunt as a qualification to hold a post. What they want is convenience, a lack of obstructionism and a willingness to play along with the pet projects that a politician may think up. Except in the rare cases where a politician knows that failure of a project may reflect directly upon his political career, they do not pay much credence to specialized interest, qualification or experience.

There are, of course, exceptions to these trends and practices on the acquiring of specializations and the posting of people with specializations in appropriate jobs. One such exception that I can think of operates at the state level, namely, the selection of officers for the finance department. The finance department scouts for talent early and picks up young field officers just out of the subcollector ship, some with the right qualifications—a degree in economics, for instance—and then posts them in critical jobs relating to financial management. One such job is that of the deputy secretary, budget: the job requires an eye for detail, an ability to agree to release funds and then deny their release later and a face that is smug enough to make others believe that the finance department is doing something profound and mysterious. It is my observation that officers who are selected during their tender and impressionable years as deputy secretaries looking after the budget in the finance department, tend to stick with finance jobs for ever. They often climb to the post of the finance secretary, with positions as joint and additional secretary in the department as stepping stones. Politicians, too, quail at the sight of these immovable objects in the finance department.

Is that a good thing? Not so, in my opinion. Those who stick with the finance department throughout their careers finally end up having the vision of a common calculator. They know very little, except what is gained by attending innumerable meetings in which they say the same things; yes, we will see, yes, we will release funds and then not release funds. I believe that financial management ought to be done by generalists. People ought not to be posted to the finance department for long durations, because they then forget what it is like to be in a department that requires a steady, predictable stream of funds to undertake their activities. They lose touch with the fact that a government's welfare activities are seriously hampered if financial management is done secretively. A finance secretary moving to some other expenditure department would do a world of good to everybody; but sadly that is not the case.

What does the IAS think overall about the idea of being generalists or specialists? It all depends upon the particular point at which one asks an officer; his opinion is always made with an eye as to whether it will further his career prospects at that point in time. The default setting for most IAS officers is that they passionately believe that generalists are better at governance simply because their own relevance depends on the entrenching of that opinion in the minds of people. However, they are also aware that while this approach might have largely sufficed in an earlier, more uncomplicated era, specialist skills are becoming key to the solving of knotty problems, for instance, if they relate to technology choices, or macroeconomic strategies. If they see opportunity in specialization for themselves at that precise moment the question is shot to them, they will argue for specialization. Looking back, I have no illusions about myself either, in this regard. In 1996, I returned after a five-year stint in an agriculture sector job and was pitchforked into the position of additional secretary of the energy department. Recalling my school physics, I grappled with volts, amperes and ohms and quickly graduated to watts, kilowatts and kilowatt hours. Problems of measurement sorted out, I took like a fish to water on the subject of generation, transmission and distribution of electricity. It was fascinating and I read voraciously, wrote some pretty decent policy notes and in two years, had a more than adequate knowledge of the sector.

I was then transferred to an ailing public sector company in the agriculture sector, which had far outlived its utility.

I was horrified and appealed to the good sense of senior officers. I am good at my job, I said. And then I made the cardinal mistake; I like my job, I said.

That was enough for the old fear of specialization to kick in. You are not supposed to like your job. If you do, you have ulterior motives. I never went back to the power sector and still consider it with the wistful nostalgia one reserves for an old lover.

All this may change soon. To the chagrin of the IAS that has so far ruled the roost as a generalist service, the higher echelons of the government are now being invaded by specialists—technocrats inducted laterally into the government and they seem to be doing quite well too. However, there is still hope for those in the IAS and their votaries. A colleague of mine once observed that IAS officers learn fast, and forget fast too. They will adapt to new realities and begin to compete with lateral entrants, with their own specialist skills, whether obtained fortuitously or by design. The IAS's innate resistance to specialization will gradually wither away. There cannot be definitive conclusions as to whether specialists are a good or a bad thing. There won't be an answer to that question that satisfies all. There are compelling arguments in favour of both and certainly in the IAS, a group of people with above average intelligence propelled by ambition, one can transform into the other.

those with the latest mobile phones.

stenographers.

8

Problem-Solving, Technology
and the IAS

Over the years, the earlier character of the IAS officer as a
wordsmith, educated well in the liberal arts, has been replaced
by that of a techno-manager—somewhat inarticulate
when compared with the earlier generation, but a whiz in
automation, IT and communication technology. However,
since the IAS spans at least two generations of officers, the
system has to accommodate the styles and priorities of the
wordsmith chief secretary and the tech-savvy but relatively
inarticulate subcollector. In between are various hybrids.
You find some oldies who have desperately attempted
to keep pace with changing times, usually equipped with
state-of-the-art mobile phones being utilized to about 5 per
cent of their capabilities and who are well educated through
WhatsApp forwards and YouTube with some of the latest
that technology has to offer. You also find others who
stubbornly cling to the old ways, who dictate their letters
to stenographers—animals that will be kept alive for at least
the next two decades by government efforts alone. Because
of the glacial speed with which government works anyway,

paradoxically, the latter seem to get as much work done as those with the latest mobile phones.

I confess to being something of a hybrid myself. At one stage, I might have counted myself as an innovator in technology and process re-engineering, but if I were in the government today, I would provide sanctuary for stenographers.

Yet, I must count myself lucky for having worked for the better part of my career in Karnataka, which has had a long history of innovation in the digital sphere. The state established a government computer centre in the early seventies and has since then spearheaded several reforms in governance, using the possibilities of e-governance. The Karnataka Government Computer Centre was a mysterious place in the eighties. It filled one with pride to walk through the centre in those early days, with their whirring mainframe computers maintained in sterile, air-conditioned environments.

Yet, one thing remains constant: the Karnataka government does not seem to have made any significant improvement in its responsiveness to people. True, certain things have dramatically changed, such as the accessibility and availability of land records, but in other ways, the state remains as non-transparent as it used to be. This ought not to be construed as a criticism of Karnataka's government, which is probably much better off than other states'. Yet, this dichotomy lingers within the government, of a certain indifference and unresponsiveness that continues in spite of remarkable successes in streamlining certain self-contained processes. Indeed, Karnataka could be an excellent case study of this kind of widespread schizophrenia that affects other governments too.

Why is it, that in spite of measures to streamline government processes through e-governance, the government is still seen as being forbidding and non-transparent? Why does the government live in parallel worlds, nay, centuries? Why do some people in the government dazzle us with visions of a cashless, paperless future in which we breeze through life with nary a thought to the burdens of transacting with the government, while the same dusty rooms, with piles of files, the same rudeness, confusion and corruption assault us daily when we visit a typical government office?

Maybe the answers lie in history.

When I joined the government in the eighties, information technology was unknown to us. However, the zeal with which we wanted to banish red tape was as strong as what one observes today in younger government officers. The first inspiration came from an unassuming gentleman named Anil Kumar Lakhina, who had undertaken some simple, yet far-reaching reforms whilst serving as the district collector of Ahmednagar district in Maharashtra. Picking up from what another district collector, V.P. Raja, had done in the Satara collectorate towards improving the friendliness of the office to citizens, Lakhina set about streamlining the Ahmednagar collectorate. He started with the record room, the equivalent of a hard disc in today's e-environment. Tons of waste paper were removed and documents classified and organized into neat bundles, easily identifiable by the colour of the cloth in which they were wrapped. With professional assistance in office design, Lakhina rearranged how more than 200 officials ranging from clerks to officers sat in their offices. Picking up from the practice in banks, he introduced a token system that enabled visitors to be attended to on a first come, first served basis. Lakhina turned offices into front offices, with people transacting over the counter with clerks, rather than having to wind their way between mountains of files to land up at some intimidating and crowded table. He simplified office procedures and prepared pamphlets detailing step by step, how to obtain various services from the district collectorate, ranging from licences to run cinemas to obtaining caste and income certificates. Dispensing old land records is an important function of the district revenue department and the streamlining and neat organization of the record room ensured that records were easily accessible. Starved of success stories and anxious for reforms, the bureaucracy embraced Lakhina's experiment and proactively aimed to replicate it countrywide. Prime Minister Rajiv Gandhi wrote to all state chief ministers to emulate Lakhina's model in all collectorates and sub-district offices.

I was deeply impressed by Lakhina when he visited the Mussoorie academy and spoke to us of how he went about improving the systems and processes in the Ahmednagar district collectorate. Suitably armed with his vision and full of revolutionary zeal, I set about implementing his reforms in the small town where I started my career in the government, Madhugiri, as an assistant commissioner (subcollector). Computers were unknown in the mid-eighties in most government offices, not to speak of connectivity. Madhugiri was served by a manual telephone exchange, with a jolly man (whom I never did meet in person) at the other end who would connect us to the outside world. A lightning call, which meant that one did not have to wait for an outstation call—sometimes the wait could be a day or more—cost a lot of money. Yet, the friendly telephone man connected government offices with each other without charging us the exorbitant lightning call fee. By the year end, he was helpful enough to connect me to my wife in Bangalore instantly, whilst charging me ordinary rates. On one memorable occasion—New Year's Eve it was—he enabled me to play an Elvis love song to my wife, oh so far away. That must have been a first of sorts for lightning calls. Yes, that telephone man caused a considerable revenue leakage in the telecom department by misclassifying calls. I do hope the laws of limitation apply and arrears are not deducted from his pension with usurious interest by some nitpicking auditor.

The Lakhina-fication of my small record room was easily done. It just took a few weekends with all the staff pitching in to classify and arrange the files, to have them all neatly arranged on newly painted racks, wrapped in brightly coloured cloth and tied in ribbons. The spring cleaning of the record room was not without its side benefits: along with desiccated rat carcasses, we discovered a single barrelled flintlock muzzle loading gun, probably seized in a long forgotten dispute. This was promptly entered in the asset register and became a property of the Government of Karnataka; it still is preserved in Madhugiri, one hopes.

It were the typewriters and the stenographers who were our window to speed and efficiency. I had two of them in my establishment: Venkatlakshmamma and Indiramma. Both engineered the transition from my monochrome English-dominated persona to someone who could swear as fluently in Kannada, and what is more, dictate court judgments in it. It helped that I had learnt typewriting formally, so on the rare occasions when a document needed to be typed in English, I could step in as well. All that stopped when the

Kannada Watchdog Committee, headed by the legendary Patil Putappa, sent lorries across the state without warning to seize and remove English typewriters from government offices. It was a very effective way to ensure that recalcitrant officers, particularly non-Kannadiga IAS officers from other states work in Kannada. Indiramma had a no-fail technique to hasten my education in Kannada. She assured me that if I did not know the Kannada equivalent for a particular official term, I could use the English term and she would immediately tell me the Kannada equivalent. That was the most efficient language class I ever took, except that my familiarity with stilted official language rarely used by ordinary people made my informal conversations in Kannada seem like I was a government circular come to life.

Speeding up decision making by just having the decisions typed out faster was, as they say nowadays, a win-win situation. My office's arrears in disposal of court cases came down dramatically and what's more, Indiramma married Sannamuddaiah, the assistant looking after my court cases. Indeed, a win-win situation in more ways than one.

In the mid-eighties, when personal computers made their first appearance, I jumped at the first opportunity to be trained in the government computer centre—an opportunity that was possibly not available to other service colleagues in other states. I was completely absorbed in the training, learning the possibilities of using Lotus 123 and MS–DOS, the pre-Microsoft offerings for spreadsheet and documentation. I felt a similar thrill when I opted for an early bird training in the centre in the mid-nineties, to familiarize myself with the first offerings of Windows. That was the time when I saw a mouse—not the rodent, but the cursor mover—for the first time. In terms of years, that was a mere two decades ago, but it could have been eons in the past, considering the strides that have been made since then in the capabilities of computers and software.

In the meantime, the winds of change were blowing through the offices of private secretaries of senior officers. The electronic typewriter, a curious hybrid between a typewriting keyboard and electronically assisted punching of the typefaces on to paper, began to make their appearance. They were horrendously expensive and their ribbon cartridges were not designed to reduce one's revenue budgets.

Yet, in spite of these tentative first steps, the efficiency gains in the government were negligible. As desktop computers began to be part of the official landscape, a few laypersons in the government began to realize that they could be used for something more than mere typewriting. To fully utilize the potential of computers to improve one's efficiency, a few enthusiasts—one cannot term them as computer experts—began to experiment with something more than mere typing.

I fell in love with spreadsheets, even as most in the government looked upon computers as nothing more than modern typewriters. The idea of bunging in formulae into columns and rows and watching them do addition and subtraction and more was fascinating. Yet, my extolling the virtues of spreadsheets with colleagues and team members—all novices in computers anyway—only drew blank stares. Why would an IAS officer be fooling around with these machines, when they had stenographers to type on them? they asked.

The stenographers were no good either, when it came to understanding the potential of desktop computers in the office space. They liked them only because they could make corrections with the text without using white fluid and because they did not have to wait for the tinkle of the typewriter's bell to ratchet down to the next line. Even when it came to documentation, they did not have any clue about storage of written records and their retrieval on the computer. I could explain all day about how easy it is to prepare tables using spreadsheets but undersecretaries and others preferred the clunky calculator to attempting to enter formulae in spreadsheets. To them, preparing spreadsheets constituted the task of programming, which was beyond their *sarkari* remit. We must hire programmers to do that, they said.

The loneliness of being spreadsheet–enlightened has its compensations, though.

I worked those days in the department of health and family welfare, looking after the murky goings on in the medical education department. I operated out of a dank, dark room, beyond which an equally dank and dark corridor was being constructed, with all its attendant delights of wet gunny sacks hanging over my windows for curing the concrete. Sure as anything, I developed a rich, throaty cough, which drove me to gulp down plenty of antibiotics, which in turn, made my tongue the colour and consistency of the concrete being laid just beyond my window. The files I dealt with were not inspiring, either; they were mostly about the shenanigans of private medical colleges, which were charging astronomical fees for 'management quota' seats and which used their leeway to provide subsidized seats to the children of politicians and bureaucrats, to wangle more concessions for themselves.

Suddenly, things began to change. Various courts began to issue orders that private medical colleges should not be allowed to operate in this way and that they must provide a percentage of seats for those clearing the government-managed entrance exam at subsidized rates. The private colleges howled in protest and complained that they were living a hand-to-mouth existence and that their earnest efforts to improve the lot of humanity by charging several lakhs of rupees for medical seats were being thwarted by an interfering government.

So the owners of these colleges came to our office in their Mercedes Benz cars to negotiate the fee structure that would enable them, in their opinion, to break even after they were done with cross-subsidizing the seats that needed to be filled by students who passed the government-conducted examination. They came well prepared, with data that showed the cost of medical education and how various permutations and combinations of fee structures for different categories of students would affect their bottom line.

My boss came from a trading background; he often proudly told me that he was the first in his family to join the civil services. Whilst medical evidence does not reveal any genetic predilection to driving a hard bargain in those who belong to trading castes and communities, my boss could drive many researchers scuttling to seek conclusions in that direction. He would stare impassively at the bejewelled boss of a private medical college, resplendent in his white safari suit and crocodile skin shoes, reeling off statistics to show that the government's proposal for a fee structure was totally unworkable. Then he would tighten the screws by asking for a lower fee for the government student than what the man opposite had used for his worst-case-scenario projection.

He was able to do that because I was Sancho Panza to his Don Quixote.

No sooner I was handed over the calculation sheet presented by the private medical college management than I would run down the corridor to the Karnataka Government Computer Centre and breathlessly enter the data myself in those beloved spreadsheets. Bingo! I ran the calculations and created my own analysis of these and prepared alternative scenarios that I would slip into my boss's hands. He, in turn, would confront Mister White Safari Suit and Crocodile Skin Shoes and apply his squeeze.

On the eve of the nineties, I escaped from my dungeon in the medical education department and took charge as deputy commissioner of a district. Known as the district collector in most other states, the posting as the deputy commissioner is the single most important aspiration for most people who go through the arduous task of appearing for the civil service entrance exams. The fifty acre forests surrounding the huge colonial era bungalows in which these worthies live, their cars with red beacons on top of them, the appearance of the deputy commissioner at most district-level functions, the automatic reference to her as the problem-solver in each district, all this drives the popular lore and mystique that surrounds the IAS.

Yet, in Karnataka, the DC of the early nineties was a piffling scaled-down version of the real thing. In 1987, the state had gone through a 'big bang' effort to deconcentrate power to elected rural local governments by setting up zilla parishads in each district. These bodies were elected and most development departments were transferred from the control of the DC and placed under the zilla parishads. What was worse—as seen from the perspective of an IAS officer who dreamt of the day when he would ride into the collectorate on a white charger (or at least pull up in a white Ambassador)—was that the administration of each ZP was headed by a 'chief secretary', a far more senior officer to the DC.

Luckily, I was not particularly worried about being dislodged from the numero uno position in the administrative hierarchy of the district. The fact that plenty of open-ended development responsibilities had moved to the zilla parishad meant that DCs could focus on their core responsibilities, the main of which was land administration.

It was then that I discovered Altaf and Raghavan, two kindred souls.

Altaf was a shirastedar, a lyrical term used to describe someone higher than a head clerk, but not yet an officer. He was one of those rare souls who still retained wit and wisdom even after two decades in government service. His ready smile hid a fanatical commitment to being systematic and a phenomenal memory for the intricacies of the laws relating to land administration.

Raghavan was another restless soul, who, finding the regular land administration work to be too boring, wandered into the National Informatics Centre (NIC) of the district and discovered that his calling lay in software. He taught himself programming—of course, this was back in the days when Office suites were virtually unknown—and his aptitude got him a job close to the DC's office, where he could be relied upon to churn out the multitude of reports that are sent every day, which is often the only tangible evidence of any governance happening.

Like all taxation systems, the land revenue laws of most states are detailed and logical. Land administration by the British, which was copied to a large extent by the old Princely State of Mysore, lived by precise data on land assets on which land revenue was assessed, charged and collected. This was maintained by an army of village accountants, displacing an earlier generation of hereditary 'shanbhogs', who wielded considerable power and influence because of their knowledge over land matters. However, over time, as the attention of DCs began to encompass several welfare programmes, the reporting protocols of land administration began to fail. Less attention paid to the daily tasks of land record maintenance, coupled with staff shortages and the expansion of welfare responsibilities, was beginning to weaken the land records system. The resultant confusion and uncertainties about land ownership had the potential to derail the entire economic base for the rural economy.

With my new-found enthusiasm for spreadsheets, Raghavan's far better programming skills and Altaf's depth of knowledge of the law and rules, we set about systematizing land revenue and land records maintenance and creating a computer-aided system that would replace the entirely manual one followed so far.

In line with the newly fashionable trend—something that shows no signs of abating three decades later—we used an acronym to describe our efforts. We called our system 'MISRA', meaning, a management information system for revenue administration.

If one individual has to be fervently thanked for initiating a national movement towards e-governance, it has to be Prime Minister Rajiv Gandhi. During his tenure, he ensured that the National Informatics Centre established an office in each district in the country. As Karnataka had established a strong rural decentralization framework with the zilla parishads as the district-level rural local government, the NIC office of the districts were not located in the offices of the deputy commissioners as done elsewhere, but were attached to the zilla parishad offices.

By the time I moved to the position of the chief secretary of the zilla parishad of Hassan district, Karnataka, Rajiv Gandhi was no longer the prime minister. But the good work he had initiated was continued: all NIC offices in the districts were connected through satellite with the national office and the capability of data passing upward seamlessly was established—not that data passed that way, but in any case, one could not grudge that the infrastructure was not in place. The World Wide Web was in the future, for laypersons such as us, so the movement of data was still in the domain of the programmer, who all behaved as if they were apostles of God.

But that was not the case with Parasher, a young gentleman just out of college, who had the bounding enthusiasm of someone who genuinely thought that the rest of his life would be like his college days. He was unsullied by government hierarchy and spoke out of turn in meetings—a trait I welcomed, even as I saw the acute discomfiture of those who thought that I must only receive filtered information. Since I was staying by myself and the evenings were long and lonely, I spent plenty of time in the NIC with Parasher, learning the ropes of the latest in computerization.

The NIC office was a quiet haven in the hubbub of my office complex. Like a temple, one left one's shoes outside reverentially and went into the sanctum sanctorum where a bunch of earnest programmers, under Parasher's watchful eye, sent data and received instructions from their mysterious masters in Delhi.

In those days when the principle of separation of the budgets of the state and local governments were more strictly followed than today, the government issued an order every month, releasing the zilla parishad a one-twelfth installment of its annual budget. This single consolidated order released funds department wise, for each of the twenty-odd departments that worked under the zilla parishad. My office sent the order manually to the local office of the treasury after the necessary authentication, following which the treasury operated the order and released funds to the departmental heads concerned at the district level.

However, there was a chronic problem that I had to face. The government system of budget taxonomy is a two stage one, with funds being allocated to 'major heads' of account, which are then further sliced into 'minor heads'. Thus, the public health engineering department receives funds for provisioning of drinking water supply under a major head, which is then subdivided into minor head allocations, for piped water programmes, drilling of borewells, maintenance works and payment of electricity bills and suchlike. The government, in its release order, only allocated funds to the level of the major head. However, if in turn the zilla parishad released the funds on that basis alone to the departments, it faced the risk of the money being diverted within the major head to some minor heads alone, starving other minor heads of sufficient money. This occurred usually due to bad planning, but corruption, which drove officers to spend more money on purchases while neglecting maintenance, was not ruled out. I, therefore, needed to put in place a system that would automatically divide the major head-wise allocations made by the government to the zilla parishad, proportionately to the minor head level. Communicating this order to the treasury would ensure that the departmental heads could not divert money from one minor head to another, thus sabotaging the zilla parishad's implementation plans and leaving it with piles of useless inventories.

It was kids' play for Parasher to design and implement a system that would do this. As soon as we received the monthly release order from the government, the data was digitized and an automatic release order subdividing the allocations to the level of the minor heads was issued to the treasury. Parasher did not stop there: he designed a system by which expenditure vouchers lodged in the treasury by the implementing departments concerned could be tracked, so that we had an idea of who was spending how much, when and for what.

We called our system GRASP or grant release and accounting software programme. Over two years, GRASP was able to introduce a level of budget discipline in the departments that executed the plans and projects of the zilla parishad. There was resistance as departmental officers lost the flexibility to play around with the money released under a major head in the past, as they could not divert money from one minor to another minor head now. But in the long term, they saw the sense in budget discipline, as their programmes did not stop and stutter for a surfeit of money locked into useless inventories, while they starved for it elsewhere.

Parasher did not stay long in the NIC. Within a few years, he joined a major software firm, one that would make waves over the next few decades. He is probably driving a Ferrari in sunny California, as we speak. That was another lesson I learnt with e-governance. The champions of e-governance usually move on, even before the systems they develop are entrenched in government processes.

Looking back on those days, nearly everything we achieved was done using spreadsheets. One could have moved mountains of red tape with them. Yet, nearly three decades later, I am not surprised when I ask data from a government office and it is often sent as a picture of a table, rather than as data in spreadsheets. The large majority of people in the government did not use spreadsheets then; sadly, they don't do so now either. Ironically, the same chaps who send me pictures of tables of data also send WhatsApp forwards of how Blockchain technology is going to revolutionize governance.

My four-year stint in the Tobacco Board as director (auctions) was where I finally saw e-governance making a big difference to the lives of people who dealt with the government.

A few disclaimers, before I begin.

The Tobacco Board is a Government of India body that assists tobacco farmers to grow and sell tobacco. Before one throws up one's hands in horror at this, let's dwell on the fact that the government is concerned with all interests of people, so while on the one hand, it actively campaigns against smoking, on the other hand, it also cannot be blind to the fact that a considerable number of farmers depend upon the cultivation of tobacco for their livelihoods. If and when tobacco use diminishes, the farmers will look for other alternatives. However, as long as people smoke, in the face of health warnings given by the government, one cannot overlook the fact that tobacco will be grown. And if it is so grown, the government takes on the responsibility that farmers don't get short-changed for their produce.

Indian policy has been that government regulates the cultivation of tobacco by licensing farmers to produce a limited quantity every year. The government does not take on the responsibility of buying all the tobacco produced; on the other hand, all it does is to run auctions where registered farmers sell to registered buyers. Tobacco is a high priced product and the proper grading and weighing of produce is the key to ensuring that farmers receive a fair price. Auction halls during the season are a hubbub of activity. At least a thousand farmers come to each auction hall daily. The halls open as early as three in the morning, so as to ensure that all the tobacco bales put out for auction are ready for inspection and auction starting from eight in the morning. An early start is necessary to ensure that the auction is finished in the morning light; experienced buyers say that afternoon light is not right for assessing the colour of the tobacco, a key parameter of quality. Usually, by 12 p.m., the auctions are over and the sellers wait to receive their payments.

In the early nineties, the Tobacco Board was one of the first institutions in the government to embrace e-governance. All bales were physically inspected jointly by the buyer, the seller and the quality assessor provided by the board. An agreed upon description of the bale, its weight, colour, moisture content and quality, were recorded in a 'bale ticket' placed on each bale. The auction commenced only after all bales were marked. After each bale was auctioned, the details of the winning bidder and the price quoted were also entered into the bale ticket. Once the auction was finished, all details on the bale tickets were entered into the auction software, which then proceeded to print out debit notes for buyers, indicating the debiting of their bank accounts by the appropriate amounts and payment cheques that were handed over to each seller. The software also churned out reports that kept tab on all essential statistics on the buying and selling, the quality, the quantities sold, the financial values, all on a daily and cumulative basis.

By today's standards, the state-of-the-art computing technology of those days was laughable. Simple PCs with no hard discs and minimal RAM were used to churn the numbers. As the auctions progressed, computing times took longer, particularly to prepare cumulative reports. By the end of the four- or five-month auction season, processing time would be more than three hours. We kept our fingers crossed, because a tiny blip in the power supply could corrupt the calculations and one would have to start all over again. When we upgraded to the latest PC-ATs in 1995, we exulted, because the computing time at the end of the season was reduced from several hours to a few minutes.

Yet, in spite of the obvious benefits of e-governance, one could not help but notice how power equations were changing within the organization due to technology. The computer operator was the key to the integrity of the system and like any other lesser mortal, he could be compromised. Since the system set quotas and imposed upper limits on what a farmer could sell, the software automatically rejected sales where farmers exceeded their set quotas. It took very little time for computer operators to hack the software. Then, for a price, farmers who exceeded quotas would be able to sell their extra tobacco.

The hacking was so elementary, that an equally elementary safeguard sufficed to snuff it out. I got a software written that would automatically scour through the sales and list out all the sales where quotas were exceeded. I carried that software on a floppy disc; it was given only to a few senior people. A few random checks discovered the main transgressors. Once caught red-handed, the erring data entry operators were punished. The software soon became an effective instrument of deterrence; merely letting data entry operators know that their bypassing of the quota rule could be instantly detected was enough to make them cautious.

Like all robust e-governance solutions, the Tobacco Board's system continues to do well even today. Regular upgrades have made matters even simpler; data entry operators have very little to do after the introduction of barcoded bale tickets. Cheques are no longer printed; the amounts paid by buyers are transferred to the bank accounts of sellers. The linkage to bank accounts also provides assurance to the Tobacco Board to raise loans on behalf of sellers to obtain fertilizer and other inputs in bulk and resell them to the buyers.

The Tobacco Board's system has features that are typical of many good e-governance solutions. It has kept things simple; it has constantly upgraded itself and worked to reduce discretion and effort. Most important, it has kept farmers and buyers at the centre of its focus, not the Board or its data entry operators.

Fast forward to today, and if one keeps aside the fact that technologies have moved at lightning speed, the same circumstances that constrained governance reforms then, operate today as well. As was in the past, any discussion on e-governance today is peppered with the same tired, self-evident assertions, which mostly focus on why e-governance is so necessary. Attend any conference on e-governance and the presentations, whether by government officers or those who collaborate with them, will dwell for long on 'disintermediation', 'business process re-engineering', 'transparency', 'accountability', and other such unimpeachable words. Technical solutions are seen as instant problem-solvers, with little thought given to the change management process that is needed to ensure that these solutions survive. This has its own drawbacks: IAS officers wedded to technology solutions tend to take too much ownership of these, leaving those less capable of handling these far behind. Therefore, technology solutions in the government often do not live beyond the tenure of the evangelizer. Early victories in the adoption of technology tend to ignore that often, the inefficiency that is aimed to be removed, continues alongside. This coexistence of the old red tape, along with snazzy computers, is akin to bullock carts on a six-lane highway.

There are three reasons why age-old inefficiency and glacial slowness can coexist with the latest in technology within the government. First, government e-governance solutions are typically department or process specific and are not designed to be interoperable. This is related to the second reason, which is that software procurement by the government is fraught with problems and risks. Third, government goes all soft when it comes to shutting down outdated legacies. There are innumerable case studies that prove these reasons to the hilt.

Turf battles are the bane of any large organization, but the government raises these to an art form. Process re-engineering and e-governance rarely succeed in overcoming boundaries of turf between departments. Karnataka's revenue department is justifiably lauded for Bhoomi, its effort in digitizing written land record information of lakhs of land plots. Bhoomi, undertaken nearly twenty years ago, remains an object lesson in how to go about computerization in government. From Bhoomi emerged some rules and strategies that ensured that e-governance efforts do not fail. Here are some that could guide us.

First, the team that planned and designed Bhoomi, headed by Rajiv Chawla, a tech-savvy IAS officer, fully understood the short- and long-term implications of computerization. They were aware of how computerization would eventually encompass radical changes in government and legal processes, even if at the outset they did not work out the precise changes of how this would be done. Second, Bhoomi kept things simple at the field level. It did not bother field-level officers with talks of process re-engineering. Government officials are creatures of habit and too much information confuses them; complete makeovers are a strict no-no; their habits are best changed one at a time. One reason for Bhoomi's success rested on its immediate focus on the simplest thing to do: shifting written data on land records from registers to the computer system. This was simple for field staff to understand and execute. Third, Bhoomi was successful because it attended to the consumer need first and not the office process. This has had a tremendous psychological impact on both the consumer and the staff involved. Consumers were immediately benefited and their satisfaction resulted in greater goodwill for the government. This built greater confidence and self-esteem in government staff. Fourth, Bhoomi proved that the volume of data to be processed is irrelevant to success. Bhoomi had a staggering scale of data entry: more than 2.5 crore land records were to be computerized. But at the same time, much of the work was repetitive and rapidly done, if people learnt the habit of doing it. Once patterns were established, given the large size of staff at the government's command, data sizes became irrelevant. Bhoomi's success also had a demonstrative effect on other government departments; it showed that large volumes of data can be computerized and updated in reasonable time. Fifth, Bhoomi managed the transition to digital land records by focusing on the younger staff at the lowest implementing level in the government. Bhoomi's strategy for training was amazingly simple and effective. The revenue department chose the youngest staff at the cutting edge for being trained, normally those who were children of government staff who died in harness appointed on compassionate grounds. These young women and men were too young to be cynical and turned corrupt. Most of them valued their jobs immensely since they got them at the expense of a parent's loss. They did not have preconceived notions or sentimental attachments to systems of the past. Bhoomi got them before the system got to them. Training the youngest also had a powerful impact on the higher staff, that were often indifferent and cynical about Bhoomi. As Bhoomi progressed, older staff were often shamed into paying more attention to developing their own skills. Computerization was a tremendous leveller; it often exposed seniors who lacked skills to the steady gaze of their subordinates. Sixth, Bhoomi did not rest on its laurels; it continued to improve and upgrade its capabilities. Bhoomi 1 dealt only with computerization of the basic land record. By declaring that the computer format is the only legal document relating to land records, Bhoomi shut the door on a reversion to the manual record. Version 2 allowed for changes in ownership of land records to be made on the computer.

Version 3 permitted the oldest cases to be dealt with first, thereby reducing whatever discretion available locally to allow some documents to be dealt with out of turn.

Yet, Bhoomi hit roadblocks that prevented it from making further impacts on land administration. One of the most corruption prone processes in land administration is the registration of sale and other land transfer transactions. After Bhoomi's success, 'Cauvery' was introduced—a software for the registration department to digitize their sale deed registration transactions. Cauvery has also gone through several improvements, but its essential focus remains on the digitization of land transfer documents, such as sale deeds through scanning and word processing. However, for many years, Cauvery was not interoperable with Bhoomi. There was no way that the former could automatically draw data from the latter, even though the land records system and the land transfer registration system both fell within the remit of the revenue department of the state. Similarly, for many years, the Bhoomi records did not automatically link up with the property databases of the local governments, namely, the gram panchayats and the municipalities. When agricultural land was converted to non-agricultural land and their administration shifted from the revenue department to the local governments, primarily so that the latter could charge property tax on them, Bhoomi ought to have automatically transferred these land details to the property registers of the local governments concerned, which it did not, for a long time. This meant that there was a backlog of local governments charging tax on non-agricultural properties. It also meant that those who wished to obtain certificates showing that their purchased lands now reposed under the administration of a local government, had to obtain their land certificates from the revenue department and then produce them in the offices of the local government for further verification and change of land title to their names.

Why do departments take loads of time to solve problems of interoperability of software, both within themselves and across departmental boundaries? Put it down to the complexities of procurement associated with e-governance. Procurement processes within the government are, even within the normal course, slow and protracted. This is eminently justified because government is supposed to spend the public rupee responsibly. There are several rules that govern how procurements are to be made—the cardinal one being that purchases of products with identical features are to be purchased from the one offering the lowest price, with 'price' not merely being reckoned as the purchase price alone, but also the hidden or downstream costs of maintenance and upkeep. However, there are exceptions to this rule too, the prime one being that if the requirement is for a particular 'brand' or exclusive service that is provided only by one or a few vendors, then the procurement offer could be limited to those that provide this brand of product or exclusive service. Several aspects of software procurement make it particularly hard for those involved to make the right choice. First, software and hardware prices vary dramatically depending upon the volume of requirement and the bargaining capacity of the buyer. Second, robustness of the software can be easily compromised by a vendor anxious to offer a competitive price, without the buyer being any the wiser. Third, maintenance capabilities of the aspiring vendor remain unassessed, particularly if it is a relatively new face in the market. Fourth, technology changes so fast that often the product being purchased may be obsolete by the time orders are placed for it. The risk-averse bureaucrat, therefore, prefers to place orders on a government entity, usually the National Informatics Centre, or a state government equivalent, to purchase or develop software for its needs.

Going to the NIC is a mixed blessing. Where the NIC state office is strong, wonders can be done by it. It is no surprise that many of the successful software suites for e-governance have been developed by the NIC. However, the NIC route is as often likely to not solve the problem; it merely distances the decision-maker from the responsibility of defending a risky choice of vendor selected through an open tender. The NIC is something of a revolving door; it does not offer the same salaries that a private software company does. Therefore, going to the NIC usually means that the buyer department has to tolerate changes in the software development team and breaks in the programming stream consequently. If the buyer is a tech-savvy bureaucrat, then this problem is easily mitigated by the officer herself stepping into the breach—I have seen IAS officers with an IT background working with the NIC to write code, but that cannot be expected from all officers.

Apart from these issues, not a day passes without any department, and in particular, the information technology or e-governance department being approached by all and sundry, ranging from ethical hackers to college projects to large IT companies, offering one or the other end-to-end solution for the department to clean up its act. No black marks to them, though, but the constant barrage of choices and quick solutions now being offered from IT companies to individual professionals, enthusiasts, NGOs and hackers can get very bewildering for any department to handle.

The third reason why governmental schizophrenia persists when it comes to e-governance is that rarely does the government do away with legacy processes. The case of Bhoomi is an exception; the Government of Karnataka legislated to make the electronic copy of the digital record a valid document, whilst doing away with the validity of manual records with prospective effect. That in turn resulted in a flood of certification services moving to the electronic mode, with digital signatures to validate them. However, the same alacrity has not been shown with respect to rendering paperless the background documentation and files.

I saw the first possibility of a paperless office in 2002, when a major software company demonstrated a software that even today, strikes me as being remarkably simple and easy to use. On the screen one saw exactly the same format as in a paper file, with the correspondence on the right side and the note sheet on the left. Each officer had to log in and check out the files that had arrived on his table, take decisions and record notes and then pass on the file to the next in line. It was as simple as dealing with a manual file; except that one did not have in and out boxes on one's table and no messengers were required to carry files from one table to another. However, the system did not catch on. We were told that Andhra Pradesh—we were in hot competition with the IT friendly Chandrababu Naidu-led government—had introduced paperless offices. But that was a false lead. In terms of scale, the conversion of the secretariat to paperless files was kids' play as compared with the roll out of Bhoomi. However, there was stiff resistance; the maximum that was possible was to introduce a paperless system of recording file movement, which was then put online so that the public could track files on it if so they wished. I could never fathom why the paperless file system did not catch on. Was it that officers did not feel that they had done something substantial, if they did not see a pile of dog-eared files in their 'out' trays? Was it that we did not want messengers to lose their jobs? Was it that we loved the smell of paper and the 'thunk' of a file as it landed in the out tray (before sliding gracefully to the floor) satisfied some inner craving for finality?

The reluctance to let go of the past pervades the entire sensibility of the government. Panchayats have implemented software solutions for their accounting and maintenance of records. However, every panchayat accountant worth his salt will still rely on registers in which accounts are faithfully written. That is used as a cross check to confirm the reliability of the digital document. As for digital signatures, they can be subverted too. I once had the experience of tracking a transaction where a piece of land was converted from agricultural to non-agricultural purposes and then the record transferred to the panchayat for entry to its records. It went smoothly thus far; the record was entered into the 'Sakaala' system, which operationalizes the assurances under the Karnataka Right to Services Act to deliver certain certifications within specified periods of time. The deadline passed with not a leaf stirring in the panchayat office, after which I received an SMS that informed me that since the transaction was complete, it was being removed from the Sakaala tracking system. Intrigued, I footed it to the Sakaala overlords in the district and was told that since it was showing up as a pending case, it was becoming an embarrassment to the system and, therefore, a manual override option was used to remove it from the pending list. 'But isn't the pending list supposed to show what is pending?' I asked the Sakaala satrap. No, not something that is pending for such a long time was the obdurate answer that I got. So I went to the panchayat and asked them why I did not get the certificate and got the answer that the digital signature was stolen, twice, and so they could not issue the certificate in time. 'Why can't you go to Bengaluru and get a new digital signature?' I asked. 'Unless there are a sufficient number of such signatures that are missing, we won't be able to place orders on the Bengaluru office for digital signatures', said the panchayat secretary. I now had a job in hand: to steal sufficient numbers of digital signatures to make it scale efficient for the district to place on Bengaluru a bulk order on renewed digital signatures. However, I just pulled rank and within a few days, a brand new digital signature was issued by Bangalore, which, by the way, was just 70 kilometres away.

Even as the galloping steed of e-governance is lassoed by a rope of shredded red tape, hope is held out every now and then, when a technocrat visionary in the government paints a bright picture of our lives being completely transformed by information technology.

A few months ago, the Government of Karnataka announced that it would make the Aadhaar number compulsory through legislation. The government said its draft law would be modelled after the ones enacted in Maharashtra, Gujarat and Haryana.

I have been walking the tightrope on Aadhaar since the time it was introduced. I see on the one hand, the possibility of using a unique identity number for easing the process of obtaining a multitude of services from the government.

Yet, on the other hand, I also see that the premature linking of Aadhaar to various services by bureaucrats and politicians driven callous by their ambition, has led to many tragedies in the lives of the poor. Stories abound of distraught parents being unable to admit their children to school under the Right to Education Act because they did not get their Aadhaar numbers in time and of ration shops being unable to distribute rations because the lack of connectivity does not enable them to update the central database, which uses Aadhaar to record the rations given to individual card holders. We even watch mutely with horror at the recent report that a child, bereft of an Aadhaar card, starved to death for lack of ration.

Looking beyond the current grim reality that faces many, particularly the poor, there is the not-so-remote possibility that an illiberal, malafide government that cares little for democratic freedoms, might use the Aadhaar to conduct surveillance of a magnitude that cannot be imagined; a horror scenario where dissidents may be electronically confined, with their bank accounts and credit cards frozen, their properties seized, their conversations tapped, their emails read and who knows, their physical location tracked so assassins can pick their time and place to pick them off.

Let us suspend for a moment, our scepticism and fear about a leviathan government running us into slavery through its ability to snoop over all of us and look closely at what the Karnataka government promises in return for making Aadhaar compulsory. The state intends to adopt an Aadhaar-based platform created by the Central government, named the DigiLocker, to enable citizens to store all their critical documents in their own virtual locker in cyberspace, thereby obviating the need for documents to be stored physically. Therefore, citizens will be able to keep virtual copies of their caste and income certificates, ration cards and other essential documents in a secure space on the cloud. The citizen, when applying for a government service that requires some of these essential documents, will be able to give access to the relevant government department to dip into the DigiLocker, extract the documents required and issue whatever it is that they want. Thus, physical documents will not be necessary.

I have no doubt that all that is promised will become possible in the near future. However, the question is whether such innovations will make the government more responsive and accountable to the people. There, I have no reason to be optimistic. Examples of this dichotomy between the technocrat vision and the reality on the ground abound.

A few months after demonetization was announced in November 2016, the government shifted the goal post and declared that the object was to achieve a cashless economy. This desperation was conveyed to the country's administration and advisors and others from the NITI Aayog, the organization that supplanted the Planning Commission, but had no idea what to do next, set off to the far corners of the empire to promote a cashless economy. District collectors posted in the boondocks, anxious to impress the Delhi hotshots, nodded in appreciation and set off to get the innocent millions who suffer their administration, to eschew cash. An outstanding young officer friend of mine, one who embellishes his multiple talents with a great sense of humour, writes thus of the efforts of the government to ram cashlessness as a target in the face of the demonetization fiasco:

'You should see the frenzy in the cashless movement in our state. Vast areas [are] unserviced with electricity, mobile network and existence [is] on the edge of survival and a large part of the administration of many districts is going hammer and tongs over making this town or that block cashless. [Instead of] efforts that could have gone into better credit for agriculture or planning for the impending unorganized sector employment crunch and batting down the hatches with NREGA [National Rural Employment Guarantee Programme], PDS [Public Distribution System] and MDM [Midday Meals Programme], we now have kiosks [being] set up in panchayats trying to teach people "apps". Slightly misplaced priorities, I would say. A target of one block in every district [is] to be cashless by 28 December [2017]. Pretty sure, we will be able to do that, given that there won't be any cash to go around.'

He continued thus: 'The marketing frenzy is becoming rather nauseating. A day when a senior government official from Delhi visited the state capital and was shown a rather exciting video mashup of our district's cashless campaign— some get rather enamoured of half decent animations and movie-maker effects—I visited a village today where a self-help group [of women] makes little items out of bamboo shavings and sells them to middlemen for Rs 4 to Rs 10 that fetch Rs 40–50 in [a nearby industrial town]. I didn't have the heart to ask them if they were thinking of going cashless using SBI Buddy or Paytm.'

The ground reality is also readily apparent in the hidebound secretariats of the government.

A couple of years ago, Accountability Initiative took up the 'Paisa for Panchayats' project. This was an exercise in fiscal tracking, which aimed to ascertain how much money is spent by all government departments put together, within the jurisdiction of a gram panchayat. The rationale for undertaking this exercise was the belief that if a citizen could easily access what each department of the government was spending in her vicinity, she might be prompted to ask them questions and take a greater interest in governance in her area. This was also prompted by the belief that efforts at fiscal decentralization had not only flagged, but also reversed, so that all the social accountability practices that the government had boasted about were being implemented only upon a tiny slice of the entire expenditure of the government; the slice sent to the gram panchayats.

Our research, conducted in the thirty gram panchayats of Mulbagal taluk in Kolar district, Karnataka, showed that the annual expenditure of the major departments of the government in the area of each panchayat was in the range of Rs 5 crore to Rs 7 crore, but the gram panchayat had effective control and supervisory responsibilities over a mere 3 to 5 per cent of this expenditure. While these findings made for a strong case to align fiscal transfers with the range of functions devolved upon the panchayats, we believed that such an exercise would require political support. As we were not sure that such political support would emerge, we suggested to the government that it should devise an expenditure information network that would put in the public domain in real time allocations, releases and expenditures under each stream, disaggregated to the level of each gram panchayat in rural areas and each municipal ward in urban areas. This we argued would make it much easier for ordinary citizens to check at a glance which department of the government was spending how much, when and for whom, in their neighbourhoods.

An expenditure information network of this nature, given Karnataka state's commitment to e-governance, required only a minor tweak to the already existing treasury management system. If all departments and their vendors were compelled while lodging their expenditure vouchers in the treasury to disclose where exactly they were spending the money—this could be done if each habitation in rural areas and ward in urban areas were given a unique locational code, as also every service delivery institution, such as a school, hospital or crèche—then a simple algorithm could gather this data location-wise and present it to any citizen.

I dare say it is an elegantly simple idea.

The reaction when we presented this suggestion to officials of the finance department was depressingly predictable. Said my friend, a senior officer in the finance department. 'You are going to make my life miserable.'

And here lies the rub. Quite often, the primary consideration of a bureaucrat is that e-governance has to be convenient for the government, not necessarily for the citizen. Thus, there is a clear dichotomy in the government's enthusiasm for e-governance. It is most enthusiastically embraced when taxation systems are automated—the government loves to make it easier for citizens to pay their taxes and file their returns. The government is a lot more cautious when it comes to service delivery. Rarely does online application for a service suffice; the government will still insist that one visits the office to physically verify documents filed online. And finally, when it comes to the disclosure of expenditure details, e-governance is given a wide berth by the government. As my friend says, it makes the life of the government miserable.

Yet, there is hope. New technologies and processes have the potential to be disruptive and in one fell swoop, the resistance to making expenditures transparent may be eroded. Blockchain technology, which has the potential to handle large lumps of data and enable their interaction much more easily than now, can replace several of today's linear processes within the government. The sequence of approvals and scrutiny checks and balances can be removed and their place taken by machine intelligence and algorithms that are less fallible, less prejudiced and faster than current manual safeguards.

Would this shift happen, and if so when and where? What could be the solutions for the future? How does one get process reforms in a fast-changing world embedded in government systems and outlive their creators' brief tenures in their jobs of the moment? And most of all, how do we, the citizens, know of whether we have reached the promised goal of a smoothly functioning government or whether the solutions announced by the governments signal false dawns?

It all boils down to how e-governance solutions are assessed for their success. Conventional ways of estimating success is to study the robustness of the software per se; its absence of internal bugs and downtime, its simplicity for its operators and the ease of retrofitting into existing systems. While each of these approaches are legitimate within their narrow spheres, they do not assess the efficacy of the system from the perspective of citizens. For that, a four-question approach may provide a simple metric of success for e-governance solutions. Of course, it goes without saying that the four questions are interconnected and weave into each other

The first question to ask is whether the solution has led to greater convenience for the public user. Surprisingly, the answer to that question may not be complimentary to some widely touted success stories for e-governance. One of the criticisms against Bhoomi is that by digitizing land records, it centralized their availability from 22,000 village accountant offices to 175 taluk offices. True, while there was no need to pay a bribe at the village level to obtain the document from the village accountant, it was inconvenient and more expensive for farmers to come to the taluk office and obtain their village records from there. Of course, at the moment, the delivery of Bhoomi records has been decentralized, with greater availability of computers and connectivity. But when it was introduced, Bhoomi did not score highly on this parameter, even if, as an early mover, it was unfairly judged. In contrast, nobody would doubt that the moving online of railway ticketing or passport application has immeasurably been convenient for the user public.

The second question is whether the e-governance initiative has reduced corruption. This is a tough standard to achieve and often overlooked. Many such initiatives would fail to meet this standard. For instance, an assessment of citizens' experiences on ipaidabribe.com[1] in 2011 revealed that the registration department was grievously corrupt. Of 527 citizen experiences recorded on the site till then, citizens had paid bribes to have their properties registered in 513 cases. Only thirteen individuals were able to successfully resist corruption and just one person reported that he did not have to pay a bribe because he was helped by an honest officer. Clearly, while the Cauvery software had changed the internal process of registering a document by creating a scanned record of the document, it did nothing to reduce the taking of bribes to get sale transactions registered.

In fairness to Karnataka, Professor Subhash Bhatnagar, who had conducted an impact assessment study of more than sixty e-governance projects in fifteen states, noted that while citizens benefited from a reduction in the number of trips to offices and waiting times, in computerized subregistrar's offices there is very little impact on bribes.[2] With respect to Karnataka, he had this to say:

> Currently the computerized service delivery system in a subregistrar's office is designed in a manner that a user is almost compelled to engage an agent to handle the movement of papers from one desk/station to another within the subregistrar's office. Unless the procedures are simplified, made completely online using work flow, a first in first out regime is implemented and any rejection of applications has to be accompanied by formally stated reasons, bribery is unlikely to be reduced. In such an efficient and transparent system the users may feel confident in registering a deed on their own rather than through an agent [. . .] the entire process is opaque, as many forms/documents need to be filled and dozens of signatures are needed. Documents are in the local language—one has to sign without understanding the contents. Many different payments are involved—why can't these be calculated in the aggregate and charged. Later, the internal posting to various heads for purposes of accounting can be computerized. The work flow is manual and difficult to comprehend by the user. Why can't the work flow be automated and handled on a first come, first serve basis?

A study in which Professor Bhatnagar had a leading part to play put numbers to these conclusions. It said:

KAVERI has lowered the travel costs significantly by Rs 116.684 per transaction. Waiting time in KAVERI offices has been halved from the 162 minutes in the manual system and the total elapsed time for registrations has come down significantly from 11.3 days to 5.2 days. Compared to the promise of registration in half a day, the performance of computerized system is poor. There has been some improvement in service quality. However, there has hardly been any improvement in the quality of governance. The proportion of transactions in which a bribe was paid in the manual system was 34.32 per cent. Though the proportion of bribe payers came down, it continues to be high at 21.61 per cent in the computerized system. A detailed study of one of the centres indicated that any type of system breakdown leads to corruption. The breakdown can be on account of an overload of demand in comparison to the capacity of the system to process registrations. Agents play a key role in promoting corruption. Private operators also exhibit rent-seeking behaviour given an opportunity. Systematizing queues by appointments helps prevent breakdown.[3]

That brings us to the third assessment question; is the workflow of the e-governance solution simple, transparent and easy to administer? This is an internal test, but the continuance of manual processes alongside the e-governed one for an inordinate length of time, the reluctance of staff to move to the new system whilst leaving the old behind, are telltale signs that all is not well. If the government cannot persuade its staff to undertake a complete changeover, then it fails to satisfactorily answer the third question.

The fourth question may sound like a technicality but it is an important one. Has the e-governance solution transcended departmental boundaries? This is super critical from the perspective of the citizen, who is not concerned with which arm of the government deals with her transaction. True, the answer to this question may not be an immediate priority when the software solution is focused on a single transaction. However, it is necessary that software solutions be stitched together to provide a complete cover to a series of related transactions, instead of existing in indifference to each other. If downloading from one software to apply afresh to another one is the name of the game, e-governance has had little effect. The sequence of progression on how to buckle together disparate pieces of single transaction–oriented software is not difficult to work out. If the front end of the particular service is tackled by an e-governance solution, the department concerned ought not to rest on its laurels. Cleaning up the back-end processes, which is the original objective, needs to start immediately. For example, if land records and local government transactions are separately computerized, the next step ought to be to link the two together. For instance, the extension of the copy issuing facility of the revenue department could be decentralized to the gram panchayat level. The availability of revenue records at the gram panchayat could be the trigger for the merger of the revenue and the panchayat systems, things that have been kept apart for too long. Revenue record computerization could converge with land registration and make possible the unification of the legal systems that govern land ownership, record maintenance and documentation. Agricultural data is available on Bhoomi, but the agricultural department hardly uses it for anything other than preparing statistical reports. This could interlock to real-time data on agricultural prices. Merger of initiatives to computerize village and municipality housing records with Bhoomi could lead to a comprehensive property database, which could be the back end for a more efficient property tax assessment system. That in turn could lead to insurance possibilities. An assessment of the extent of convergence and the revealing of the lost potential to do so will compel the government to measure itself to a higher standard.

The important thing is to not stop; a healthy scepticism of e-governance and a refusal to take government reports at face value would do the government a lot of good.

9

Ethics and the IAS

ETHICS, CORRUPTION, ACCOUNTABILITY AND THE CIVIL SERVICE

Perceptions of the lay public about the civil service range from envy through consternation all the way to admiration. Popular beliefs are also bipolar: they range from bestowing complete faith in the civil servant to fixing grievously dysfunctional systems and the conviction that they are responsible for all the ills that plague governance. However, civil servants who are punished for their alleged misdemeanours rarely receive understanding, not to speak of pity. More often than not, when a civil servant is punished, the public is quietly elated, serves him right, they say.

How corrupt is the civil service? Is corruption a default setting; would all civil servants turn corrupt unless they are placed under the most stringent of curbs and vigilance over their decision-making? How wide-ranging does vicarious liability have to be to ensure that civil servants perform at their best? Do oppressive looking-over-the shoulder tactics against the civil service do more harm than good; does society at large benefit if the law is so oppressive as to scare bureaucrats from being proactive and decisive? Does the civil service have protection against character assassination and malicious prosecution?

From the haze of memories of one's training stint in the Lal Bahadur Shastri National Academy of Administration, there is one recollection that stands out. It was the day that we congregated on the lawns at Mussoorie to take an oath to abide by the Constitution of India. We laughed and joked, stood in our appointed places dressed in our black bandhgala suits, raised our right hand and took the oath read out to us. This was followed by the photograph of the entire batch, taken those days on an old wooden box camera. For some reason, that day is crystal clear in my mind, more so as one gets older.

During recent training sessions that I conduct for fresh entrants in the Academy, I sensed an improvement in the quality and commitment of officer trainees since the ethics paper was introduced in the civil services examination. I spoke about that to a senior officer in charge of training at the academy, but she was dismissive of it. 'Doing the ethics paper well is a technique,' she said. 'The private training academies have now got the hang of it, of how to crack the ethics paper. They can game the exam now,' she concluded. However, I still continue to lecture on the subjects of ethics, corruption and accountability at the Academy. The sessions are usually for half a day and one races through the content, which remains substantially the same for fresh recruits as also those who return for refresher training. My impression still is one of hope; I see the current batches of recruits more willing to question, more concerned and more diverse in social and economic character than before.

When it comes to fighting corruption, there are two schools of thought that differ on the relative importance of a sound ethical foundation in an anti-corruption strategy. One believes that if sufficient attention is paid to building a strong ethical base in government officials, then such an attitude will become a strong bulwark against corruption. The other believes that ethics are not as important as hard-nosed administrative strategies; systems reforms that iron out the deficiencies in government processes can achieve a great deal of the discretion and lack of transparency that enable corruption to prosper. In reality, a combination of the two works best; institutions with a good ethical culture create a strong social sanction against corruption. Yet, examples abound of how institutions that are known to be corrupt still manage to clean up and reform. When a good minister and good officer can form a wholesome collaboration, they can significantly clean up corruption-prone processes with which they deal.

Yet, what constitutes a good ethical culture? In a workshop of the faculty in the LBSNAA, I ran an exercise in which participants were asked, off the top of their heads, to write down five ethical attributes that they admire, uphold or wish they could uphold, and five that they disparage, abhor, or wish they did not have. When we toted up the results, predictably, many had listed honesty as a good ethical attribute. Others that found resonance were empathy, leadership or leading by example, responsiveness and an ethic of hard work. The ethical attributes that were disparaged were dishonesty, selfishness, laziness, unreliability. Some found place in both lists, such as ambition. I also noticed that courage did not find a mention. That was interesting.

In the discussions that followed, the class came to the realization that honesty alone, particularly a certain kind of pecuniary honesty, was not sufficient to constitute the universe of a value system. We then went on to discover that an ethical framework ought to constitute a much more diverse set of attributes than financial integrity. A distinction was also made between personal ethics and institutional ethics.

What do we mean by an institutional culture of ethics? Simply put, institutional ethics comprises strong rules, strong scrutiny and strong enforcement. That builds a strong organizational culture, which in turn, hopefully diminishes the usage of, if not obliterates the requirement for, strong rules, scrutiny and enforcement. Yet, the rules set have to drive compliance to a larger attitudinal approach, a commitment to a set of values that are held dear by the organization. For instance, for every government institution, there could be three facets that are non-negotiable components of a value framework. These are integrity and impartiality, a commitment to promote the public good and a commitment to uphold a certain system of government that is defined by a constitution and the law and rules that flow from it. Integrity is paramount because every public office involves the acceptance of public trust. Government officers have to deal not with their money; they deal with taxes collected from people. Thus, they have to deal with public money with unimpeachable integrity. Impartiality is important because every citizen has equal rights. Even the exceptions in the form of positive affirmation are a drive towards equality, a strategy to bring those who have suffered handicaps for centuries to catch up with those more privileged. This impartiality is to be manifested in the form of equal respect to all individuals, whether they are clients of the government or employees.

How does the government promote the public good? This is by adopting responsiveness as an overarching ethic, even as the primacy of public interest is not disturbed. There is no point being concerned about what serves the public best if it is not backed up with speed and efficiency, if there is no access of the public to the government, or if there are no mechanisms to engage the community in collective decision-making. Transparency is often considered as a block to efficiency, but in reality, it comprises a facet of it. While processes of transparency may look inefficient and wasteful, they ensure community ownership of decisions. Cloaks of secrecy are to be worn only as exceptions, when it is beyond dispute that such secrecy is itself in the public interest.

All this sounds fairly esoteric, as also self-evident. However, in practical terms, these ideas have to find expression in the Constitution, laws and rules. In the ultimate analysis, a high standard of public administration reinforces public trust in the government. And this is built through two overarching imperatives. First, government officers have to commit to acting responsibly so their actions and decisions can be explained. Second, they need to be open and candid so their actions and decisions can be easily understood.

The LBSNAA exercise, in which participants were asked to list out five each of the most desirable and undesirable attributes, led to animated discussion that we were loath to end. The first discovery was that not all these attributes automatically went hand in hand. People usually were a combination of some desirable and some undesirable attributes. Thus, an officer who was honest in a pecuniary sense might be arrogant, unsympathetic, slow at work or completely unresponsive to the people. On the other hand, one who is prone to bending rules, even taking a few bribes, may have a way with dealing with people, have a sense of what matters, and may be super-efficient in doing plenty of right things, even as she gets away with a few heists here and there.

That discussion led us to another aspect of what constitutes financial integrity. What exactly can be considered to be a bribe, particularly when India does have a culture of gift-giving, where it is considered rude not to accept something given in good faith, without a quid pro quo involved? John Noonan, in his book *Bribes*,[1] wrote about 'those who take them [bribes], give them and condemn them in a variety of cultures from ancient Egypt to modern America'. He described two interesting insights: first, that the core of the concept of a bribe, namely, that of an 'inducement improperly influencing the performance of a public function meant to be gratuitously exercised', is remarkably constant across cultures. Of course, what constitutes an 'inducement', 'improperly influencing', 'a public function' and meant to be 'gratuitously exercised' changes with culture. Noonan goes on to say that every society has at least four definitions of a bribe, namely, that of the 'advanced moralists', that of the 'law as written', that of the 'law as in any degree enforced' and that of 'common practice'. The bureaucracy is a diverse body and comprises people who are advanced moralists, those that strictly implement the law as written, those who enforce it, often selectively, and those who follow practice or convention in defining what amounts to bribery or otherwise.

As a joint secretary in the Ministry of Panchayati Raj, I had plenty of discretion in the release of funds to states on a few critical schemes meant to benefit panchayats. As I travelled a great deal with my minister to various states, I had a cordial relationship not only with the secretaries of the state departments of the Panchayati Raj, but also with the ministers concerned. One minister, of a hill state, was well into his eighties. A well-heeled gentleman, he was in the habit of sending a few senior officers in the ministry a generous gift of a basket of apples from his personal orchard, just before Diwali. I dare say I did take the gift; sharing it with my office staff. Clearly, I was not an advanced moralist, nor a follower of the law as written, which prohibits me from taking gifts beyond a certain pecuniary value. The value of the basket of apples might have been more or less than the limit, depending on where it was sold and in what number. I suppose I assessed the extent to which the law is enforced and decided that taking a fruit basket during Diwali was a common practice that would not fall within the ambit of bribery as I understood it.

Another officer and mentor, the late M. Sankaranarayanan, the former chief secretary of Karnataka once recollected an incident from his early days in service. Back in the fifties, assistant commissioners (subcollectors) did not have official transport. The only jeep in each taluk was courtesy the Union Ministry of Community Development and was in the custody of the block development officer. Sankaranarayanan was posted in the town of Nanjangud, south of Mysuru. On a weekend, a staffer from his office developed a serious infection of his appendix. Sankaranarayanan, after assessing the gravity of the situation, commandeered the BDO's jeep and drove to Mysuru with his staffer. An emergency operation was performed and the latter's life was saved. Sankaranarayanan dutifully wrote up this unauthorized journey in the jeep's log book and received a show-cause notice from the deputy commissioner's office a few months later, questioning him as to why disciplinary action may not be taken against him for misusing the government vehicle and driving it out of its jurisdiction, without taking permission. Shankaranarayanan wrote back to the DC's office that were such circumstances to arise again, he would do the same thing that he did. I did not know whether Shankaranarayanan was punished, but considering that he did rise to become the chief secretary of the state, he might not have been.

A simple and obvious way out of this conundrum is to follow the rules prescribed to the 'T'. Many honest people follow the written word, which is contained in the conduct rules for civil servants. Though there are separate rules for the IAS and the central services respectively, there is hardly any difference between the two when it comes to prescribing the standards of the conduct they are to follow.

The civil services conduct rules, enacted in 1968, after defining the categories of the civil service to which it applies, starts with some broad mandates on how civil servants ought to conduct themselves. Rule 3 says that all officers shall always maintain 'absolute integrity and devotion to duty' and shall do 'nothing which is unbecoming of a member of the service'. The last mentioned is a broad and open-ended directive that is open to subjective interpretation. I have often wondered whether sweeping the public road in front of my house, something that I used to do occasionally, is 'unbecoming of a government officer'. Or posting a selfie in a frivolous costume, say a swimsuit? I have not done that, but in the days of Instagram and Facebook, the day is not far off when such instances happen.

The conduct rules also direct every official to 'take all possible steps to ensure integrity of, and devotion to duty by, all government servants under his control and authority'.[2] It also says that every officer shall be courteous and shall not adopt 'dilatory tactics'[3] in his dealings with the public, or otherwise. The ethic of being responsive is, therefore, covered quite early in the rules.

The next rule has a bearing on the quality of the work done by an officer. She is mandated to always act in her 'own best judgment to be true and correct',[4] whilst performing official duties or exercising powers conferred. There is an exception when directions are given from above in writing, where obedience is the norm. All such directives are to be in writing, or to be consigned to written form at the earliest.[5] The duty to both issue written orders, as also to seek confirmation of oral orders in the form of written orders, is the responsibility of the officer concerned. Slackening of duty, habitual non-performance and seeking directions unnecessarily even though adequate power are delegated to the officer concerned, are all deemed to be considered as 'lacking of a devotion to duty'.[6]

Rule 4 prohibits nepotism and the use of influence to seek positions for family members in private undertakings or non-government organizations. Prior permission is to be taken before an officer permits a family member from taking up employment with an undertaking that has official dealing with the government.[7] However, considering that such a rule may be unduly strict, for example, the family member may militate against any directions given by the officer concerned; the government relents in the absence of prior sanction, the duty to inform the government as quickly as possible if any such event of employment happens.[8] Conflict of interest is closely connected to the issue of nepotism. Thus, an officer shall not deal with any matter or contract between the government and a private undertaking if any of her family members is employed in that undertaking.[9]

When it comes to politics, Rule 5 prohibits government officers from taking part in politics and elections save for the fact that he may cast his vote and not disclose for whom he voted. Here too, there is a grey area. The rules say that government officers shall 'endeavour to prevent any member of his family from taking part in or subscribing in aid of or assisting in any other manner, any movement of, activity which is, or tends directly or indirectly to be subversive of the government'. That is a pretty tall order; why would any such relative agree to such restriction, and why should an officer be blamed if his relative disregards his advice? The rules therefore recognize that the official may not have any influence over a family member, in which case the officer is obliged to report the fact to the government.[10] Finally, an officer cannot canvass and bring any political or other influence to bear upon any superior authority to further interests in respect of matters pertaining to his service under the government.[11]

There are several rules that provide guarded permission to the officer to express her views over the media, in stark contrast to the desirable ethical value of transparency. While sanction of the government shall not be required when the member of the service in the bonafide discharge of his duties or otherwise, publishes a book or contributes to or participates in a public media,[12] he has to make clear that the views expressed are of his own and not those of the government.[13] In any case, the officer cannot criticize the government or any of its policy or make any statement that could embarrass the relations between the Central government with any state government or with a foreign country.[14] Rule 9 virtually prohibits whistleblowing, with just a tiny window of opportunity left open, that of communication in good faith. An officer shall not communicate directly or indirectly any official document to any person to whom he is not authorized to communicate, except 'in the performance in good faith of duties assigned to her'.

Officers are mandated to be aloof to the outside world. They cannot be part of any fundraising effort regardless of its objectives.[15] When it comes to gifts, they may accept gifts from near relatives or personal friends with whom they have no official dealings on occasions, such as wedding and anniversaries if such is the custom, with a stipulation that they must inform the government if the value of the gift exceeds Rs 5000.[16] A gift is said to include free transport, boarding and lodging. No gift shall be accepted without the sanction of the government, if its value exceeds Rs 1000.[17] Officers shall not accept lavish and frequent hospitality from those with whom they have official dealings.[18] They shall not demand, receive, give or abet the demanding, receiving or giving of dowry.[19] They cannot receive honours without the prior sanction of the government, with the exception of farewell entertainment, which is informal, personal, simple and inexpensive.[20] They cannot force anybody else to contribute to an event of farewell entertainment.[21]

Yet, the private life of the officer is not fully stifled. While they cannot engage directly or indirectly in any trade or business, or participate in or associate themselves with a sponsored media event, (with the exception of participation in Doordarshan programmes),[22] they can, without the previous sanction of the government, undertake honorary work of a social or charitable nature, occasional work of a literary, artistic or scientific character, participate in sports activities as an amateur or take part in the registration, promotion or management of a literary, scientific or charitable society, club or cooperative society (for the benefit of the members of the service or government servants).[23] While government servants are prohibited from accepting fees for their out-of-office activities without the sanction of government,[24] income from literary, cultural, artistic, scientific or technological efforts and income from participation in sports activities as an amateur are exempt.[25] Officers need to take the prior permission of the government before contesting election to sports bodies and holding elective office in them.[26]

On the economic freedom front there are several restrictions. Obviously, government officers cannot sublet government accommodation allocated to them.[27] But in addition, they are prevented from speculating habitually in stocks and shares, have relatives who make investments that are likely to embarrass or influence them in their official duties or lend, borrow or deposit money in any private company with whom they are likely to have official dealings, without the previous sanction of the government. Officers are expected to manage their private affairs so as to avoid habitual indebtedness or insolvency.[28] They must take prior permission before acquiring immovable property[29] and inform the government within a month of such acquisition, when acquiring something of a value of more than Rs 15,000.[30] They shall submit a return of their assets and liabilities to the government, in accordance with detailed instructions in this regard, in a format given to them by the government.[31] The government can seek additional information on the acquisition by the officer of jewellery, insurance policies, shares, securities and debentures, loans advanced or taken, motor cars, motor cycles, horses, or any other means of conveyance, and refrigerators, radiograms and television sets.[32] The government is even more careful when it comes to transactions regarding property outside India and transactions with foreigners. Nothing can be done without prior permission.[33]

Horses?

Yes, you heard right.

According to the strict wording of the conduct rules, you cannot buy horses without having to report them to the government.[34] Yet, from the strict wording, an officer could buy a really expensive mobile phone, iPad or computer and not report it to the government.

Now we turn to the personal character of the officer. No officer can go to court for the vindication of an official act that has been the subject of adverse criticism without the previous sanction of the government. However, she is not prohibited from vindicating her private character or any act done by her in her private capacity. Every officer is to strictly observe existing policies regarding age of marriage, preservation of the environment, wildlife and cultural heritage, observe the existing policies regarding crime against women and also observe the two-child family norms. Bigamy is prohibited, unless the government gives permission on the basis that a second or third marriage is permitted under the personal law of the religion to which the officer belongs. Officers shall strictly comply with all laws regarding the consumption of intoxicating drinks or drugs and are prohibited from being under the influence of any intoxicating drink or drug during the course of their duties. They are enjoined to take due care that the performance of their duties is not affected by the influence of drinks or drugs. They cannot consume intoxicating drinks or drugs in a public place.

Doubtless, there are grey areas in the conduct rules. These days some dogs are pricier than horses and yet, they are exempt from being reported. The rules are silent about officers using social media; would selfies constitute non-officer-like behaviour? There have already been slanging matches between officers who have posted material of a personal nature on Instagram and Twitter and trolls intent on embarrassing them. Facebook and Twitter pose problems that are not addressed adequately by the rules. Would the forwarding by an officer of an article that criticizes the government be impermissible under the conduct rules? How can one be sure that such yardsticks are applied fairly? We have seen recently that an officer who posts toxic material that spews hate on a particular community is allowed to go scot-free, while another, who forwarded a post on the plight of SCs and STs following the suicide of a Scheduled Caste university student, has had a show-cause notice slapped on him. Yet, one must underscore the fact that even though the rules are outdated, they provide a basic underpinning of a framework that nurtures an organizational culture based on sound, desirable values. They can be improved, but they exist.

Yet, nobody will agree that the rules drive compliance. There is a wide gap between the law as written by Noonan's 'advanced moralists' and its enforcement. That has led to common practices that amount to a wide deviation from the value framework within which the government functions. Sometimes, even advanced moralists fall prey to the temptation of securing a quid pro quo for their actions. Some of them fall unknowingly into the trap, others convince themselves that there is such a wide gap between their decisions and the eventual benefit that they receive, so as to not constitute an act of bribery. The Bangalore Golf Club is a case in point. To the west of the runway of the HAL airport was a marshy land that was a haven for water birds. This constituted the watershed of a network of lakes that dotted the eastern part of the city. Of course, to the untrained eye, a marsh is a useless place and is better filled up and put to use. The Bangalore Golf Association put in an application for the land to establish a new golf course. The file was handled by officers of unimpeachable personal, financial integrity. The land was handed over for a low price. The civil service got a quota for accelerated admission into the club. Low fees, keeping in mind that with their low salaries they would not be able to afford the higher fees fixed for lesser mortals.

Bribery?

You bet. But not in a singular, pinpointed way; instead an artful negotiation without a whiff of scandal; a useless piece of land put to good use by a club formed to promote a renowned game, tourism ostensibly to prosper and a quiet little place for civil servants to relax in the same manner as their colonial forebears.

The absence of pecuniary corruption does not automatically mean that all other ethical attributes are in place. Honest people need not necessarily be open, transparent, efficient or empathetic. Typically, therefore, the young officer is confronted with people who display a mix of good and bad attributes whilst on the ground. One boss may be financially clean, but could be incredibly sexist and condescending. Another is sweet, very nice, very accommodating, but everybody knows that he is also on the take. A third may be domineering and sanctimonious, but is known to bend the rules to suit the nefarious purposes of corrupt politicians. A fourth is honest, but a dour plodder. He remembers a time when he was a dasher, but bitter experiences have driven him to now just deal with what comes to his table and not take the risk of standing up to corruption. It is rarely that one comes across someone who ticks all the boxes as far as the components of his value systems are concerned.

At the Mussoorie academy, as we debated the significance of each of the desirable and undesirable attributes, the one growing realization was the importance of empathy. Most officers, particularly honest ones, have a reputation of being rule-minded and rigid. Politicians, good and bad, complain about them constantly; why, they ask, doesn't this officer realize that we have a serious problem that we must solve in order to bring succour to the people? Innumerable case studies could be quoted of poor people suffering injustice and inconvenience, their lives thrown into disarray, as the larger picture of public welfare is forgotten and problems sink into a quicksand of contradictory rules and instructions. Anybody who has dealt with issues such as the problems faced by sanitary workers, slum dwellers, domestic and unorganized-sector workers realizes these problems. Empathy is important and officers often diminish its worth in a value framework. This has a lot to do with a misreading of the overall spirit of the conduct rules. While the right things are said at the outset, that officers shall be responsive and conduct themselves keeping public welfare uppermost in their minds, they also convey the strong message that a good officer must be an aloof officer. The consuming obsession with being impartial and the need to avoid conflict of interest sometimes drives the impression amongst officers that disinterest is a good value to imbibe. Aloofness turns, at a practical level, into disinterest, into the lack of an ability to act urgently, communicate openly and seek counsel if there are knotty problems to solve.

How does one retain sensitivity, whilst at the same time, keeping in mind the need to be impartial, be open and work effectively? One of the ways is to be aware that one's work life will be replete with instances where one must tackle ethical dilemmas, often with little time to weigh the pros and cons of one's actions. A textbook approach would be to equip oneself with the skills to identify an imminent ethical dilemma before it happens and identify the risks of situations where a value principle may be breached. Then, one will need to apply the non-negotiable value framework principles described earlier, namely, integrity and impartiality, a commitment to promote the public good and uphold the Constitution, laws and the rules to the situation in hand, on the basis of which one can define and execute an appropriate response to an ethical risk or breach. A good way is to have a simple checklist of questions that one asks oneself; the screenplay for a little conversation with one's conscience. The questions to ask oneself are, is this the right thing to do? Am I doing the right thing? How would the public view this? How will this impact those affected?

How would I feel if this were done to me? Does this demonstrate ethical leadership?

As I lectured on these lines, drawing from literature around the subject of ethics, I sensed inwardly that this would not make much sense to young people who go to their field postings full of good intent, energy and a naïve belief in the inherent goodness of people.

Let's go a bit more practical, I said. What are the real-life ethical dilemmas that an officer faces when she goes to the field for a year of training? What impressions do officers return with, about the organizational culture of their district offices in which they serve? If we ask officers to prepare case studies based on their real-life experiences, what are they likely to say? That line of approach broke the ice. The faculty of the Academy had already done a lot of work on hearing the experiences of officers and distilling from them case studies that are thought-provoking accounts of the kind of ethical dilemmas that officers have to face on the field.

The most common dilemma that a young officer faces in her first posting is the one of providing free hospitality. Government officers travel a great deal within their jurisdictions and so do politicians. People retire to inspection bungalows and circuit houses; quaint names for government guest accommodation in district headquarters and small towns, and food magically appears on the table. If the inclination of the officer or politician runs in that direction, a bottle of liquor is also produced. Nobody asks who pays for all this. That is considered bad form. Typically, these expenses are met through an informal local flexible corpus of funds, collected by diverting a sum of money from the local accumulation of bribes. The police station's bribe kitty pays for the SP's evening meal in the circuit house, the Kasbah revenue inspector, namely the middle-level revenue official posted to the taluk or district headquarters, arranges the thali for the deputy commissioner and the assistant commissioner. Occasionally, there are *bada khanas*—a minister decides to review all development work in a taluk and food has to be provided to fifty participating officers. The expenses can be considerable. In the years past, we were cautioned by senior officers who were reputed to be honest, to always pay for our meals and make a show of it. Some of us did; others did not, a few did and then did not, because they were considered as impolite deviants who could not accept a bit of modest, decent hospitality provided by a solicitous revenue inspector.

The simple fact of the matter was that no officer, however zealous or meticulous, could take a strong stand on eliminating corruption if she conceded and acquiesced to the practice of free meals being organized for her, or other officers or ministers, by the junior staff. Let's forget the elimination of corruption; one cannot seek greater efficiency from local staff if one turned a blind eye to these informal payments, funded, as clear as the daylight, from a working capital account fuelled by corruption.

One of the faculty at the Academy spoke feelingly of how her father, an honest officer in a department notorious for its corruption, refused to toe the line of a district collector, who set quotas for collection of hospitality funds to bankroll a political jamboree that a minister wanted to organize. He paid for his blunt refusal with punishment from the district collector, who felt that his authority was being slighted in full public view. The officer's surliness was also accentuated because he knew he was doing the wrong thing, and did not take kindly to a subordinate officer, and one from a corrupt department to boot, who refused to collect money and contribute to the funding of a political circus.

Many honest officers finally accepted these practices as ones driven by custom. Very few eventually continued to insist that they would pay for their meals.

I reflected on this feedback.

The more I thought about it, the more it made sense. The problem of boarding, lodging and entertainment expenses being borne by local officers informally was one that had destroyed the ethical foundation of field organizations for decades. It might have seemed like a relatively minor thing, but it was an all-pervasive system. A young officer who militates against this practice would be ridiculed as an impractical nitpicker. Yet, if this problem was indeed faced by a large number of officers returning from their field training for the second phase of reflection in the Academy, it was as good a story as any to discuss ways and means of solving the problem. I thought to myself, how would one find solutions to this problem. Would making all meetings public and putting up collection boxes for payments for meals work? Would an instruction from the top that all officers must pay for their meals from their travelling advances send the right message? Would the giving of an adequate imprest to each office solve the problem? The amount could be reimbursed from deductions at source from the travelling allowances of the officers who travel. A thousand solutions would spring up, if the problem statement was articulated well. I heartily endorse the idea of preparing case studies as a way of getting officer trainees to think through ethical dilemmas.

The other practice that destroys the faith in officers that ethics has a place in governance is the system of transfers and postings of officers. Over the years, politicians have totally taken over the system, in every adverse sense. On paper, the political executive is to determine broad policy and at best make choices as to who would people the upper echelons of the bureaucracy. The posting and transfer of officials down the line are to be managed by the bureaucracy themselves. However, over the decades, this practice has eroded to a point where bureaucrats have virtually no say in where officers are posted; politicians alone decide this. While it is popular for the civil service to lament the current state of affairs, such a situation would not have come to pass if the bureaucracy itself were objective and reasonable in their transfer policies. But bureaucrats are themselves not free from prejudice and partiality. Their insensitivity and capriciousness led subordinate officers to go to politicians above for recourse, in violation of the conduct rules, which states that canvassing for postings and transfers would amount to misconduct that is punishable. Since bureaucrats, including honest ones, were duty bound to implement instructions given from above, the power to post and transfer was quickly usurped by the political executive. In most states now, MLAs rule the roost. They decide who has to be posted and who transferred. Lists are sent to officers, who either meekly implement them or send them upward to ministers to take action. Sometimes they sit back and watch the fun, when two or more aspirants for a coveted post bring political pressure that is equally influential and watch ministers and chief ministers squirm as they work overtime so as to not offend anyone. From an ethical perspective, the transfer industry is a grim, in-your-face retort to anyone who thinks that the government has a strong ethical foundation. Yet, sometimes, problems do resolve themselves. Some states, faced with the runaway stampede that happens during the transfer season as officers vie with each other to bring influence to seek transfers, have brought in laws that put in place norms to control them. These laws have minimum and maximum permitted tenures and have legislated categories of valid reasons for seeking transfers or retention. Counselling centres are organized where officials can openly discuss with counsellors where they wish to be posted, based on the vacancies that are available. However, while such approaches might systematize the way transfers and postings take place in relatively less corrupt departments such as the teaching faculty in the primary education departments, the 'lucrative', corruption-prone departments are kept outside the counselling system. Here, the law of the jungle applies; prepaid and postpaid arrangements are the norm. A lump sum payment by an aspirant gets him a post, but for retention there for a sufficient period of time, a regular postpaid monthly instalment has to be made to higher levels.

All in all, the informal hospitality arrangements and the transfer system are two examples of phenomena that can accelerate the disillusionment of the young officer who goes to the field. The message that goes out to the young officer is that following ethical behavior paths means going against the grain and being considered an impractical idealist. The system screams out to the officer; if everybody else is doing it, why not you? The thinking officer is tormented by questions that insist on answers. What are my ethics? What are they based on? How important are they in the performance of public service? And then, the officer realizes that effectiveness is often dependent on permanency, which raises a fresh set of ethical dilemmas. How much will one compromise? At what cost is permanency achieved? Does not success fuel greater ambition, which in turn leads to greater ethical compromise? Does strategic behaviour drive further compromise and will compromise eventually snowball to the extent that the conscience will be forever silenced and the comfortable life of the one with low or flexible value systems be achieved?

I ended my rhetorical questions by asking the faculty to ask officer trainees to reflect on where they would see themselves in the future. There are three categories of corrupt officers, namely, demanders, takers and the intellectually dishonest. And three categories of honest officers as well, namely, the honest doer, the honest non-doer and the honest un-doer. The demander is a rare species; India's anti-corruption system barely functions, but it produces enough of illusory effectiveness to ensure that only few officers demand money openly. The takers are more frequent; those who drop hints as to how much is the payment for a deal made and are often open to a bit of bargaining. The intellectually dishonest are the most favoured by corrupt senior officers and politicians; these are people who will bend the rules, write up well-reasoned file notes, undertake the laundering of the trail of corruption, look the other way when bribes are taken and make unconscionable compromises. In fact, it is possible that the intellectually corrupt individual may not be corrupt in the financial sense; a good posting where one can wield influence and power, the stoking of their ambition, is sometimes all they seek as reward for their dealings. On the side of the honest, we have the honest doer, someone who by accident or design ends up having a charmed life; this individual has not lost the idealism that characterizes one with a good base of values, but has also had the benefit of permanency and ended up working collaboratively with good politicians. These officers are able to back their honesty with the ability to empathize, work hard, be responsive and, therefore, deliver well on their objectives. Then come the honest non-doers. These are people who may have been more industrious and effective in earlier days, but probably having suffered a bitter experience, are now more cautious and worse, and have become reactive. They will not take initiative as that carries risks and they are more than happy to just push what comes to their tables. They are honest, but their honesty is something they are insecure about and they wish to protect it by avoiding all ethical dilemmas. The best way to do that is to do, well, nothing. Then come the honest un-doer. This individual lives for his honesty. They are often the advanced moralists that Noonan[35] speaks of: people so steeped in the study of honesty that they have little time for work. As they strive to preserve the high standards of their honesty, those proximate to them become their targets and enemies. When they take up a new assignment, their first task is to dismantle everything done so far in order to seek evidence to nail their predecessor. If that predecessor is a corrupt person and the politicians at the top wish to punish him, an honest un-doer is the best person for the job. But if the predecessor were an honest doer, then good systems can be dismantled in a trice by an honest un-doer and replaced by chaos.

However, even as we ask officer trainees to look into the future and speculate about where they see themselves in a few years, it is necessary to keep their spirits up and buoy them for the fight to preserve their ideals and execute their ideas. What would be a safeguard that not only provides solutions to such problems, but also builds the spirit of the young officer and prevents her from slipping into a grey fog of indifference, or worse, being drawn into the seductive embrace of corruption? One way could be to have a system of ethical coaches, mentors who are outside the system, but who can provide a non-judgmental and non-threatening space in which the officer can reflect upon her ethical dilemmas. In all my conversations with officers who have been through the torment and loneliness of fighting a corrupt system, I see them seeking solace from someone who is not in competition with them, yet knowledgeable enough about the system to ensure that the officer is protected and given the right choices of action. Funnily enough, even corrupt officials can become coaches in their later avatars, in case they have the one positive attribute of empathy. Curiously, I have seen enough instances where corrupt officers have stood up and protected the honest in their fold, as compared to officers who are honest in a pecuniary sense, but are so taken up with self-admiration that they have no time to offer solace or assistance to another honest officer stuck in a predicament.

If governments were to experiment with ethical coaches and create panels of people external to the system who can be completely trusted and who can offer mature advice, it may be possible for us to preserve a culture of honesty and help it fight back the rampant corruption that has overtaken the civil services.

Now to move on to the issues of the bureaucracy and corruption. I had started with the premise that there are two schools of thought with respect to the most effective way that corruption can be fought. The first underscores the importance of a strong ethical base in combating corruption and the other avers that a focus on systemic and process changes will bring about significant changes, rather than a fuzzy emphasis on strengthening ethics and value systems. Let us look at the second approach closely. For that, it is necessary to digress into a systems analysis of corruption before coming to the question of what bureaucrats have to do with it.

Corruption is derived from two Latin words 'cor', which means comprehensively, and 'rupt', which means ruptured. Corruption is, thus, much more than bribery. Having said that, how corruption is defined in the law as a crime is important. If one does not define corruption in the law comprehensively, then certain acts that seem to the layperson to be corrupt, slip through. For instance, if one goes to a hospital and bribes the security guard, it would amount to the criminal act of corruption in a government hospital, but won't in a private one. In India, corruption is defined as a crime that is committed only by public servants and those who bribe them.

Everyone has their favourite fix when it comes to finding solutions to corruption. Those who spearheaded the agitation for a Jan Lokpal believed that the answer lay in creating a strong Lokpal with wide powers to detect, investigate, prosecute and punish the corrupt. They are right, too. India's oversight of higher-level government, including high-level politicians, bureaucrats and judges is weak and fragmented. The result: very few of them have lost their jobs or faced criminal action for corruption. That justifies the belief that a strong Lokpal might remedy the situation.

Then we have the lamenters, who burrow into history to extract stories of perfidy and intrigue, of deserting armies and spies bought over, to justify their case that Indians are chronically and incurably corrupt. If we are to believe these purveyors of the thought that corruption is culturally determined, then surely we have a pro-corruption gene lurking somewhere in our south Asian DNA.

Yet, the experience across the world shows that many countries have been able to drastically reduce corruption, so fast that we cannot attribute its demise to a sudden improvement in morals and ethics. They did this mostly through a series of system improvements and simultaneous crackdowns on the corrupt.

There are several rigorous theses that have been built around a 'systems' view of corruption. One respected model is by Robert Klitgaard,[36] who presents an understanding of corruption in a simple yet powerful formula, C=M+D–A (corruption equals monopoly plus discretion, minus accountability). Wherever these conditions exist, be it the public or private sector, corruption tends to happen.

The solution to corruption is self-evident in the formula. If we reduce monopolies and discretion and increase accountability, corruption can come down dramatically. De-monopolization of the telephony sector shows how corruption has been eliminated in retail telephony services. The filing of e-returns for income tax, automatic assessments and sending of tax refunds directly to assesse bank accounts are examples of reducing corruption through the elimination of human discretion. Seen through the filter of this formula, the positioning of a strong Lokpal within an overarching anti-corruption system is in increasing accountability.

Klitgaard's approach to reducing corruption makes sense because it does not look upon corruption through the lens of morality, as the lamenters do. He terms corruption as a crime of calculation, not one of passion. Nobody is

born corrupt. However, as long as people anywhere find
that rewards are high and punishments are unlikely, they
will continue to drift into corruption. The taking of a large
kickback on a contract or cheating on medical and transport
bills is prompted by the same calculation: temptation and
the secure knowledge that one won't get caught. That is
why many government and private officials start off being
honest, then become corrupt over time.

In practical terms, a strong oversight agency alone cannot
reduce corruption. The most important shortcoming is that
it focuses only on corruption involving public servants;
private-sector corruption is typically left out from its
purview. Moreover, even in the public sphere, the effect of
an anti-corruption agency is multiplied when its actions go
hand in hand with systemic reform that simplifies procedures,
reduces discretion and de-monopolizes whatever can be de-
monopolized, so citizens can have a choice between service
providers. In such situations, it is expected that the corrupt
service provider will be competed out of the market.

The lamenters do play a useful role, though. Their
depressing dirges about the corrupt culture of Indians
may hurt national pride enough to spark an upsurge of
societal disapproval of corruption. However, we cannot
expect this to rise spontaneously; it has to be spurred by
an initial concerted and successful effort in anti-corruption
reform. It is when we stop and reverse corruption through
systemic reform that society will quickly change track
from celebrating corruption or standing by helplessly to
disapproving it.

What we need not waste our time on is in wishing that
morals will improve or that messiahs will arrive magically
on the horizon to rid India of corruption. Nobody is going

to descend from heaven and banish corruption by waving a magic wand.

Corruption takes many forms and each manifestation requires a distinctively nuanced treatment. An effective systems approach to combating corruption begins with a classification of its different forms, which helps one to identify the characteristics of each type and thereby find solutions. A rough and ready classification comprises seven categories, based on the nature of the transactions of which they are a part. These are: corruption in over-the-counter transactions, public procurement and privatization corruption, natural-resources-related corruption, private-sector corruption, regulation and adjudication corruption, political corruption and policy corruption and state capture. Most of us have experienced petty corruption, the kind that one experiences in over-the-counter transactions with the government, for obtaining a ration card, a passport, a driving licence, for registering properties, for filing FIRs and for a host of other services that citizens are to get from the government as a matter of course or a matter of right. Then, there is the corruption that takes place at a higher level, the corruption in procurements of goods and services by a government, ranging from office supplies to road construction, from consultancy services to buying aircraft to privatization of a public sector undertaking. Natural resources corruption touches transactions in the granting of mining leases, in the assignment of airwaves and myriad transactions relating to urban land, from outright sale to leasing to the change of land use to the issue of licences for construction. Private-sector corruption in countries where it is criminalized comprises corruption within corporates, such as bribes paid for recruitment, clearance of travel or medical bills or of contractors in private companies having to pay bribes to procurement agencies within companies, between corporates, such as kickbacks for deals, professional corruption, for example, bribes involving lawyers, chartered accountants or doctors, and those between corporates and governments. Private-sector corruption also includes the taking of bribes for admission of students to schools and bribes for appointment of teachers in private educational institutions.

Regulation and adjudication corruption is a vast area with serious ramifications and has become a critical generator of misgovernance with the burgeoning increase in the number and nature of regulatory institutions. The corruption in police investigations would also find place here. Political corruption could be about bribing voters, bribing other political parties either to provide support or to slacken their campaigns. It could also be about the funding of expensive election campaigns, including through the securing of funds into private coffers, ostensibly for funding campaigns beyond financial limits set. It could be to bribe the media to produce paid news, to engineer defections or prevent mid-term destabilization efforts by bribing elected representatives or to channelize money into the private pockets of politicians. Policy corruption and state capture is again a vast area of a diverse number of shady transactions, including the use of insider information to gain an unfair advantage, the granting of a business favour, a tax rebate to a favoured business house, granting an import or export licence and permitting large-scale evasion of taxes and duties due to engineered policy loopholes. It goes without saying that many of these categories flow into each other, thus rampant corruption in the handing out of mining leases (natural resources corruption) may be catalysed by mining companies bribing political parties (political corruption) or mining magnates buying themselves political office, influencing members of Parliament and ministers (policy corruption and state capture).

Different kinds of corruption requires different strategies for effective tackling; but hyper-corruption adds another dimension

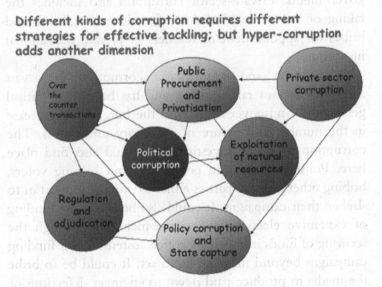

Klitgaard points out that while most corruptions start as the acts of a few corrupt freelancers who see an opportunity to make money when the going is good, if these are condoned and allowed to flourish, corruption can steadily ramp up to a distressing state termed 'syndicated' or 'hyper' corruption. This is when corruption becomes a well-oiled chain of business with linkages that run from the top to the bottom. Individual freelancers are interlinked and syndicated into networks where money collected below moves up the bureaucratic and political chain. For instance, the bribes collected from the ration card system or while registering one's property is governed by specific rates accepted by all, promoted by middlemen and distributed at all levels of the government through quotas. Powerful syndicates devise means of passing tainted money upward and hiding it.

Liberalization at first sight may look like a good policy antidote to corruption because it is supposed to be anti-monopoly. A free market, in theory, is supposed to improve fair competition and, therefore, act as a strong disincentive to corruption. After all, liberalization is expected to reduce corruption, by de-monopolizing service delivery to people and giving them a choice of products. Capitalism spurs competition, which drives efficiency and lowers costs, improves access and betters the quality of services. However, in reality, economies that have liberalized have seen an increase in corruption rather than a decrease. Even as liberalization de-monopolizes some sectors, we also witness other phenomena that raise their ugly heads: of cronyism, of oligarchs, cartels and others who thrive in a climate of poor regulation. Contrary to popular notion, good competition is a result not of 'freeness' of the free market, but of careful and nuanced regulation. However, a robust regulatory system that ensures quality, fair competition and restriction of monopolies takes time to stabilize. Till that happens, capitalist economies cannot prevent rogues from making piles of money through corruption—sometimes, the very same that made a killing in the socialist era. At the very border, the line that separates corruption of this kind and sharp business practices is a blurred one. India is particularly hard hit by both socialist and capitalist corruption. On the one hand, poor Indians do not have access to good quality of essential services. So they suffer the shortages that ought to have died with the waning of socialism. Yet, even as they do, we see the birth and growth of capitalist corruption.

Policymaking is a natural monopoly and discretion exercised in the highest echelons of the government can tend to be very wide. Therefore, there is a much greater role for accountability mechanisms to play in curbing it. Currently, India's oversight of higher-level government, including high-level bureaucrats, politicians, the political executive and the judiciary is weak and fragmented. The result is that not one judge has been impeached yet for corruption. As regards MPs, a few sting operations (such as in the MP's local area development fund case) have forced some to resign, but corruption prosecutions have not succeeded. One of the reasons is a weak investigation mechanism. The Central Vigilance Commission and the CBI together are unable to provide the deterrence to curb wholesale corruption. The recent controversies surrounding the character of those who head these institutions have done little to enhance the reputation of these institutions.

There is no doubt that we need strong laws that empower investigating agencies and provide for deterrent punishments. However, many more measures are required to build an effective anti-corruption regime. A strong Lokpal alone will not suffice, if the definition of what constitutes corruption under the law is narrow. India's Prevention of Corruption law has a very narrow and restricted meaning of the word 'corruption'. This law only recognizes a few actions of public servants, such as the taking of bribes or the misuse of public office to amass wealth, as corruption. We need amendments in this law to ensure that the wider definitions of corruption, as recognized in the UN Convention against Corruption

2005,[37] are operationalized in India. This is a legal reform that is of equal significance to having a Lokpal Act. If we do that, then several actions that are not considered crimes in India—such as bribery in the private sector, an Indian bribing a foreign national in another country, concealment of wealth, exercising undue influence and obstruction of justice—will be punishable. If we wish to control the corruption that flourishes in capitalist economies, then we will also need to tackle the corruption rampant in the private sector. Recent amendments to the Prevention of Corruption Act only solve part of the problem. An amendment to Section 9 of the Act criminalizes the bribing of government agencies by the private sector. It says that if any person associated with a commercial organization gives or promises to give any undue advantage to a public servant to obtain or retain business or an advantage in the conduct of business that amounts to corruption. However, the act still does not criminalize bribery wholly within the private sector.

The reasonably honest and practical-minded bureaucrat, caught in the midst of this hyper-corrupt environment with few legal instruments to use to combat it, is an insecure, unhappy and sullen individual. Caught in the political crossfire over corruption are many members of the permanent civil services, who at all levels are governed by conduct rules that direct them to keep their mouth shut. Under the conduct rules of the civil services, officials are not allowed in normal circumstances to speak to the press, even if it is to clear their names or defend themselves when undergoing a trial by the media.

Even though bureaucrats cannot speak of their good work in public or defend themselves against such extreme and unwarranted observations, in private circles, there is plenty of disappointment against bureaucrat bashing. In my email group of former colleagues, during the height of the victory of civil society following Anna Hazare's fast, one wrote:

Dear Anna,

Congratulations on your 'victory'. But you are encouraging anarchy. Your 'victory' was achieved through blackmail. This is no different. Your movement was peaceful with an unquestionably noble end. But your means have subverted the democratic and legal process.

You cannot go and assume every politician or bureaucrat is corrupt. They too are Indians and are from the same stock as you. And if you believe they are bad, go and defeat them/ encourage your supporters to have their children appear for the civil services exam and get into the IAS and other civil services through merit! Our elections are free and fair. The civil services exam is fair. The majority of the urban supporters in Jantar Mantar do not even vote.

This is no victory. For every taker of a bribe, there is inevitably (not always) a more–than–willing giver. The root problem is our national character or lack of it. We sell our votes, our testimony (on oath!), our conscience, our principles but do not hesitate to criticize the government, the politicians, bureaucracy, etc., for corruption and inefficiency. We behave like animals on the road but talk about civil society.

We have no work ethics—our productivity is among the lowest. It would have indeed been fitting if you had begun and ended your fast with a pledge by you and all the millions you have galvanized swearing by all that is precious to them that they would NEVER give or take a bribe, that they would pay all their taxes, no under/over invoicing, not evading a traffic challan, not tampering with the water and electricity meters to avoid paying the full bill . . . the list is endless. In essence that they would themselves be good citizens and bring up their children to be good citizens too. Ask not what your country can do for you but what you can do for your country.

Jai Hind.

The truth, as always, lies somewhere in between the extreme view that nearly all of government is corrupt and that the problem is our national character alone. For instance, there is plenty of evidence to show that elections might not be fair, particularly if electoral rolls are grievously inaccurate. Similarly, if national character were the central problem, then we would not have had remarkable success in reducing corruption through changes in systems, like with income tax refunds, railway ticketing and a host of other services that are available over the counter without corruption.

There is no doubt that one of the significant reasons why India is progressing is because there are large numbers of honest bureaucrats, who go about their work diligently and honestly, but are constrained not to speak about the changes they have brought about, because they are trained to be self-effacing.

Yet, bureaucrats are not trained in the fighting of corruption. There are hardly any training programmes that are focused on anti-corruption, and even if they do exist, they focus on the action to be taken after the corrupt incident happens—how the corrupt may be nabbed and punished. Thus, bureaucrats become anti-corruption fighters, if at all, by accident, often straying there as they handle random instances of corruption and fight back with reform tactics such as transparency, technology, process change and greater oversight.

There are several instances of how corruption has been curbed successfully. However, even as we celebrate these, there is a need to keep our critical faculties open to how these solutions may be subverted. Yamini Aiyar and Salimah Samji's study of the stellar success of the Andhra Pradesh Society for Social Audits in curbing corruption in the payment of NREGA wages,[38] showed that while the Society's processes were remarkably effective in getting public accountability over wage distribution in NREGA, it was not as nimble and effective in curbing the corruption that took place over a large number of procurement transactions to obtain building material for NREGA works. This is not to disparage the work of the Society, headed at different times by driven individuals of high integrity from both within and outside the bureaucracy, but to flag the point that those who fight corruption have to always be on alert because the corrupt never rest.

What might a broad strategy that can anticipate some success in fighting corruption consist of? There are five components that have to work in concert to ensure that countries have an effective anti-corruption strategy. First, corruption must be regularly assessed and measured through frequent studies. Such analytical rigour leads to more efficient strategies of fighting corruption. They move from being the random efforts of a few well-meaning people to a systems approach to fight corruption, transaction by transaction, sector by sector. Second, there must be a strong whistleblower protection regime that gives assurance to those willing to speak out about corruption, whether a bureaucrat or anybody else (that they will be protected, if not rewarded for their courage). This has to be backed by an effective and swift system that investigates, proves, prosecutes and punishes transgressors for corruption. Third, there must be an overarching emphasis on the ethics of organizations and those that people them. Such an ethical regime cannot be imposed on public services alone but also equally on the private sector.

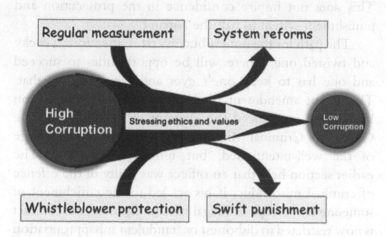

India is struggling to get its anti-corruption strategy right. It does not have a regular measurement system to gauge the extent and the constantly changing nature of corruption. Most measurement studies of corruption are too narrow in their focus, not rigorous in their investigative approach and tend to come out with results that are unreliable. Systems reforms are, therefore, based on the notions of individual champions, who rarely stay long enough to ground the reforms that they push and ensure their success. India's draft whistleblower law is a disaster, it is more intent on punishing whistleblowers who are found to be wrong rather than incentivizing people who come forth with the details of corrupt actions that they witness. To compound the problem, India's system for legal recourse against the corrupt is dysfunctional. Politicians get away with murder in long, dilatory legal exercises. And often, bureaucrats who are known to not have committed any corrupt act or did not have any corrupt intent are punished as scapegoats. This does not inspire confidence in the prosecution and punishment system to nab the corrupt.

The path for the honest bureaucrat is, therefore, a rocky and twisted one. There will be opportunities to succeed and one has to keep one's eyes and ears open for that. The recent amendment to the Prevention of Corruption law, which introduced the element of intention into the Offence of Criminal Misconduct, will be to the advantage of the well-intentioned, but unlucky bureaucrat. The earlier section held that an officer was guilty of the offence of criminal misconduct if his act led to the enrichment of someone by corrupt or illegal means. Criminal misconduct is now restricted to dishonest or fraudulent misappropriation of any property entrusted to the public servant or if the public servant intentionally enriches himself illicitly during the period of his office. It is defined as the obtaining of 'undue advantage' (meaning gratification other than legal remuneration) intending that in consequence a public duty would be performed improperly or dishonestly, either by himself or by another public servant

The final hope for the honest bureaucrat may lie in the formation of networks with honest civil society. For that, the bureaucrat will have to give up the long held notion that aloofness is a virtue in all circumstances. The personality trait of empathy will have to stand hand in hand with that of financial honesty and effectiveness. It is only when the bureaucrat is able to empathize with the people, even those who have cooperated in corruption, they can find solutions to the latter.

Between 2010 and 2011, just after I left the IAS, I had the unique opportunity of heading ipaidabribe. com as the programme coordinator. This Internet-based effort, started by Janaagraha, a Bengaluru-based not-for-profit organization, aimed to crowdsource experiences of corruption from ordinary people. It was a hit straightaway and within a year, we had sufficient numbers of reports from citizens under three categories of transactions, where people paid bribes, where they did not pay bribes because they fought back and where they did not have to pay bribes because they were helped by a good and honest officer. Since people were not constrained in relating their experiences, they ranged from the short and brusque to long accounts of the circumstances in which they paid bribes. From the bribe payers, which sadly accounted for about 85 per cent of those who responded on the site, the following emerged as the key motivation for paying bribes. Many paid bribes because they wanted to finish their transactions quickly, a hint of delay and they readily paid speed money. They found that convenient. Others paid due to fear of the unknown or just a sense of relief that a much-anticipated transaction, say, the buying of a flat, had gone through without a hitch. Many people paid bribes because they did not take the trouble of reading up beforehand on reforms that aimed to help them. Thus, they did not check out the citizens' charters of the departments concerned, which guaranteed service delivery within prescribed periods of time. Such people were only too willing to be persuaded by middlemen or agents or even their peers or mentors that corruption was inevitable and it was prudent to submit to it. Thus, the agents and lawyers of building companies were the ones that arranged for the 'service charges' for registration of properties, even though the registration department had publicly committed to completing registration within a few hours of the transaction being commenced. It was particularly sad to listen to the experiences of teenagers who paid bribes to obtain their learner's licences for driving, probably their first transactions with the government. They were often persuaded by their parents to pay bribes and not get into 'trouble'. A few colluded with bribe-takers, because they profited from the bribe, such as a reduction of property tax by the municipality or the issue of a business licence without fulfilment of all the conditions.

Why do people pay bribes? (Answering this question, leads to the appropriate solution)

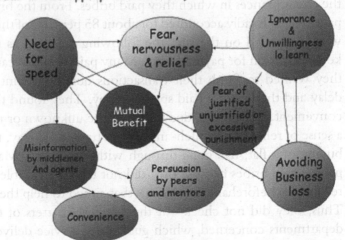

Clearly, an understanding of the mental state of the bribe-giver is a key input for the honest bureaucrat intent on reforming systems, even as they fight indifference, hostility and loneliness within the government. An effective bureaucrat will hopefully find that ability, even as she may compromise to a reasonable extent to remain in one place long enough to design, implement and make irreversible changes that are possible.

The battle against corruption can be won, but one cannot rely upon one's own wits for success. Networks and strategic approaches will signal success. It's not going to be easy, but it is inevitable if the bureaucrat has to retain relevance within the government.

Afterword

QUO VADIS?—THE INDIAN ADMINISTRATIVE SERVICE

'The petty done, the undone vast'

—Robert Browning,
'The Last Ride Together'

Recherche du temps perdu

Many of us, who have spent half a lifetime in the closed confines of the Indian Administrative Service, eventually discover how it transforms our way of life, thoughts and outlook on domestic and global events. When we started off, a career in Indian administration offered young people permanence, comfort, reasonable income and prospects of worthwhile public service. Four decades later, we are faced with a harsh, painful reality. We discover how our plans for development only distorted economic incentives and spawned corrupt intermediaries. Our half-baked notions of how to improve the lives of citizens were often too little and too late, since they were based on ancient theories and built on obsolete data. Our schemes to change the behaviour of producers, consumers and intermediaries were overdesigned and micromanaged. The handouts we invented to raise the incomes of the poor only fed the appetites of rapacious middlemen.

But this was what I had wanted to do since my teenage years. Where did it all go? Around me lies the detritus of hopes and plans. Today, in India, one out of every four male adults is still illiterate. A third of our women do not read and write. Almost thirty-four of the children born in every thousand live births do not survive. As many as 178 out of a hundred thousand women giving birth do not survive. And one-fifth of our children under five are wasted, with the percentage going up and not down!

We are at the very bottom of almost every global list. Even optimists admit that close to a quarter of the population earns less than a dollar a day. Our marks for governance are just as poor—we rank among the lowest in Transparency International scales, always sinking lower. It sometimes seems that every public service is at the mercy of fixers and middlemen, a fast-growing occupation accounting for a substantial chunk of the national income. What went wrong?

Mea culpa. I am to blame. We are to blame. We were there when conditions were analysed, our theories of development drove the policies and we brought them to fruition. And these are the inadequate and perverse results. The conclusion is inescapable. What was inherent in the structure of the civil administration that brought us to this pass? What went awry? Why and how did it fail so badly?

THE BUREAUCRACY IS NOT A MERITOCRACY

Is the selection process muddied and the wrong persons selected to run the government? In India, recruitment to the higher civil service is done through a competitive examination, an ancient method favoured by Confucian China. Not a perfect system but not totally flawed either. The British adapted it to local needs to provide them with enough babus to run a sprawling empire. After Independence, the arrangement was retained to hold together the disparate masses of the vast country. There is little evidence to suggest that the wrong kind of person is entering the civil service. There is no slackening in the number of applicants to the examination; it is still a highly preferred career option for talented, patriotic young people. There are more than 11 lakh applicants for around a thousand posts in the higher civil services, 1100 plus for each place. And numbers increase every year. Civil service aspirants come from the most educated groups—professionals like doctors and engineers as well as academics and managers with years of study. The magnet of career permanence, prestige and power and the dream of public service still draw them in inexorably.

There is cynicism about leaked papers and external meddling in most selections done on 'merit' in our country. Yet, the civil service examination has escaped such cynicism. Of course, we may demand, in the manner of jesting Pilate: 'What is merit?' This is, after all, a concept defined at a specific place and point of time by dominant social groups to suit their interests. Whenever we prescribe qualifications for professional courses and the best-paid jobs, we do make profiles in our own image, choosing book learning over manual dexterity and aptitude: our engineers are rarely children of weavers, masons or mechanics! Within these limitations, however, over the years, the UPSC, guided by changes suggested by think tanks and commissions, has conducted civil service examinations objectively and transparently. And those who clamour at its gates do believe in its relative impartiality, even when they approach courts to demand relief. Which is one reason why aspirants make the attempt relentlessly year after year, determined to somehow storm the portals. And the selection methods are achieving their aim. Every year, the managing class appoints meritorious people of diverse backgrounds, with high technical qualifications, well-versed in Indian languages, from rural areas, poorer families and backward groups.

We cannot then blame poor induction policies for civil service failures. The rot sets in later, within the stultifying, elitist habitat of top management. And its totally dysfunctional personnel management framework.

I was a mere juvenile with four years of civil service experience when I realized that April was the cruellest month. This was the performance-appraisal period when we misjudged our personnel and were paid back in the same coin by our bosses. We still believed then that quantitative parameters could be applied to correct the subjectivity of the dreaded ACRs for some jobs at least. We laboured for months to develop predetermined targets for every job so that year-end achievements could be evaluated and performance graded in sliding scales from one to ten. The inevitable happened. As a (slightly inebriated) colleague once concluded, civil servants continued to work and shoot at random. Now, however, every year, they draw circles around their hits and call them targets. Thus, working backwards, targets were derived from achievements.

Appraisers, too, avoided responsibility. Out of timidity and a desire for peaceful coexistence, they bunch appraisals together at the middle or top ends of the scale.

Within the government, familiar words acquire new meanings. The oddest example is the use of the word 'select'. Technically, no one in government can expect promotion by passage of time to 'selection' posts. In actual fact, everyone jumps the selection hurdle with aplomb; only independent thinkers and troublemakers are penalized with deselection. Most entrants to the IAS can safely assume that they will rise to the top of the ladder, if they remain anonymous and sign on dotted lines.

The cruellest ACR joke is the empanelment process. To be posted at positions under the federal government, panels of state officers are prepared after scrutiny of recent ACRs. The whole procedure is beautifully gamed: a boss management manual could advise how to get around a boss (by toadying, entertaining or overawing him or by sheer persistence) to elicit annual 'outstanding' ACR ratings, which get counted mindlessly, when empanelment season comes around. The largest number of outstanding officers often comes from the poorest-governed state administrations, from which they flee to shelters in Delhi corridors. The fact of having risen through various empanelment fiascos to the rank of secretary confirmed for me my own mediocrity: I looked at the final list and noted that the best of my batch mates, the one most committed to the welfare of the poor, had not been empanelled. At one time, four secretaries to the Government of India picked meticulously by such meaningless shenanigans ended up in adjacent cells in the country's prisons.

Beneath the charade lie the real facts of selection: how prestigious posts and training opportunities are always reserved for private secretaries of ministers, the role of caste, religion and region in key postings, how cronyism and nepotism operate. For those who meet these selection criteria, the overt rules are twisted and reinvented. Ministers of personnel routinely compel their unfortunate secretaries into paroxysms of creativity to find legal justifications for arbitrary choices. In recent years, it is amusing, though not surprising, to see how safeguards against reemployment built into statutes for top level regulatory posts, like chairman of the Telecom Regulatory Authority of India or even the Comptroller and Auditor General, have been blatantly violated to favour loyalists. Rot at the top that will only seep to other levels!

Relentless undermining of innovation and creativity by unkind and unfair personnel policies also takes its toll on the morale of enthusiastic newcomers. No wonder the civil service has in some ways become a large pool of underperforming cynical and lethargic managers.

But, there is a bigger issue: what should be the civil service ideal, how do we define high quality public service so that we may promote and reward it? Awareness of and responsiveness to citizens' needs are rarely noticed or incentivized. Neither the department of personnel nor successive administrative reforms and pay commissions have focused on keeping administration citizen-centred and in close touch with the ground reality of poverty and corruption. There is also no encouragement for innovative thinking and behaviour, the kind which leverages public participation at every level and produces positive developmental outcomes. All because civil servants live in a bubble of their own making, which distorts their professional gaze and seriously affects their ability to cater to people's needs.

DISTANCE FROM REALITY

I had noticed and experienced the lure of civil service appointment for a long time, but its full implication sank in only when I saw the movie *Nil Battey Sannata* (a fairy tale about a maid's determination to give her daughter a glorious future: her dream is realized when the daughter becomes a Very Important Person, an IAS officer!). The determining incident behind the selection of this career is when the maid is helped by a kindly (and lordly!) district collector; she cajoles and bullies her way into his highly secure bungalow to discover the secret formula behind his elevation. Power and distance from the poor—this is what attracts our maid; the harsh reality today is that these account for much of the attraction of the civil service. Which explains why induction policies that successfully favour diverse and disadvantaged groups still fail to bring the administration closer to its poorest citizens. The norms and practices of the system overawe new entrants, not surprising when many of them have chosen this career precisely because they wish to distance themselves from the *aam janata* (the common herd) and enter the exclusive IAS club.

Colonial administrators were sheltered from their subjects in exclusive residences, modes of transport and places of entertainment. Many of these practices were continued after Independence, at first only to provide houses, halting places, medical and (official) transport facilities for touring officers transferred at short notice. Over the years, however, these have become protected entitlements, perks and privileges, fiercely fought over as symbols of precedence. Everyone joins in the 'keep up with the Jones' rivalry. I have seen uniformed and police staff, judges, and even

politicians line up to compare who has the largest house
(with ample neglected grounds), priority in invitations to
presidential ceremonies and 'black cat' security for personal
protection. A posse of vehicles with red lights and sirens is
de rigueur to authenticate one's standing. And norms are
thus established: never use public transport, never stand in
a public queue (unless, sometimes, if you are in the more
egalitarian Kerala cadre), never drive your own vehicle if
you can avoid it, never go through security in an airport and
never ever, after retirement, go gentle into that good night
of thankful anonymity. Within offices, attached restrooms
are reserved for senior staff; in the Reserve Bank of India
and the State Bank, there are lifts only for the privileged few,
government medical institutions make special arrangements
for senior personnel, which continue after retirement.
Some allowances are disgustingly petty. In Karnataka, the
government pays the cost of a maid in every officer's house;
recently, this was extended to retired officers too! The
lure of perpetual vehicles, subsidized accommodation and
telephones keeps many pegging on forever in government
posts after every retirement.

Perhaps, as Indians, we are at ease with such hierarchical
rigidities, because we have always believed in social
and religious inequality. The exercise of economic and
regulatory power by government employees in post-
Independence dirigiste India has also distanced 'rulers'
from the 'ruled'. We may ape the West in most things,
but politicians and senior government officers will never
imitate their counterparts in developed countries and use
public services or join public queues. Such attitudes have
serious professional consequences: by cocooning themselves
in exclusive enclaves, civil servants never experience how

schemes and plans really work nor how they are gamed and distorted.

In all my IAS years, it was only in the initial months of training, when I was attached to field staff as a probationer, that I directly observed the behaviour of local officials and the reactions of citizens to government policies and directives. Later on, feedback came from secondary sources: through anecdotes, rumours, academic studies. It was difficult to gauge the reliability of information presented by complainants at the official podium and one always feared that large public enquiries were being managed or hijacked.

One area that I continued to be familiar with was road transport. Having chosen to drive my car to office and back, I quickly learned about both what government drivers went through on their daily rounds and the venality of traffic police towards commuters. Indeed, I hardly know of a single traffic incident, which has ever been legally, honestly and courteously dealt with by police personnel! The process of re-education after retirement often throws up pleasant surprises. On government buses today, I admire drivers for their dexterity in avoiding accidents, conductors for handling crowds of commuters and fellow passengers for their courtesy and kindness.

THE BUREAUCRAT IS NOT A DEMOCRAT

It is universally acknowledged that permanent civil services are hostile to people's representatives and will seek to subvert fresh ideas and change in any form. Which is why civil servants recognized themselves as milder manifestations of Sir Humphrey, when the BBC television series *Yes Minister* and its equally entertaining Indian version *Ji Mantriji* were aired. Indian bureaucracy is also a rump service, rooted in colonial practices. One consequence is the perceived dichotomy between politicians and officialdom. Some political figures believe that bureaucrats are not entitled to speak in the name of democracy, as they are paid employees of the state, not direct descendants of the democratic tradition. I had a taste of this perception, when, as managing director of the Karnataka State Cooperative Marketing Federation, I recorded my dissent on a board resolution to repeatedly postpone internal elections, because I believed it was undemocratic, I was roundly attacked by many elected directors for overstepping my limits and daring to use the D word. This is not, however, the sense in which I make my case here about the senior bureaucrat's relationship with democracy. I am referring to something more fundamental, something that is inherent in our reaction to the democratic notion of the equality of all citizens and the submission of public servants to the will of the people.

As a good citizen, the bureaucrat's first democratic duty is to participate in governance by exercising his vote. The entire electoral process is managed and run by the bureaucracy, but few of us actually vote! Look at the miniscule number of postal ballots in any election and we get a whiff of this huge anomaly. The civil service exhorts citizens to register and vote, civil servants list voters, organize elections, count the ballot and announce results. And they never vote. It would be instructive to discover how many election commissioners at the Centre and the states, how many district election officers and electoral registration officers, have ever voted. What underlies such behaviour is, at its worst, a frightening contempt for democracy and all its notions of equality and participation. At its best, it is a supreme indifference to the realization of the popular will. The causes and results are far-reaching.

In some ways, shying away from the ballot box is a middle-class malady. In India, after the few early years of heady patriotism, professionals and salaried persons mainly stayed away from the pollution of politics. My parents instructed me to shun student politics because they believed that political parties were corrupt and violent, and when carried over into adulthood can lead to a profound dislike of the democratic process itself. But, are there even deeper roots?

For democratic instincts to become embedded, we must routinely accept that, in some matters at least, all citizens are equal: at a polling booth, votes have the same weight; before the law, we are on the same level. The functioning of Indian bureaucracy is rooted in age-old habits of inequality, which take for granted levels of priority in access to temples and social acceptability. Much of this pervades bureaucracy too. Visitors to public buildings are not received as equals— there are the few who are offered chairs and the very few for whom the officer might even get up for a welcome. There are three gradations of language: second person singular will suffice for the poor, a politer version for the hoi polloi and extreme unction for VIPs or PLUs (people like us). At its heart, choosing not to vote is part of the elitism and sense of privilege that suffuses the bureaucracy, the sense that it is somehow above normal citizenship requirements and responsibilities. And this is dangerous, like all the other distancing methods routinely embedded in civil service comportment.

Election supervisors who have never voted never experience the rottenness and corruption that every citizen finds at the core of the voter registration process that wastes their time and energy in endless visits and disputes with election staff to ensure that their names are put on electoral rolls and remain there. It is only by themselves undergoing the same soul-searing humiliation that a chief election commissioner or chief electoral officer can discover the mechanics of managing elections, if, of course he cares passionately for democracy and believes in its preservation.

How deeply the civil service despises the democratic route can be measured in the way it manages its own associations. Service associations are rigidly calibrated hierarchically—the senior-most person (outside the official channel) must head the body, irrespective of whether it suits his inclinations or those of his colleagues. After the Karnataka IAS officers association amended its byelaws to provide for democratic elections, the innovation was easily stifled in the bud; none would ever propose a candidate for election against the senior-most officer. It was astonishing to see how a senior turned against me for merely suggesting that an election might actually strengthen her arms with the formal support of members. An eye-opening encounter that taught me how unaccustomed bureaucrats are to democratic behaviour.

Indian bureaucracy is profoundly undemocratic in another sense too. The seventy-third and seventy-fourth amendments to the Constitution formally legalized at the highest level a key tenet of democracy, the people's right to self-government. The concept had already been around for ages. It was this philosophy that Mahatma Gandhi and other early leaders had developed when they spoke of Swaraj. The western states derived from the old Bombay Presidency introduced advanced self-governing structures by devolving political power to zilla parishads and below from very early days; others were expected to follow suit after the amendment came through in 1993. But this has been successfully foiled by bureaucrats marching side by side with the political establishment. Why would anyone who already enjoyed power give it away voluntarily? Politicians at higher levels forced themselves on to all local fora; civil servants recaptured control over transferred functions.

A good method for destroying a scheme is to build the form and eat away the substance—this was done for Swaraj too. In Karnataka, for example, Abdul Nasir Saab recreated the structure of zilla, taluka and village panchayats and formally moved key developmental activities to popularly elected bodies to determine for themselves how to run schools and medical institutions and manage common lands, water supply and sanitation. These brave attempts were undermined and destroyed in two ways. Funds required for financial self-sufficiency were neither allowed to be freely raised or devolved nor were they allowed to be easily spent. And political and administrative control over the transferred activities never shifted to local bodies. Today, local representatives are a frustrated lot, starved of personnel and authority.

The key figure in colonial administration was the district officer—he was a magistrate and regulator, who, over the years, took on 'developmental' functions too. A civil servant, who holds this post, gets a heady taste of concentrated power and all kinds of diffused responsibility. Before Independence, the district magistrate reigned as the local symbol of the state itself, but his supremacy was undermined when a senior was made the chief executive officer of the elected local body and 'development' departments shifted to local bodies. The old guard hit back by working at all levels. Every departmental head at the state and Centre reworked his programmes creating silos outside local body control, to which they summoned the district collector/ deputy commissioner as their local representative, relegating the local body to the fringes of decision-making to perform the role of mere observers, uninvolved in implementation or even feedback. This process is almost complete today. And we, the bureaucracy, have actively and successfully connived at the destruction of local democracy. No, we are not and have never been democrats.

THE UNSKILLED BUREAUCRAT

The bureaucracy is a house divided against itself, whenever it debates the generalist-specialist issue. We can expect this sort of (un)civil war, when generalists are treated as better managers, more suitable to head professional departments and the promotion prospects of internal candidates are affected. (I have heard French officials too refer sarcastically to the énarques chosen to manage their departments as 'les petits genies')! In the early years after Independence, liberal arts education was universally favoured for civil service positions in India. Engineers trained in IITs, RECs and the like and doctors from prestigious medical institutions were expected to hone their professional skills; scientists headed research and academic facilities; economists were drawn into government to advise all departments and particularly the Planning Commission to formulate policies and evaluate achievements. Technical expertise within the government was well anchored only at lower levels and in advisory capacities while decisions remained in the hands of 'unskilled' civil servants. In our dirigiste economy, financial stability and advancement were largely assured in the public sector alone. Unable to rise to the top in government positions, highly qualified professionals from all areas streamed out of the country to make careers overseas, picking up fortunes and honours in the process.

The absence of specialist professional knowledge at top levels was offset to some extent when selection processes were modified to induct persons with technical skills. Engineers flocked to the civil service and so did doctors and scientists. The quality pool today within the bureaucracy is extensive and deep, so that it is perfectly possible to find technically qualified persons appointed through the one time examination for most departments. Today's conflict could even be between professionals now embedded within the civil service who have been taught or have acquired managerial skills versus those who have developed within technical departments and picked up administrative acumen on the way.

No happy marriage of technical and managerial skills has, however, resulted from the arrival of doctors and engineers within top management. Government departments still do not deliver services professionally nor manage their tasks with technical proficiency. Clearly something in the bureaucratic process freezes technical skills and makes them inoperative. Private offices undertaking similar tasks are always far more pleasant and accessible and always work more effectively, with greater courtesy to clients and probably even at lower cost. We might have used technical tools to build a compassionate society and responsive public services. This has not happened. Professionals who enter government either imbibe the government culture or introduce systems which overlook the real needs of the poorest groups.

When children turn three, they learn to say no. In the same way, a person who qualifies for government service becomes an expert naysayer. The civil servant who is rapidly shifted among jobs learns to cope by turning to official bibles: manuals of procedure, procurement policies, lists of administrative and technical powers and disciplinary rules. The pity is that most civil servants rarely stray beyond these limits. Successful careers are built by merely stemming the flow of public needs and demands with a stern no. In India, bureaucrats who can stay focused on the main objectives of their departments are very rare indeed. The commissioner for public instruction, for example, forgets that his main function is to bring and keep all children of the state in school; he spends far more time in regulating admissions and inspecting schools. No wonder elected people who are mandated by voters to provide improved services complain about negative bureaucrats.

Lasting damage has been done to the country by official obstruction of many kinds of commercial behaviour without providing proper facilities for legitimate development at the same time. In the '70s and '80s, when Bangalore was the fastest growing city of Asia, attracting homeowners and developers, the bureaucracy was never able to anticipate growth trends and requirements or formulate quick and workable procedures for meeting the swelling demand. Transfers of many kinds of property were prohibited and city development concepts and approvals always lagged far behind construction plans. The result was that buildings were built in violation of norms or by taking advantage of the interstices between regulations. The system only bred fixers of all kinds and created ineradicable layers of corruption. We live today with the consequences of this technical and administrative failure.

Changes in recruitment and training methodologies have not made a dent in such authoritarian behaviour. Mindless application of rules is justified on the ground that it is essential to satisfy auditors. Except for the fact that the bureaucrat who interprets a rule is also adept at advising how it can be subverted. But such advice is offered only in return for a favour, in cash or in kind, to powerful and influential clients. Audit for its part has also developed into a mindless checking of rules. Auditors rarely have the capacity to see the larger picture of departmental failure; I remember one of them catechizing me on marginal increases in sumptuary costs for board meetings while never asking why a once profitable organization was sharply losing revenue. Audit and the judiciary too often pin the blame on the wrong actor, without appreciating the causes and effects of poor judgments. The CAG report[1] on the telecom scam had far-reaching effects on political and economic developments in the country. Eyebrows were naturally raised when the same CAG was subsequently 're-employed' by the government that benefited from his comments. An unfortunate and innocent victim was the top civil servant who headed the Ministry of Coal (a civil service topper with a blameless record of honest service). Incidents like this reinforce the natural conformism and cowardice of civil servants and encourage them to pass the buck and avoid innovative and effective management.

How did the two areas of technological transformation of the seventies and eighties—computers for automation of processes and the Internet for communication—alter government when the IAS was inundated by engineers? Quickly, of course, the internal dichotomy surfaced. Seniors, who made and managed policy were uncomfortable with computers while new recruits, who were eager to use their skills to transform systems, were refused access to them. For laptops, like other amenities, were doled out strictly on seniority to decorate the offices of personal assistants, to be brought out and adorned for the annual ayudha puja. As planning secretary in Karnataka, overseeing the Karnataka Government Computer Centre, I ended up lending my laptop to everyone who could use it; changing internal attitudes seemed far too exhausting. Over time, though, the benefits of computerization have filtered upwards and outwards. Many effective initiatives for satisfying clients are in place today—Bengaluru One outlets for single window service delivery, computerized issue of records of rights, online payment of taxes and utility bills etc. Except for one fatal flaw.

Systems have always existed to organize government tasks. Some excellent classifications like those formalized in *Anderson's Manual*[2] used throughout the Bombay Presidency during British days made sense of the data collected by scrutiny of records and village visits as well as those that turned up at offices. A well-oiled system that picks up only essential information and churns out required outcomes should work without a whisper, taking care of all contingencies and meeting all public needs. Unfortunately, many computerized systems are superficial overlays, with no relation to the underlying connections with real transactions. This is particularly the case with systems of land management like Bhoomi, which has now become ubiquitous in Karnataka.

Village records have been organized for decades around twelve or eleven forms that link the nature of a particular piece of land, its quality and use to ownership, produce and a score of relevant indicators, all of which are available during periodical land surveys and from ongoing transactions and alterations. This was kept updated by an annual audit process called jamabandi. The symmetry of the system ensured that every critical entry was validated by data captured in another format, so that all anomalies are noted and corrections could be made. It was also reasonably accurate and reliable before it fell into disuse through poor administration and was overwhelmed by rapid changes. Bhoomi should have simplified and modernized the system; instead, it is churning out printouts of one village record, the RTC or pahani, in which several key items of individual information are entered, treating it as a standalone document. The result is a classic case of GIGO—garbage in garbage out—since all methods of validation have been removed and errors cannot be discovered or remedied. No wonder that all over Karnataka today, land records are totally out of touch with the real situation and there is almost no hope of ever setting them right.

Another blatant and widespread way of papering over cracks and presenting a rosy picture is the use of PowerPoint. We are all adept today at reducing our programmes, ideas and performance to a few dramatic slides that pass for the truth. Except that figures given in such statements are often hollow and baseless. They are not drawn from documentation systematically maintained and collected. When we are told that 2000 persons were employed on a rural work guarantee project in a village, a little healthy scepticism is advisable. Is it validated by a muster roll recorded day after day on the site, by measurements of work done during the period and matched with payments made for materials and labour (at the prescribed minimum wage)? Statements trotted out on PowerPoint are valid only when they are sourced directly and backed up by field records. What we get today is often only the perfect slide, which has replaced reality.

When government systems are superficially modernized disregarding the harsh truths of ground-level work, things only get worse. The seduction of a technical tool dazzles promoters into overlooking its dangerous consequences. Insistence on Aadhaar ID cards for admitting poor primary school children to highly sought-after seats in private schools, without examining how flawed and inadequate the Aadhaar database is, has resulted in excluding the poorest and most vulnerable from the best educational opportunities. The education department exists to find and include every child in the schooling process. Insistence on Aadhaar has had exactly the opposite effect and the evidence is all around us. Such shortsightedness blinds even the most concerned bureaucrats so that today no one in the department cares any longer about what Aadhaar has done to the poorest parents and their children. This experience is being repeated in the midday meals programme for schools. Mindless adoption of a technological product has become more important than outreach to the neediest.

Communications technology has transformed our world and invaded government. Social media is one bright area within the general scenario of government departments distancing themselves from the public. Complainants who can use it have found direct access to official departmental heads. Many of us know how a Facebook or Twitter comment or even one on a

WhatsApp group in which government officers participate can trigger instant corrective action and lively debate. Far more can be done to link public feedback to appraisal and reward systems for government personnel to judge contractors and renew contracts and even to assess the effectiveness of elected corporators.

WOMEN AND THE CIVIL SERVICE

The experiences and choices of women IAS officers are in some ways distinct from those of the men. If asked why they wished to make a career in the civil service, women of my generation might give the same answers as the men; as for beauty contests, there are the standard acceptable replies (public service) and the standard unspoken ones (job security, pay, perks, prestige; a higher dowry is a reason that applies to male officers alone, since being in the IAS was often a deterrent in the marriage stakes for women!). For my part, the decision to prepare for the IAS was taken in high school when I began to sense the shades of social constraints falling across my future. I longed to participate in exciting things happening in my country and society, but my history books were full of only male protagonists. I also fretted against the constant reminder of relatives that a mere girl like me could only get married and submit herself to the future of some man somewhere. I learned that the very few women who were then in the IAS were not allowed to marry. Entering the civil service would give me a good excuse to avoid the compulsion of marriage. I could also become a participant in public affairs, not remain an observer on the sidelines in a teaching capacity, the only other career open then to women like me. And these incentives motivated me to work hard for the civil service examination. Perhaps other women entrants sensed the same things. Certainly, we learned that a woman who got into the IAS would seldom be pressured by family and friends to resign and become a fellow traveller (cook and homemaker) to a man or stay at home to bring up children and adopt other unpaid nurturing roles. All around us, we also knew highly intelligent women, whose families had actively prevented them from competing in the civil service examination, so that they could fulfil their roles as submissive married women, always moving a step behind spouses and other male relatives. I had succeeded partly because many brilliant women could not compete in the examination because of family pressures. The need for a woman to play second fiddle to a man was brought home to me rather brutally, when a close relative who had qualified for the civil service interview was told by a prospective groom that he could agree to their marriage only if she withdrew from the examination. (As it turned out, she didn't!) To add insult to injury, in the training academy, women civil servants are treated by their colleagues as husband-hunters, seeking spouses among their own kind, because no one would marry them now that they were in the IAS. For, in the public mind, IAS male spouses were as desirable as IAS female spouses were undesirable.

Once part of the administration, women officers continue to face constraints imposed by spouses, families and society. Field postings with 24x7 responsibility are essential to lay the foundations of a sound career as a civil servant. In general, women were allowed to pursue careers only if they did not neglect spouses and children, which meant that they had to attend offices only between

9 a.m. and 5 p.m. Transposed to the IAS environment, this meant that women officers could be posted only in the metropolis, not work in or even travel to rural areas without spouses or other suitable male escorts and return home at a decent hour to attend to household duties. Effectively, they had to have lifestyles as close as possible to what they might have had as lecturers or officegoers. Such thinking is so ingrained in the popular mind that a chief electoral officer of Karnataka, while appointing senior civil servants as election observers in various constituencies of the state, put every woman officer on his list in a district adjoining Bengaluru, so they could all be within touching distance of home and family! He was astounded when I told him that I would prefer to observe the election at a spot distant from the capital, where I could always meet representatives of political parties who might want to complain about election malpractices.

Gender bias was also rampant in postings and career development. Although higher civil services were in theory open to women since Independence, the first women officers who joined the government (Chonira Belliappa Muthamma to the foreign service in 1948 and Anna George to the administrative service in 1951) were inducted with reluctance and with the caveat that they must leave if they ever married. At that time, patriarchal and misogynistic ideas about the unsuitability of women at higher official levels were widely prevalent among colleagues, bosses and members of the public. But these women remained role models, inspiring some more to reach for the stars. The first woman to top the IAS list was Anuradha Majumdar in 1970, the year in which a record number of women became civil servants. What happened to Anuradha within the Gujarat cadre of the service perhaps exemplifies how gender bias operated within the system.

Meena Gupta and I authored a first assessment of what was happening to women after they entered the higher echelons of government, using quantitative data and referring to the notions and prejudices that shaped postings and careers. The idea of such an article was conceived when more than half of the thirteen women of the 1971 IAS batch who gathered in Delhi in the early eighties discovered how similar their experiences were during the first working years. Most of us had fought our way to gain the right to be posted to districts and everybody had faced sexist comments and behaviour from bosses (political and administrative) and colleagues. Stereotyping linked to gender alone was rampant—aptitude, performance and preference were never the criteria which determined career paths for women. We knew that conduct rules prohibited criticism of government policy. But an academic analysis was still possible if biases were reflected in postings at the Centre and across states. With a school-going daughter as a willing worker and a friend in the department of personnel who supplied us with civil lists for several years, cards were prepared listing the postings of every woman in the IAS. An explicit pattern soon emerged to match the anecdotal evidence—refusal of district collectorships and stereotyping in 'soft' departments like health, welfare and education, departments focused on nurturing activities entailing supervision of large numbers of women employees. Equally apparent was the almost exclusive reservation for men of jobs in economic ministries like industry and finance or heads of prestigious public sector undertakings. The newly created department of women's welfare and its controlling ministry were, of course, always handed over from one woman to the next. The message was clear. High-profile women would be allowed to exercise power and responsibility only if they presided over other women, looked after women's issues or performed nurturing jobs for which they were best suited by gender.

Our article which called attention to sexism and stereotyping in IAS postings created waves within the system. I learned later from a woman colleague within the department of personnel how the then minister of state, Chidambaram, wanted the legality of our article examined with reference to the conduct rules and how he was told after lengthy study that the piece was based on solid data from civil service lists. Not every male colleague or boss, however, reacted with denial. Vaidyanatha Iyer, then resident commissioner for Andhra Pradesh at Delhi, told me how much he had benefited from reading about the perceptions of women officers in the article; he later served as a very effective secretary for women's welfare at Delhi.

Statistical evidence apart, two decades after the first woman entered the civil service, I experienced many of the same attitudes and biases—from bosses, colleagues and staff, far less from the public. And I watched biases inform policies and behaviour. It began early, with the National Academy itself. At a dinner held by the director, D.D. Sathe, attended by several secretaries of the government (all male), on a visit to the Academy, women trainees, decked up to the nines, were moved around like pieces on a play deck, while the men tossed dice and decided whose piece had moved up and won the game. I was there as IAS probationer and even have a photograph of this event. (This was apparently a game that was quite popular in clubs of the armed services). At that time, after twenty-three years of a sheltered upbringing, I had secured a place in the civil service by competing on equal terms with male contenders. This experience at the National Academy shattered my illusions of equality of treatment within the IAS. I sensed that something was badly wrong, yet everybody took such behaviour in their stride! I felt as deeply violated by this tawdry game as I felt when watching beauty contests that degraded the mind and focused on the female torso.

The public perceptions of our traditional society prevented me from getting thorough hands-on district training. Like all women then posted to Karnataka cadre, I was sent off to Mysuru district, considered most 'suitable' for women trainees. The deputy commissioner for form's sake took me around on tour just once to all talukas, but I could never learn the job by staying beside him continuously, as all my male batch mates did. An unknown woman beside him would compromise the deputy commissioner's reputation in the district. On the job too, the playing field was never level for men and women officers. Yet, like the rest of my women counterparts, I made my own way, travelling at all hours alone (and later with a three-month-old baby and a nanny) in a bumpy jeep, visiting villages and tramping through fields, attending meetings and dispensing justice, briefing ministers and on rare occasions the chief minister himself. Knowing that women would not be posted as deputy commissioners in the normal course, I publicized my desire to head a district when I became due for the posting and did in fact achieve my goal. After acquiring a doctorate in public finance, I requested a posting (any posting) in the finance ministry, which was almost totally the preserve of male officers. When Prime Minister Rajiv Gandhi was elected, he chose a woman, Sarala Grewal, as his secretary, a first that evoked smothered chauvinist comments in many civil service fora. Caught in the wave of that liberal tide, I found my way through an obscure byway of the department of expenditure into my preferred field of federal finance and was finally offered a prize posting in the department of economic affairs. Only to watch the bias crop up again and again. When I qualified for promotion as joint secretary, the then finance secretary, G.K. Arora, feared that as a woman I would not be suitable to oversee the critical balance of payments situation, as it would entail round-the-clock monitoring. Yes, seventeen years after I had tramped around lonely villages, working through the night to handle emergencies as assistant commissioner, I was still found unfit for 24x7 jobs, because I was a woman! It took much self-restraint to patiently convince yet another boss that late nights did not frighten me. I did persuade him to try me out on the job and I hope he never regretted the decision.

Are biases past and how have things changed? Many women of all backgrounds have topped the civil services since then. Almost all departments at the Centre have been headed by women. No woman has still served as secretary in the defence ministry and home ministry, formulating policy and handing down decisions to the male bastions in the armed forces and the police. Nor has a woman yet headed the civil service as cabinet secretary. There have been male heads of women's welfare departments. Perhaps all women entrants do work in subdivisions and head the district administration as a matter of course. Are sexist comments still made and do sexist perceptions affect postings? A follow-up study might update the matter. Certainly, biased perceptions have not gone away, among political bosses and perhaps even colleagues and staff.

What is the impact on government and on society of the increase in the number of women in the higher civil services and their visibility in top positions? Specifically, what have these women done for the disempowered and oppressed sisterhood? At the start, it was a lonely furrow indeed that we ploughed, often a sole women's presence in meetings, conferences and official functions, the cynosure of curious and malicious gazes. As others became accustomed to having us around, many wondered if the women in their own lives, (daughters and perhaps sisters but not wives!) might not also make similar careers for themselves. It is quite common to meet old friends who declare that our examples have inspired them to encourage their daughters to enter the civil service. Women pioneers in government were my role models and we played the same role for those who came after. In the early days, we were viewed with curiosity and disbelief. Visitors would ask us to take them to the real bosses; they found it difficult to accept that we were in charge and were available for discussion. Often we were taken for stenographers or personal assistants of the great men sitting next door. This happened to me frequently in the finance ministry in North Block, the sting being that my neighbour was a busy batch mate. When I was promoted to an office adjacent to the finance secretary, I resigned myself to being taken for a member of his personal staff. When I drove myself to office, I received inappropriate and intrusive advice from all and sundry about the 'most suitable car for a woman driver'! Nobody would dare to make a similar comment to a male officer. A police commissioner (who later became an MLA from Karnataka and had a movie made about him) publicly declared that women were not suitable for certain police jobs! There were favourable stereotypes too, the belief, for example, that women were not easily 'approachable' for bribing and could therefore be expected to be less corruptible than men. At one point of time, women officers of Karnataka were also apparently considered less malleable to political inducements. So much so that one chief minister, J.H. Patel, was taken aback when his minister for women and child development wanted a male officer to be posted (for the first time) as secretary, women and child development, since she found the dozen senior women officers then available too independent for her taste!

But, over the years, within and outside the government, by and large, colleagues, staff and bosses began to take the presence of women officers for granted. The novelty of a woman participating in high power decisions seems to have worn off now, though it probably lingers in the few sanctums, still sacred to masculine control, like home, defence and some high-profile public sector undertakings, particularly those in engineering and technology.

It was impossible to take on a chauvinistic establishment and society as a lonely and very junior presence in the early days, but many of us used public platforms and official correspondence to speak up for disempowered women and point out discriminatory practices. Some may have appeared trivial, but they were symptoms of deeply ingrained gender biases, which needed eradication. For example, an internal manual for magistrates suggested that it was a woman's role to hand out prizes and bouquets to distinguished visitors. Or the insistence of the governor's aide de camp (ADC) that I should wait upon the governor's wife, when, as district magistrate of Dharwad, I was briefing the governor on current issues. The annual observance of International

Women's Day highlights this dilemma, with the focus shifting away from real empowerment and equality for women to celebrating their decorative and nurturing functions alone.

Women officers also promoted important policy initiatives affecting women employees, women clients of public services and the general discriminatory treatment accorded to women in society. A lone woman secretary faced an uphill battle in taking on these challenges, but as more faces appeared around senior tables, battles became somewhat easier. As in the case of Dalit officers, women officers were more sensitive to problems plaguing their own group and often succeeded in providing support for affected individuals. Policy change was, however, more difficult to push through in the face of the gender biases of ministers, colleagues and the system as a whole. The prevailing tendency was to cover up cases of domestic violence or abandoned spouses involving senior persons. The general attitude towards sexual harassment was to take a 'boys will be boys' approach and advise the women involved to learn how to handle it. This was the reaction of many male colleagues when I led the effort to mobilize civil servants to protest about the Rupan Deol incident (an inebriated, very powerful police officer, K.P.S. Gill, harassing a senior IAS officer at an official party). I was stunned when a close friend, and father of a daughter himself, justified the incident as normal adult behaviour, almost the perquisite of uniformed men, which women must accept meekly. To their eternal credit, however, senior police officers, like Julio Ribeiro, Kiran Bedi and Kanwaljit Deol, supported our protest staunchly. And, soon enough, statutes were voted to define and end sexual harassment.

Due to efforts made by women officers, some policy changes to empower women were pushed through; a large number were also shot down by entrenched interests. Registration of property allotted by government agencies in the joint names of spouses was staunchly resisted, although all women secretaries in Karnataka supported the move. Automatic deduction from the salary of a government employee to provide for the maintenance of abandoned wives and children was opposed by employees' unions. Compulsory registration of marriages has also not become the norm. And there are still occasional cases of polygamous marriages by senior officers, which are not penalized as required by rules. Women activists often found their demands being encouraged and supported by women officers. Some of us joined hands with the voluntary organization Vimochana to wage a long battle for transparent investigation of deaths by domestic violence; with the support of male and female colleagues the inquest rules have been revised, but to the eternal shame of Karnataka government, these have never been implemented! Realizing how important mobility was for empowerment, a woman officer of Tamil Nadu provided training and free bicycles for girls in government schools. It worked its magic as I observed when my route was blocked by waves of cycling girls on a visit to my old university in rural Tamil Nadu. After an outburst of attacks on women at a Dharwad college function, I was overwhelmed by public support, when I found funds for free self-defence training for young girls—an extension of this scheme to metros would control this public menace, but the spectre of militant women is, somehow, too dampening for the public and for most policymakers. Training and sensitization programmes also became mandatory, although they were often mindlessly targeted: the department of personnel tended to pack gender sensitization programmes equally with men and women trainees, since there are far fewer women in government jobs than men, women found themselves slotted for gender sensitization programmes repeatedly to fill up the seats meant for women! As managing director of the Karnataka State Finance Corporation, it was possible to focus effectively on altering the prevailing mindset within the financial institution of supporting male entrepreneurs with alacrity while distrusting the capacity and solvency of women. While occupying that position, I learned the lesson that women's empowerment was often better achieved by placing women heads in powerful positions, not by merely creating an exclusive women's ministry and ghettoizing its demands and policies.

The list of failures is perhaps just as instructive as the few successes. There are still vast swathes of government activity where discrimination is rampant. Most engineering and scientific establishments fall within this category. The Government of Karnataka had reserved 30 per cent of fresh recruitments for women when I took over as managing director of the Karnataka Power Corporation. The number of women civil, electrical and electronics engineers in the corporation were far below this level and everybody in the organization expected that the government order could not be made applicable to them—what would we do with all the women engineers? They would be superfluous, because women were not suitable for shop-floor jobs or field tasks, they must all remain in offices designing and planning, and sometimes called on to hand out bouquets to visiting dignitaries. I struggled with the issue for the very few months that I stayed at the organization. Nothing much has yet changed in the engineering milieu within government and private engineering firms during the following two decades.

Clearly, women officers did make a difference to improving the lot of women in a few areas and failed spectacularly in others. They helped to formulate and implement some policies and programmes as well as to support individual oppressed women. Yet, what remains to be done is immense. In the last Karnataka cabinet, there was just one woman minister, who was in charge of women's welfare. Assembly discussions and public pronouncements of politicians are often as sexist and misogynist as they were in the earlier decades, but thankfully there are more critical observers to pull up offenders. Colleagues who theoretically are expected to promote the government programme to empower women will tell you in their unguarded moments that they expect wives to cook every meal for them daily. Social messages are mixed and success in supporting women is mixed too.

THE FAUSTIAN BARGAIN

Even with the inherent failures of Indian civil servants, we cannot pin the blame for poor governance only or even mainly on them. Mea culpa, then, but not mea maxima culpa. Those most responsible for betraying the Indian dream are their elected representatives. They have over the years handed the country over to exploiters and middlemen. Voter intimidation and capture are the only techniques honed by them for winning elections. 'Cheat the voter' is the name of the cynical game that surfaces before every poll. The idea is to rouse sentiments of hatred that polarize people so that they overlook the real problems that plague them. Civil servants are dominated, manipulated and co-opted into this sport. When a few are coerced and bullied, others get the message and silently capitulate, while those who collaborate with fixers rise to the top easily. All this undermines original thinking, candid advice and independent action. The first to be manipulated were departments like the police; others who hand out lucrative contracts or regulate land transactions were infiltrated and subjugated. Public procurement legislation and audit checks introduced to ensure accountability and transparency have all been nullified today. Vigilance bodies have been removed or enfeebled. The citizen retains one recourse, the right to information, but this bulwark is being rapidly eroded through restrictive amendments. The ambit of action for an honest civil servant has been considerably reduced.

Sooner rather than later, today's civil servant comes up against the Faustian bargain. Our dirigiste government has endowed employees with extensive authority; those who seek government approvals and services proceed on the principle that everyone has a price. And they are often right. For the political people who oversee administration also demand the wrong outcomes. Pressures are often almost impossible to bear. The demand is to sell your soul to those who undermine the system in return for prime postings and promotions. The allure is irresistible especially when penalties for integrity (transfer to the boondocks and worthless sinecures) stare one in the face. But there is also a price to pay. Sins do often catch up with collaborators (sometimes innocents are also harmed, as in the case of the former coal secretary, Harish Gupta). If and when there is an inquiry, the civil servant who signed on the dotted line takes the rap, while his political (tor) mentor escapes.

What can a mere civil servant achieve within this often-perilous ambience?

- Offer advice for systemic reform, although the best ideas are doomed to languish unimplemented
- Collaborate with social activists, sharing official data and integrating civic society demands into government programmes
- Work enthusiastically to fulfil the ideas of honest, pro-poor politicians, if lucky enough to work with them
- Perform regulatory functions, professionally and independently, as for example, in bodies like the Election Commission of India
- Train others in the country's core ideas of secularism and commitment to the poor and share and disseminate methods of resisting corruption and intimidation

There is not much else to offer to the hordes of aspirants who yearn to enter the higher echelons of government. Is the higher civil service an anachronism? Should it have a future at all? At its best, we find a rare civil servant, who speaks his mind and works for the poor. At its worst, there is the time-server, who has sold his soul for the mess of potage. Most of the others cluster in the middle, slogging from day to day, succumbing to daily pressures, avoiding risk at any price. Not the ideal agency to transform the country and realize its full potential.

Renuka Viswanathan

Acknowledgements

This book would not have seen the light of the day had it not been for my colleagues at Accountability Initiative (AI) and the Centre for Policy Research (CPR), New Delhi. One of my commitments as an adviser to AI is to write a blog every Friday, something on which I often default. AI, indulgent as it is to me, tries to make the best of my spurts of writing. In one of my frenetic bursts, I wrote about leadership in the IAS, provoked by self-indulgent reflections of some civil servants at a seminar on the subject that I had attended. Those blogs were resurrected by Richa Bansal, director of communications at the Centre for Policy Research, and her team and published online as a collection. It went viral—in the modest manner that boring stuff on the bureaucracy is capable of going viral—and caught the eye of Manasi Subramaniam, senior commissioning editor and head of literary rights, Penguin Random House India, who thought they could become the nucleus of a book for lay persons on the bureaucracy. Apart from Richa, Yamini Aiyar, president of the CPR, Avani Kapur, director of AI, and Avantika Shrivastava, senior communications officer at AI, egged me on whenever I was consumed by writer's block and I am thankful for their encouragement and support.

Most written material on the bureaucracy fall into two categories. Dull as ditchwater research tomes that are meant for the seriously masochistic reader, which includes those who choose to write the civil services examination, and reminiscences of bureaucrats that can be interesting, but are usually topical and confined to the era in which the author served. In a decade, such books lose their interest value. The world moves on. Manasi and team did not want me to follow either genre. Yes, they said, please get into detail, but write in a mode that holds the interest of the interested, lay reader. Please reminisce, they said, but not so much as to stretch facts and experiment with the truth. I tried as best as I could to stay within the confines of that advice. The fault for any exaggeration and inaccuracy that might have crept in, is entirely to be laid at my doorstep.

My blogs were a good place to start and the first versions of the book looked exactly like that: a collection of blogs stapled together. I then realized that writing a book meant much more than cutting and pasting a bunch of clever blog-worthy statements. I benefited a great deal from serious writing about the IAS by my former colleagues in service, K.P. Krishnan and T.V. Somanathan. Milan Vaishnav's take on big data and the IAS also provided excellent food for thought; all these inputs feature in Chapter 1.

I approached Renuka Viswanathan with the idea that she could write a guest chapter on women in the IAS. She is one of the most accomplished IAS officers that I know and has both mentored and browbeaten me over the years, by virtue not only of being my senior in service, but also my sister. With the casual disdain that older sisters muster so easily for the suggestions of younger siblings, she refused to confine herself to that canvas and has written as only she can, about the travails and challenges of the service. Hers is a grimmer section than mine; together I hope we have provided enough food for thought.

Zulfiquar Haider, chief strategy and programme officer, Azim Premji Philanthropic Initiatives, had introduced me to Heifetz's concepts of adaptive leadership and 'acts of leadership'. Swaroop Iyengar, management consultant, introduced me to the idea of 'bridging leadership'. I have relied on these, while writing on leadership and the bureaucracy in Chapter 6. Lant Pritchett, till recently professor of the practice of international development at the Kennedy School of Government, Harvard University, graciously allowed me to flesh out some of his ideas in Chapter 4 on Postings, Transfers and Government Dysfunctionality.

In a few conversations, my former colleague Ramani Venkatesan reflected a great deal upon the examination system and its changing contours over the years, which helped me write Chapter 3 on how to get into the civil services. He knows how that system works, having stood first in the entrance examination and followed up that blazing entry into the IAS with a stellar career. His blog, https://vramani.com/, is a hugely educative one and strongly recommended to anybody who wishes to know more about the civil service, administration and reforms in that direction.

A young officer of great promise, with a delightful sense of humour to counter the dour landscape of life in the service of government, filled me in on the bizarre details of promoting cashlessness in remote rural areas. I have elaborated upon that in Chapter 8, on Problem-Solving, Technology and the IAS.

I owe a debt of gratitude to Manasi Subramaniam, who bore all my quirks and moodiness with pleasant fortitude. Indrani Dasgupta edited the text with efficiency and speed.

I do hope the book entertains the reader; as much as I enjoyed writing it.

Annexure I

Gardens or Garbage

When a fast-growing city generates mountains of garbage, it often pays legally contracted people to collect and remove them. Once upon a time (please be patient, this is not a fairy tale), there were such contracts in Bengaluru, which has been among the fastest-growing cities of Asia from the 1970s. BVG India was one of the last of these contractors to be terminated. What the city now has are orders issued to persons (not selected through open tenders) for supplying a specified number of workers and vehicles to perform garbage collection and street-sweeping functions. From 2011 onwards, Bengaluru has been unable to complete the tendering process to appoint garbage contractors, even though concerned citizens have approached the high court to monitor the process. Suppliers of workers and vehicles are close relations of corporators. BBMP officials have forced several women's self-help groups, who were collecting garbage in many parts of the city, to work as subcontractors to relatives of corporators. Here is what has happened to the oldest of these groups.

The Saagar DWCRA group based in Kadugodi village is a self-help group of twenty women registered under the development of women and children in rural areas programme of the department of rural development in 2000. I work personally with them. It was given the task of garbage collection from households and street sweeping in one portion of Mahadevapura in Whitefield, Bengaluru, by the City Municipal Council, which was absorbed into BBMP in 2007. It received government grants and bank loans under government sponsorship to purchase handcarts and tractors for transporting garbage. When BBMP decided to use suppliers of labour and vehicles to handle solid waste management, local officials informed the self-help group that it was not eligible to become providers of vehicles and persons for garbage collection, since it did not have compactors and lorries. They forced the group to continue to do their work as subcontractors for the corporator's brother at rates lower than they were being paid then. This continued for years. Payments made to the women fluctuated according to the whims of the contractor. Contractors claimed that these women and those who worked for them were persons being supplied against the BBMP order. Since they were not paid the minimum wage, BBMP issued ATM cards so that payments could be made directly to workers. The Saagar DWCRA group has not seen their ATM cards since the contractor retains them and draws money in their name. I have seen and heard of this first-hand, and many have sworn affidavits to confirm this.

Walking the streets of Doddanekundi ward as a volunteer, I observed that segregated waste was remixed by collectors and dumped and often burnt in open areas. No protective gear was given to garbage collection staff and child labour was used. Householders could be persuaded to segregate waste, but they rightly complained about remixing and dumping. All of them knew only the members of the self-help group (not the contractor) and appreciated its work.

In 2015, on high court directions, BBMP called for tenders for garbage disposal after drafting a monumental tender document (sixty pages long with three schedules and seven appendices and a draft services agreement covering another sixty-one pages!) providing for all kinds of safeguards and qualifications. Volunteers, who discovered that the best bet for high-quality segregated solid waste management without dumping, plastic-burning or child labour and with fair wages and protection gear for garbage collectors was the women's self-help group, decided to assist Saagar DWCRA group to bid for the tender. The ensuing saga records the continuing failure of civil servants to provide effective and cost-efficient public services quickly and fairly, even in areas where they exercised power and discretion.

Collection and transportation of garbage is not rocket science. Unfortunately, the wordy tender document sought bids from all categories of legal persons, except those actually doing the work everywhere in the city. Tender conditions and requirements were tailored to companies (public and private limited), partnerships, individuals, cooperatives, voluntary organizations, non-profit societies; self-help groups, promoted, registered and aided by government for this task were not recognized. Undeterred, a method was devised by volunteers to make the bid through the self-help group federation, which could produce the documents required for bidding. After completing formalities, the self-help group needed an experience certificate from the corporation for the work that it was doing and had been doing for over a decade. BBMP local officials refused to give the certificate and, when the high court directed them to do so, they produced a mangled document, deleting the period for which the group had been exploited by the contractor.

A formal appeal to senior levels was ignored. The tendering process, forced on BBMP by activists who had approached the high court, floundered again and again, as existing contractors refused to bid and other willing persons, like the self-help groups doing garbage collection, were prevented from bidding. BBMP has, therefore, shelved the tendering process, and, under the influence of the pernicious garbage mafia, built a tangled knot of unsustainable and patently illegal processes for garbage collection, which do not and cannot ever provide a workable solution to the problem.

At first there was pressure from the government for BBMP to hand out garbage-collection orders to self-help groups in areas where they exist. For the areas serviced by this group, and I have a full file of these orders, BBMP reluctantly issued orders in its favour, but not a simple one allocating to them the work they were doing with a proportional share of the total payment. Instead, street sweeping was removed from their list of tasks and the group was arbitrarily divided into six entities of four to five members each with its own order. By introducing this Kafkaesque procedure, BBMP has effectively warned off all genuine self-help groups from ever seeking to obtain BBMP garbage collection contracts. Since, each five-member group can only get Rs 43,000 per month for servicing 750 houses in ward eighty-five. With this amount, it must hire one auto with a helper and driver, leaving every member with remuneration far lower than the prescribed minimum wage. By removing street sweeping from the order, the total gross amount earned by the six groups will cross Rs 2 lakh (Rs 2.58 lakh)—not much of an increase from the Rs-2-lakh level reached by them in 2010. The injustice is palpable when we consider that between 2013 and 2017, the amount paid to the contractor more than doubled from Rs 23 lakh to Rs 52 lakh. The benefit of the increase given to the contractor did not percolate down to the group, which did the real work. The number of houses actually serviced by the group (at one auto for 750 houses and one lorry for ten houses) also entitles it to thirteen–fourteen autos and one lorry. By keeping the number of autos at six, no lorry can be allotted to the group, which has been directed to dump its waste in the lorry of a hostile rival—the present contractor.[1] A perfect recipe for disaster!

BBMP's arbitrary division of the existing group into six blatantly contravenes an order of the women and child development department issued in 2000, which prescribes a minimum membership of fifteen to twenty for such groups. By arguing that six groups must be separately registered and produce independent PAN cards, BBMP delayed paying this group for several months, openly defied the order of the senior most government secretary (who is now chief secretary) and eventually broke up the group and destroyed its morale. Three years of battle by the group and volunteers who supported it have not succeeded in increasing its emoluments in any significant way. It has still to be paid for months of work!

Meanwhile, citywide, after bitter internal combats with interested parties, a new procedure for solid waste management has been put into place. Since the beginning of 2018, unable to ignore the proof that waste collectors were not being paid their full wages and benefits by contractors, BBMP has begun to directly pay them by transferring money to their bank accounts. But the process is riddled with unsolved issues. Street sweeping and garbage collection have been separated—a bad idea, since garbage collectors continue to collect unsegregated garbage and sort it on streets already cleaned by street sweepers! Who is responsible then for the fetid piles of garbage? Both or neither? There is no visible documentary relationship between BBMP and the street sweepers. The latter are not BBMP employees with their own service books and government benefits and obligations (pay scales, housing and medical allowances, pensions and the rest as also the applicability of conduct rules—they can for example be added or dropped without enquiry). They just receive wages as fixed by the labour department directly from BBMP. But the person who determines who should be paid, that is, the person who maintains the muster roll, is still the supervisor (subcontractor of sorts?) of the contractor, which means that he can drop or add a name at his will and pleasure. And escape all legal consequences, since he no longer has any kind of contract with BBMP, not even to supply manpower and certainly not to ensure that sweeping is actually done! How is the auditing department condoning money being paid out by BBMP with no documentary relationship with the payee? As for house-to-house collection, one auto with a driver and two helpers is still expected to service 750 houses. This task is given out on contract as before through work orders.

Why is BBMP working in such a deliberately confused and illogical manner? Qui bono? Who benefits and who has benefited all along from these shenanigans? The pre-January 2018 arrangement had been carefully crafted to hand over this lucrative business of garbage collection without tendering or selection of any kind to close relatives of corporators for indefinite periods, who could not be removed by legal process, since they were only suppliers of vehicles and personnel and could easily prepare and produce bogus muster rolls for inspection, while keeping their areas filthy. These contractors never trained their personnel and there still is no link between public complaints and feedback and contractor monitoring. Without bids, there is no way of knowing the market price for the service of garbage collection and BBMP can easily apply some internal formula to periodically raise the rates of contractors without actually discovering whether it can be done more cheaply, because it has not tested the market through a bidding process. Since January 2018, this arrangement has been tinkered with, creating further chaos and lack of accountability, offering only limited guarantee of payment of full wages for street sweepers, but keeping them still at the mercy of supervisors picked by the earlier contractors, who are generally close relatives of elected corporators. And, most of what has been done and is still going on, openly violates laws and principles of financial and administrative propriety. What is apparent is the inability and unwillingness of senior officials to see their way through this maze to a sane and logical conclusion. When will we revert to the only workable alternative, an enforceable composite contract for street sweeping and garbage collection executed with the best bidder through a quick and honest bidding process (yes, this is still possible in these dishonest times!) selected by tendering in which the best present workers (contractors, self-help groups and good NGOs/corporates, of which there are a few in the metropolis) are allowed to freely participate? A contract, with safeguards and accountability, that provides for specific outcomes (a clean locality, for example) and removal if outcomes are not realized, after notices to the contractor? Even garbage mafia participants could bid and pick up such work orders, in free and fair competition and earn legitimate profits. Thaler might appreciate how important it is for all players to get the right incentives and disincentives to keep the city clean. I can provide the city fathers with a seven-page draft contract that might serve the purpose.

Annexure II

The Vanishing Vote Trick

The best proof that India is a democracy is my right to vote to elect municipal corporators and members of the state assemblies and Parliament. And I share this right with every adult citizen, which means that all of us (except for the very few exceptions provided in the Representation of People's Act) must be included in voters' lists. The electoral process is outside the political hierarchy, supervised by an independent Election Commission, with its own officers in states. It is controlled by civil servants. Those in the Election Commission have almost always been retirees from the civil service, those heading state offices are deputed from state cadres, enumeration is done through local bodies in towns and the district administration in villages and supervised by district-level officers, freed from political control and protected from political interference. There is substantial independence to ensure free and fair elections, although elected persons have long memories and offer favours to or persecute those who have helped or harmed them at election time. Yes, this is among the most independent assignments for a civil servant, a task in which they can fulfil the oath of fealty to the Constitution, which they took when joining the government.

Here, if nowhere else, the IAS officer can follow his conscience as an independent and patriotic professional. But, after several years of walking the streets of Bengaluru to enroll rich and poor voters on electoral lists and after recently contesting state assembly elections, I have discovered that the system is badly broken, even though it is perfectly possible to manage and run a reasonably accurate mechanism.

Any resident of the city can personally test the accuracy of the current voters' list. Please verify against the Election Commission's website whether the first ten adult citizens that you meet any day, (whom you know to be normally resident in your area) are in the list. You will get a very unpleasant shock indeed! The electoral registration system uses publicity on all media to remind voters of their rights, but it alone has full responsibility for proactively locating and listing all voters. Every missed out or inaccurate name is proof of its failure and bungling.

Election manuals give elaborate guidance on voter registration and there are circulars and training programmes galore. The application process is always available and it couldn't be simpler. A voter fills up Form 6, which is available online or (theoretically) in the municipal office, and they only add date of birth and address proofs. The reality of voter registration is, however, pretty scary. Citizens who use the online application process and upload scans of relevant documents must also send hard copies to municipal offices, a clever manoeuvre giving ample scope for mislaying papers, even when postal acknowledgements can be produced by harassed voters. Online applicants are appalled when their names are missing on the published rolls or when (as usually happens) they turn up to polling booths and find themselves disenfranchised.

Those who file paper applications are, of course, never given the acknowledgements, printed on their forms. Voters depend on the tender mercies of agents of political parties, who use the process to control the entry of names on electoral rolls and the voting choices of applicants. Such people corner the 'voter IDs' of the applicants sponsored by them and distribute these to bogus voters on election day, while actual ID-holders, falsely believing that they are disenfranchised, stay away from the ballot.

Over the years, the voter enumeration system has been beautifully gamed to *prevent* fresh registration, as everyone who deals with it knows very well. Names are deleted willy-nilly from the rolls. Applications are refused behind the citizen's back without cause or reason. Electoral registration staff have invented their own methods, contrary to Election Commission rules, to pick and choose voters for the rolls. They demand every kind of additional documentation to ensure that fresh applicants stay off the list. One example: applicants who reveal that they are already registered in another constituency are regularly asked to provide notarized affidavits.

I have watched an electoral registration officer in a Bengaluru municipal office scrawling rejections on scores of online applications, by using his own criteria to violate every direction of the Election Commission. It was his practice to reject the applications of citizens, who were not first-time voters, if they did not mention where they had been registered earlier. (Had you, therefore, for some reason, failed to register when you came of age, you could never make the list; you would forever be refused your democratic right). This officer also arbitrarily eliminates names of relatives, children and others in the same residence, if their surnames are even slightly different, without making any verification. Attempts by militant citizens to bring order to the system have been effectively blocked; one officer complaining that if he processed their applications as required by the rules, the list would be overrun by 'outsiders'. The mission of municipal officers in this, as in most municipal services, is to exclude as many applicants as possible and include only the chosen few, who come to them with political or other pressures and inducements.

And then concerned citizens hit back. A bunch of determined voters of Whitefield Rising, led by the redoubtable Anjali Sawhney and Ajit Sequeira, negotiated a collaboration between electoral registration officers and local communities— they offered access to the records of apartment managers for verification of the accuracy of online applications and marshalled scores of applications at registration camps to which they invited municipal staff for spot verification of forms and documents. When their efforts evoked a thunderous response, municipal staff chickened out and avoided verification. After months of confrontation with dodgy officials, Whitefield Rising went to court. These and other complaints finally forced the chief electoral officer to inspect the delinquent office just before the 2018 assembly election, resulting in restoration of the names of more than 8000 wrongly deleted voters to the rolls. The discovery of wholesale elimination techniques has not, however, led to the inescapable conclusion that there is deliberate collusion between venal officials and some elected representatives—that battle is still on.

At the other end are the techniques widely used for the wholesale removal of legitimate voters. Often enough, this happens during 'summary' cleansings of electoral rolls, undertaken from time to time. Several rules of thumb are applied to avoid actual ground-level verification. The names of older persons or of those who have lived at the same location during several elections suddenly disappear from the rolls. Election IDs are issued in waves; one cleansing technique rumoured to have been used before the 2018 election is cancellation of IDs bearing older numbers. And, as usual, this is done without notice to the hapless voter, who discovers the disenfranchisement only at the polling booth. Naturally, voters, who feared polarization on religious grounds in the charged atmosphere before the 2018 polls, now wonder whether some religious minorities were deliberately dropped from lists.

Loopholes in the electoral registration process facilitate, even promote voter fraud. Election IDs (commonly known as EPICs) are expected to be issued to every voter as soon as they get on the roll. But, municipal officials rarely do this, citing non-receipt of holograms as the cause. Instead, they hand the IDs over to agents of political parties, who retain them for distribution to bogus voters. A common complaint encountered during the 2018 election campaign was non-receipt of EPICs. When we took time off to chase up such applications, a horrifying number of duplicate entries came to light on electoral rolls—of applicants who had repeatedly been put on the lists, but had not received their EPICs, leading them to reapply again and again (today there are many applications of the same applicant on the rolls, which were not removed as duplicates). Such double entries are used for bogus voting, as can be easily discovered if checked against marked copies of the rolls used in polling booths.

Therefore, when IAS officers trot out the alibi of political meddling to excuse the ineffective functioning of their offices, citizens are entitled to ask them why they have failed so miserably to ensure accurate voter registration, even when they work in a politically independent Election Commission, headed by formal civil servants. The real reasons for failure do not lie in political interference; they go back to the civil service's own legacy of distrust of democratic processes, its elitism and distance from ordinary citizens. Election Commissioners never see the anomaly of exhorting others to vote while staying away from polling booths themselves. Charity, evidently, doesn't begin at home! No wonder they never realize how inaccurate voters' lists are nor empathize with the travails of those who exercise their political rights.

It is still true that state-level staff of the Election Commission are drawn from local departments. And municipal officers are nominees of politicians who have their own agendas. But, the Commission itself is above such compulsions. Its members are free to do a professional job and lay down simple systems to make democracy workable to verify the accuracy of electoral rolls and control misuse.

Here are some things that they could easily do:

- Test the accuracy of electoral rolls frequently by asking random questions to city residents about voter registration
- Independently generate the number of online applications filed during a control period and verify how many have actually made it to the electoral roll. I sought these figures for Mahadevapura ward in Bengaluru for 2015 and discovered that only 2645 of the 11,450 online applicants had actually made it to the voters' list. Yet, the chief electoral officer of Karnataka took three years to admit this glaring anomaly and restore more than 8000 rejected names. And, even today, online application

data is not being used to identify the offices, which are prone to large-scale misuse, so that they can be inspected and improved

- In fact, congruence between online data and actual voter registration could become a useful yardstick to judge and award electoral registration performance at all levels. Today, the Commission rewards electoral officers by applying estimates of first-time voters drawn from census data to existing rolls. As always happens in offices, these estimates have now become performance targets. When actual application figures approach this imaginary figure, fresh applications are blindly rejected. And, when there is a gap, election staff ask voluntary agencies to collect more applications to achieve targets. No wonder Karnataka wins prizes for voter registration, while citizens' groups clamour and complain about chaotic performance!

1. Proliferation of duplicate IDs in voters' lists and their misuse is an open secret. Yet, the most obvious ways of discovering and controlling this have not been tried out. Like apps to scan booth-wise rolls for repetitive entry of the same names, relatives' names and addresses so that duplicated are eliminated before election day.

Similar methods can reduce the rampant doctoring of electoral rolls, which has become endemic in cities like Bengaluru over more than a decade. Ten years ago, the Bengaluru-based voluntary agency, Janaagraha, after a ground survey of the electoral roll in Shantinagar constituency,[1] discovered that only 55 per cent of the names on the list were genuine voters. The study was sponsored by the chief electoral officer of Karnataka, but it was never used for analysis or reform.

There are other knottier problems of voter disenfranchisement to be tackled: for example, enumeration of offline voters and low-income itinerant households, facilitation of voter registration for urban migrants of all classes and income levels and wholesale disenfranchisement of defence personnel and election staff, due to breakdown of the postal ballot facility.

Unfortunately, for the bloodless civil servants of the Election Commission, electoral procedure is just another box-ticking exercise, a series of mechanical motions. They hardly notice the link between their routines and the core concepts of Indian democracy. Unlike similar commissions in nascent democracies, they are not staffed by passionate votaries, alert to subversion and distortion of the people's will. Low voting percentages, proliferation of candidates and the first-past-the-post electoral system make it impossible to ensure that elected representatives are actually the first choices of citizens. When this is linked to dangerously flawed voters' lists, electoral choices no longer reflect the will of the people. Democracy is undermined, political institutions captured and the legitimacy of leaders compromised. Here, for example, are some of the chilling implications of the Janaagraha study: if only 55 per cent of the voters on the Shantinagar electoral roll is genuine, the voting percentage of 55 per cent in 2018, where the winner received 26 per cent of the registered vote, implies that the elected representative was chosen by only 14 per cent of legitimate voters. How far can the decisions of a minority government elected in this fashion, be binding on citizens in any democracy? The crisis point is long past for citizens to wake up and reclaim their democratic birthright.

Annexure III

Identity Crisis

Many reasons lay behind the search for a national ID card for Indians, which began a decade back. The home ministry wanted to locate and deport illegal migrants, particularly those from Bangladesh. The Election Commission sought to cleanse electoral lists of bogus voters and those who were not citizens. And many departments, who disbursed grants and subsidies, wished to weed out duplicate drawals—of food rations, midday meals for children, jobs under the employment guarantee scheme, old age pensions, need-based scholarships etc.

The argument was that every existing computerized list was partial (even though some were reasonably accurate or had not been gamed). Voters' lists covered only adult citizens, PAN cards were only for income earners, kisan passbooks were held by farmers and members of rural cooperatives, not everybody had a ration card, since subsidized grains were targeted for families below the poverty line, driving licences were for those who drove vehicles, bank passbooks were carried by those who were welcomed into banks, passports were issued only to those proposing to travel abroad. Many existing lists were riddled with errors and often patently false. The most notorious is the list of those below the poverty line, which is often longer than the list of families living in many areas. Every time the list is cleaned up, vested interests swiftly restore the status quo so that they can profit from the difference between market prices and the subsidized ration rates. And this black economy is nourished by a flourishing ecosystem of mediators, who channel bribes to appropriate quarters.

The solution to all these flawed lists was to create a supreme list after going through another bout of counting. This one was expected to be beyond manipulation, because IDs would be confirmed using unique digital data like fingerprints, which cannot be tampered with. It was expected that, over time, this would become the bedrock ID document, which every department could customize for its own purposes. Here is the genesis of the infamous and controversial Aadhaar card.

These seductive arguments for Aadhaar were, however, based on wilful disregard of the Indian reality of administrative chaos and corruption in service delivery to the poor, on fuzzy definitions of who was to be counted and for what purpose and, as we now know to our cost, on undependable technology.

When discussions were in full swing on the matter, I had two serious worries and neither was about identity theft. Many fascist regimes have manipulated centralized lists to target groups marked for hate crimes; I feared that our list could also be used to inflame mobs, whenever divisive rhetoric is used for political purposes. I also shrank from putting our long-suffering poor through one more exercise of counting and validation, with all the harassment and corruption this would entail.

Naysayers like us were, however, overruled. And we all turned out to be counted once again. To create the overweening monstrous master list against which every public and private transaction now has to be validated.

Here is one experience of how the Aadhaar requirement was used to subvert a pro-poor programme. In 2014, the Karnataka government computerized the application process for poor children seeking admission to private schools under the 'free' 25 per cent quota of the Right to Education Act (RTE). Applicants had to be resident within the municipal ward where schools were located and applications from the poorest categories like street children, orphans or migrants were given priority in the selection process. A key requirement in school selection was local domicile; to prove this, applicants were allowed to use any of the documents used by the Election Commission as residence proof for voters.[1]

A group of volunteers offered to help the children of migrant slum dwellers to get migrant certificates from the labour department and apply online for admission to prestigious local schools. The migrant status of these applicants was confirmed from the bridge school run by a voluntary agency in which the children were already enrolled, a school recognized by the education department, a school which also gave them daily transport, meals and free tuition. Regular and frequent inspections by the education department ensured that only migrant children from local slums were enrolled in these schools, while school staff and volunteers who interacted with the children had visited and knew each home.

In 2016, the RTE scrutiny system was further computerized. It was refined by linking RTE applications online with the database for caste and income certificates. But now, residence proof was limited to the Aadhaar card alone. The result has been a drastic drop in applicants, particularly among the most disadvantaged. Many applicants, resident in an area for years, ran from pillar to post, forgoing work and wages, unable to get addresses or telephone numbers modified on their cards and many were eventually disqualified from applying. Volunteers required several sittings over many weeks to complete a single application online because of these Aadhaar complications. But the tragedy was far worse for the migrants.

Munnekolala slum is an eyesore in the heart of the poshest Bengaluru locality, Whitefield. But it is an essential link in the chain of garbage removal from the exploding metropolis. It is crammed with migrants, who have lived there for six to seven years in shanties without numbers on lanes filled with their only wealth, the garbage meant for recycling. The education department insisted that Aadhaar cards must be produced by these migrant children, who were in any case supported by its own recognized bridge schools. And the commissioner of public instruction put the school staff and volunteers in touch with the UIDAI so that the cards could be prepared. In the process, they discovered three unpleasant details:

- Aadhaar cards are obtainable only at a price; government officials take no responsibility for counting every resident or confirming his residence
- the Aadhaar software cannot be operated in areas like slums which do not have street and house names
- Aadhaar cards need to be authenticated using other documents, which, in their turn, can be prepared only

if they are authenticated by the Aadhaar card. A neat circular requirement that effectively excludes anyone who is not already within the magic circle!

After three sessions of waiting for Aadhaar certification with migrant families (who had sacrificed their daily wages), breastfeeding babies and hungry children, volunteers gave up the impossible attempt. Local officials of the education department inquired why we could not help migrant children this year, their numbers in RTE applications had plummeted.

Thus, mindless extension of Aadhaar has, as I once feared, made life impossible for the poorest persons. The most purposeless use of Aadhaar is for children's programmes. As we have seen, without it, they cannot get midday meals, they cannot enter schools and they cannot get scholarships. Even the most hardened defender of digital recognition would admit that fingerprints of children change as they mature. Meanwhile, parents fear to lose admissions, volunteers struggle to promote schemes and NGO friends cry when they watch poor children denied meals and benefits. While government agencies watch unmoved and indifferent.

The government's responsibility for doing a near-perfect head count has been conveniently forgotten. The citizen gets himself counted or loses everything. The application process is a nightmare, even in the heart of Bengaluru. My Dalit housemaid is eligible for a scholarship for her son only with an Aadhaar card. Three days in a row, we stood together in the queue at the nearest municipal booth, some kilometres away from home from 7 a.m. on to find that when the booth opened 3 hours later we were not early enough to be served that day. The fourth time, I was at the booth at 5 a.m., long before daybreak, just ahead of another fellow sufferer; joined by my maid and her little son at 9, and we finally succeeded in putting in the application for his ID! Would Nandan Nilekani, the inventor of this torture who defends the process on TV day after day join me in Munnekolala slum, Whitefield, in the heart of India's Silicon Valley to complete the process of obtaining this perfectly useless piece of paper?

For, the bitterest irony is that Aadhaar has not delivered on any of its promises. It does not identify illegal entrants, because it is not confined to citizens; the Aadhaar website does not make citizenship a criterion for the card; foreign residents are entitled to hold these IDs while non-resident citizens are not. Aadhaar does not eliminate double counting of beneficiaries of government schemes, because of serious technological flaws. It has only added one more layer of misery to our miserable poor, as some of us had once feared that it might.

How have civil servants become partners in such schemes? Nandan Nilekani may have little knowledge of how things work for the poor, even though he was the parliamentary candidate for a Bengaluru constituency. Surely, civil servants, drawn from poorer backgrounds and trained to administer programmes for the poor would know which technology would serve the purpose behind their schemes? Or, have they all become so addicted to the philosophy of regulation that they miss what their schemes are meant for? How could an education department, whose only purpose is bringing every child to school, foster a method which did the very opposite, exclude children with the maximum disabilities and find no way to reach or assist them?

Notes

Chapter 1: Overview or Lay of the Land

1. *Rethinking Public Institutions in India*, eds. Devesh Kapur, Pratap Bhanu Mehta and Milan Vaishnav, (New Delhi: Oxford University Press, 2017).
2. K.P. Krishnan and T.V. Somanathan, 'Civil Service an Institutional Perspective', in *Public Institutions in India Performance and Design*, eds. D. Kapur and P.B. Mehta (New Delhi: Oxford University Press, 2005).
3. The paper looks at data up till 2013, so some aspects of their assessment may be outdated, given recent efforts to change certain aspects of the recruitment and career progression of the civil services.
4. Carnegie Endowment for International Peace, September 2016.
5. Rikhil R. Bhavnani and Alexander Lee, 'Local Embeddedness and Bureaucratic Performance: Evidence from India', working paper, department of political science, University of Wisconsin-Madison, 26 August 2015, https://faculty.polisci.wisc.edu/bhavnani/wp-content/uploads/2015/09/BhavnaniLeeEmbeddedness.pdf (accessed 23 October 2015).

6. Jonas Hjort, Gautam Rao and Elizabeth Santorella, 'Bureaucrat Value-Added and Local Economic Outcomes', working paper, department of economics, Harvard University, 24 November 2015 (on file with authors).

7. Lakshmi Iyer and Anandi Mani, 'Traveling Agents: Political Change and Bureaucratic Turnover in India', *Review of Economics and Statistics* 94, no. 3 (August 2012): 723–39.

8. Anusha Nath, 'Bureaucrats and Politicians: Electoral Competition and Dynamic Incentives', IED working paper 269, Boston University, 6 October 2015, https://www.dropbox.com/s/a5n7jldtqw6gza9/AnushaNath_BureacratsAndPoliticians.pdf?dl=0 (accessed 26 October 2015).

9. Writ Petition (Civil) No. 82 of 2011.

10. There was an intermediate tier, the panchayat samiti, but this was not directly elected and consisted mostly of presidents of mandal panchayats.

11. Also known as assistant commissioners or subdivisional magistrates in some states.

12. Report of the Committee on Restructuring of DRDA, department of rural development, Ministry of Rural Development, Government of India, January 2012.

Chapter 2: Files, Red Tape and the Art of Confusion

1. *Karnataka Government Secretariat Manual of Office Procedure (Revised)*, Government of Karnataka, department of personnel and administrative reforms, training, 2005.

Chapter 3: How to Get into the Civil Services

1. Report of the Committee on Recruitment Policy and Selection Methods, 1976.

2. Report of the Civil Services Examination Review Committee, Union Public Service Commission, 2001.

3. Report of the Committee on Civil Service Reforms, 2004.

4. Report of the Committee to Review the Scheme of the Civil Services Examination, 1989. Luckily, the recommendations of this committee are summarized in the report of the Yogendra Alagh Committee report.

5. This was done nearly a decade after the Alagh Committee's report, after yet another committee, the Khanna Committee, reiterated the same recommendation.

6. For those with an eye for detail, the Satish Chandra Committee recommended a five-year relaxation for SCs and STs, while the Alagh Committee recommended three years for OBCs, five for SCs and STs and ten years for physically handicapped candidates.

7. The Satish Chandra Committee suggested six attempts for SC and ST candidates. The Alagh Committee recommended five attempts for OBCs, six for SCs and STs and seven for physically handicapped candidates.

8. There has been snipping and changing of the range of optional subjects too. The Satish Chandra committee recommended that an essay paper for 200 marks should be introduced and candidates permitted to answer in either English or any Indian language. It also recommended that French, German, Russian and Chinese literature ought to be deleted from the list of optional subjects and education, electronics, telecommunication engineering and medical science ought to be introduced.

9. At the time of going to press, the UPSC's sixty-seventh annual report for 2015–16, had not yet been put in the public domain.

Chapter 4: Postings, Transfers and Government Dysfunctionality

1. Lant Pritchett, 'Is India a Flailing State? Detours on the Four Lane Highway to Modernization', HKS Faculty Research

Working Paper Series RWP09-013 (John F. Kennedy
School of Government: Harvard University, 2009).
2. Karnataka State Civil Services (Regulation of Transfers of
   Teachers) Act, 2007.

Chapter 6: The civil service and leadership

1. Eric Michael, 'Defining Leadership', The Leadership
   Institute at Harvard College, 18 November 2011, http://
   harvardleadership.wordpress.com/2011/11/18/defining-
   leadership/.
2. Dean Itani, 'A Different View of Leadership', The Leadership
   Institute at Harvard College, 5 December 2011, https://
   harvardleadership.wordpress.com/2011/12/05/a-different-
   view-of-leadership/.

Chapter 7: Generalists versus Specialists

1. Praveen Kishore, 'Grappling with Foxes and Hedgehogs of
   India's Senior Civil Services,' *Economic and Political Weekly*
   vol. LIII, no. 38 (22 September 2018).
2. Para 3.2.4.1.4 Second Administrative Reforms Commission,
   Fifteenth Report, State and District Administration
   Government of India. April 2009.

Chapter 8: Problem-Solving, Technology and the IAS

1. Jana Mahiti report, department of stamps and registration,
   Janaagraha Centre for Citizenship and Democracy, June
   2011 (based on citizen reports on ipaidabribe.com).
2. Subhash Bhatnagar, 'Bribery in Public Services: Need for
   Multi-Pronged Action', 10 March 2011, http://www.
   subhashbhatnagar.com/2011/03/.

3. Impact assessment study of e-government projects in India prepared by Centre for e-Governance, Indian Institute of Management Ahmedabad, submitted to the department of information technology, Government of India, January 2007.

Chapter 9: Ethics and the IAS

1. John T. Noonan Jr, *Bribes: The Intellectual History of a Moral Idea* (Berkeley: University of California Press, 1987).
2. Rule 3 (2).
3. Rule 3 (2A)
4. Rule 3 (3) (i)
5. Rules 3 (3) (ii) and (iii)
6. Explanation 1 to Rule 3.
7. Rule 4 (2) (a).
8. Proviso to Rule 4 (2) (a).
9. Rule 4 (3) (a).
10. Rule 5 (2).
11. Rule 18.
12. Rule 6.
13. Proviso to Rule 6.
14. Rule 7.
15. Rule 10.
16. Rule 11.
17. Rule 11 (2).
18. Rule 11 (3).
19. Rule 11-A.
20. Rule 12.
21. Rule 12 (2).
22. Rule 13 (f).
23. Rule 13 (2).
24. Rule 13 (4).
25. Exception (b) to Rule 13 (4).
26. Rule 13 (5).

27. Rule 13-A.

28. Rule 15 (2).

29. Rule 16 (3) (a).

30. Rule 16 (4).

31. Rule 16 (1).

32. Explanation 1 to Rule 16 (5).

33. Rule 16-A

34. Explanation 1 (c) to Rule 16 (5).

35. John T. Noonan Jr, *Bribes: The Intellectual History of a Moral Idea* (Berkeley: University of California Press, 1987).

36. *Controlling Corruption* (Berkeley and Los Angeles: University of California Press, 1988).

37. https://www.unodc.org/documents/treaties/UNCAC/Publications/Convention/08-50026_E.pdf.

38. 'Transparency and Accountability in NREGA: A Case Study of Andhra Pradesh', Yamini Aiyar, Salimah Samji, AI Working Paper No. 1, February 2009, http://environmentportal.in/files/transparency%20and%20audit-nrega.pdf.

Afterword

1. CAG report on telecom scam, Reference Report No. 19 of 2010, https:cag.gov.in>audit_report_files, issue of Licences and Allocation of 2G Spectrum by the Department of Telecommunications.

2. Francis Geoffrey Hartnell Anderson, *Manual of Revenue Accounts of the Villages, Talukas and Districts of Bombay State* (Government Press, 1965).

Annexure I: Gardens or Garbage

1. The correspondence relating to the above case study comprise the following:

Letter CAE 88 MSY 2016 dated 14/3/2016 of Under Secretary, Urban Development, Government of Karnataka.

Letter MME 12 MMA 2016 of 2/2/2016 of Additional Chief Secretary, Women and Child Welfare Department, Government of Karnataka.

Letter of Saagar DWCRA self-help group to Joint Commissioner BBMP Mahadevapura zone of 10/12/2015.

Various letters written to the Saagar DWCRA self-help group from CMC Mahadevapura giving them the contract for garbage collection and payments made to them.

Subsequent correspondence with the same group from BBMP Mahadevapura zonal office regarding work orders for garbage collection, particularly those dated 24/5/2017.

Certificate dated 20/3/2017 from Women and Child Welfare Department of the Bangalore North Zilla Panchayat confirming that the Saagar DWCRA group has been in existence from 13/5/2000 and working to collect garbage in AECS layout and Kundalahalli colony from 2002.

Letters written at different points in time by Saagar DWCRA self-help group to BBMP zonal and head office as well as to Government of Karnataka.

High Court of Karnataka proceedings in WP 58176 of 2015.

BBMP tenders for garbage collection in ward no 85 Doddanekundi in Mahadevapura zone from 2015 onwards (put on web site from time to time).

Annexure II: The Vanishing Vote Trick

1. Civil Citizens Initiative on Voters' Identification List, a Janaagraha initiative under the Vote India campaign to have a clean voters' list in urban areas, 2005.

Annexure III: Identity Crisis

1. Section 3A, recently added to the Aadhaar legislation after a long court battle, prevents the government from denying any child subsidy or service for not possessing Aadhaar identification. Yet, the Government of Karnataka continues to insist that admission to private schools under the RTE Act must only be done through the Aadhaar channel. So much for respecting the laws of the land!